T0311078

The Elements of Visual Grammar

Skills for Scholars

The Elements of Visual Grammar: A Designer's Guide for Writers, Scholars, and Professionals, Angela Riechers

Writing with Pleasure, Helen Sword

The Grant Writing Guide: A Road Map for Scholars, Betty S. Lai

The Secret Syllabus: A Guide to the Unwritten Rules of College Success, Jay Phelan and Terry Burnham

The Economist's Craft: An Introduction to Research, Publishing, and Professional Development, Michael S. Weisbach

The Book Proposal Book: A Guide for Scholarly Authors, Laura Portwood-Stacer

The Princeton Guide to Historical Research, Zachary M. Schrag

You Are What You Read: A Practical Guide to Reading Well, Robert DiYanni

Super Courses: The Future of Teaching and Learning, Ken Bain

Syllabus: The Remarkable, Unremarkable Document That Changes Everything, William Germano and Kit Nicholls

Leaving Academia: A Practical Guide, Christopher L. Caterine

A Field Guide to Grad School: Uncovering the Hidden Curriculum, Jessica McCrory Calarco

How to Think like Shakespeare: Lessons from a Renaissance Education, Scott Newstok

The Craft of College Teaching: A Practical Guide, Robert DiYanni and Anton Borst

Will This Be on the Test? What Your Professors Really Want You to Know about Succeeding in College, Dana T. Johnson

The Elements of Visual Grammar

Angela Riechers

A Designer's Guide for Writers, Scholars & Professionals

Princeton University Press
Princeton & Oxford

Published by Princeton University Press
41 William Street, Princeton, New Jersey 08540
99 Banbury Road, Oxford OX2 6JX

press.princeton.edu

Library of Congress Cataloging-in-Publication Data

Names: Riechers, Angela, author.
Title: The elements of visual grammar / Angela Riechers.
Description: Princeton : Princeton University Press, [2024] | Series: Skills for scholars | Includes bibliographical references and index.
Identifiers: LCCN 2022058388 (print) | LCCN 2022058389 (ebook) | ISBN 9780691231235 (hardcover ; acid-free paper) | ISBN 9780691231228 (pbk ; acid-free paper) | ISBN 9780691231211 (e-book)
Subjects: LCSH: Information visualization. | Visual communication. | Composition (Art) | Composition (Photography) | BISAC: DESIGN / Graphic Arts / General | LANGUAGE ARTS & DISCIPLINES / Writing / Academic & Scholarly
Classification: LCC QA76.9.I52 R54 2024 (print) | LCC QA76.9.I52 (ebook) | DDC 001.4/226—dc23/eng/20230724
LC record available at https://lccn.loc.gov/2022058388
LC ebook record available at https://lccn.loc.gov/2022058389

British Library Cataloging-in-Publication Data is available

Editorial: Peter Dougherty, Matt Rohal, and Alena Chekanov
Production Editorial: Terri O'Prey
Text Design: Heather Hansen
Cover Design: Heather Hansen
Production: Erin Suydam
Publicity: Jodi Price and Kathryn Stevens
Copy Editor: Cindy Milstein

Cover images Diane Picchiottino and Bit Cloud / Unsplash

This book has been composed in Bely with Bely Display and Calling Code

Printed on acid-free paper. ∞

Printed in China

10 9 8 7 6 5 4 3 2 1

The hardest thing to see is what is in front of your eyes.

—JOHANN WOLFGANG VON GOETHE

Contents

blue

premiere issue

$3.95 display until october 15, 1997

Introduction

0–1 *Blue*, designer David Carson, 1997.

This magazine cover fulfills one of the most important requirements for design: it fully captures a viewer's attention and makes them intrigued to find out more. The diver is strangely static (and headless, which is always disturbing) in the frame, frozen in an odd horizontal position rather than moving downward toward the water. What's going on? The image is simultaneously evocative and mysterious.

Literacy begins in early childhood with the building blocks of reading and writing: letters, words, sentences, paragraphs, and complete texts. Once these skills are mastered, we begin to focus on the complexities of assembling and structuring these elements. The rules of grammar create a shared understanding and set of tools for writing and speaking with clarity, directness, and precision.

How odd, then, that most of us are not taught these same skills as they relate to images. Without visual grammar, the conflict between written content and images can be jarring, akin to a formal black-tie dinner served on paper plates. When images are a good match for both the feeling and content of the text, the words and pictures merge to become an inseparable narrative. Together they unite to tell the definitive story.

Our brains take in and process images faster than they can read words. A team of neuroscientists from the Massachusetts Institute of Technology discovered that the human brain can comprehend entire images seen by the eye in just thirteen milliseconds. Even the

JEANS LONDON
PEPE JEANS LONDON

← 0–2 ***Side by Side*, photographer Joseph Ford, n.d.**

Point of view can be a thought-provoking tool to show readers a familiar object from an entirely new perspective. Combining a close-up of a sneaker with an aerial view of an industrial zone allows a viewer to see both a macro- and micro-vantage point as a single image—a harmonious composition made up of two unlikely parts.

U.S. retailer looks at foreign design

→ **0–3 Spread from *Design Research: The Store That Brought Modern Living to American Homes*, by Jane Thompson and Alexandra Lange, designer Michael Bierut, 2010.**

The large photo on the right-hand page has a few flaws, most notably the looming shadow behind the figure at the left. The image of two men looking down at a chair, however, perfectly mirrors the literal meaning of the text subhead "U.S. Retailer Looks at Foreign Design." The subtle ping-pong relationship between text and image reinforces both and ties the content together.

fastest reader can't plow through sentences at that speed, meaning that images make an impression that sets the tone and expectations of what is to come before a reader scans even a single word of text.

Understanding the structure and meaning of visual language aids our ability to both communicate and comprehend. Worldwide visual culture has never been so rich and varied, and at the same time so cluttered with images that are poorly deployed, ill-chosen, or just plain ineffectual. Careless image choices diminish the impact of written content and sometimes operate at cross-purposes to its intended message, sabotaging the author's best intentions and weakening their intellectual position. On the other hand, well-chosen images capture attention, pique curiosity, reel viewers in, and inspire them to stick around to read the text.

Just as there are rules of grammar for written language, there are rules of visual grammar for images. This book establishes a baseline structure to guide the broad array of scholars, professors, and graduate and undergraduate students—and the extended community of professionals including librarians, journalists, publishers, and others who surround them—who increasingly rely on graphic material to supplement their written work and want to feel more confident in their image choices. This volume lays out the fundamentals of visual style to impart a solid understanding of the underlying basic principles for image use, leaving deeper analyses of semiotics,

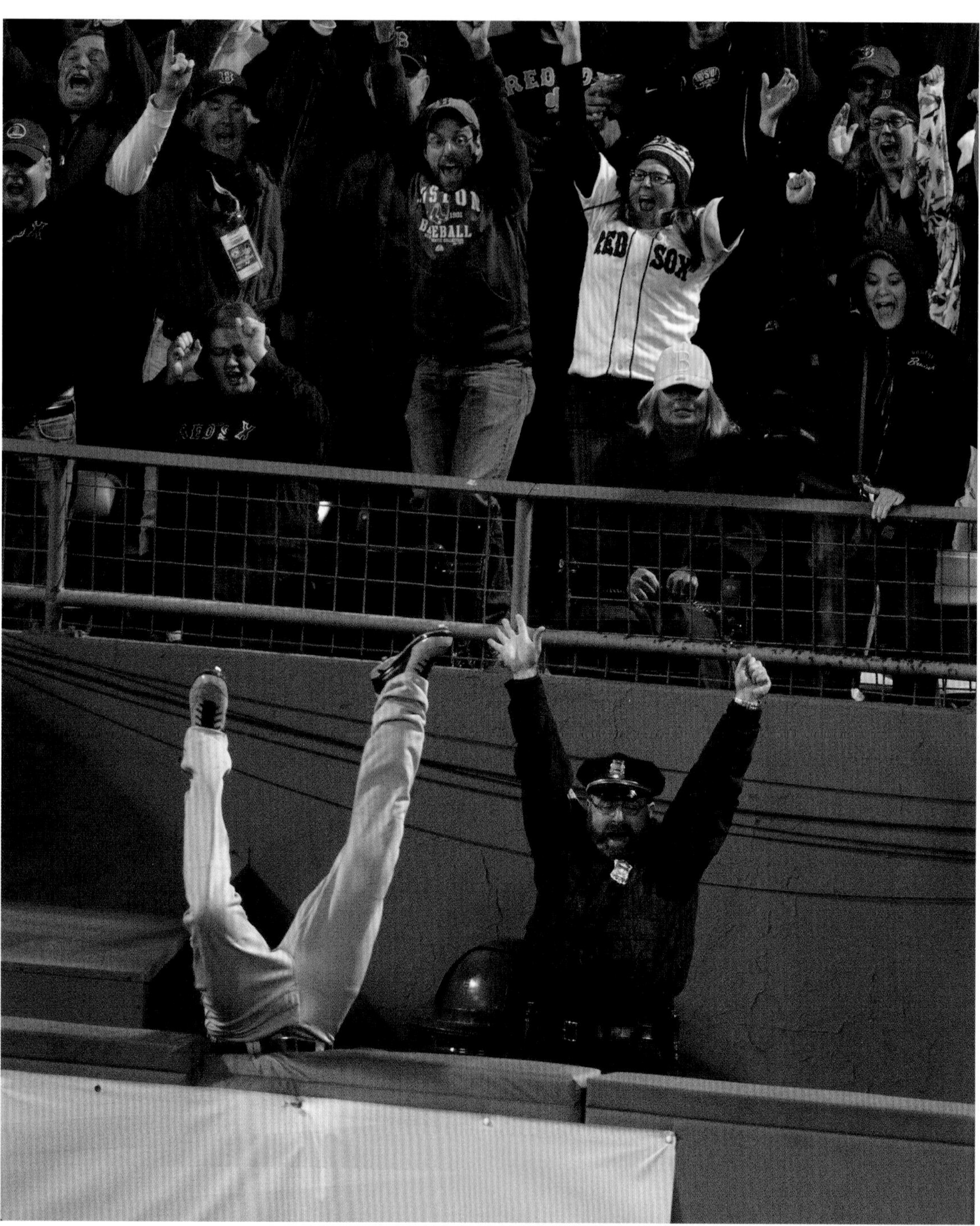
RED SOX

← 0–4 *Boston Globe,* photographer Stan Grossfeld, 2013.

This serendipitous shot perfectly captures the exuberance of a crowd at a Red Sox game reacting to a grand slam. What makes this photo completely wonderful, apart from its joyfulness, is the formal contrast of the V shapes of arms raised in victory in the crowd and the police officer in the foreground, and the same V shape formed by the upside-down ballplayer's legs as he dives for the missed catch.

→ 0–5 School of Visual Arts, Louise Fili, 2014.

Some images seduce viewers through sheer loveliness. The hand-painted artwork and lettering inspired by flower seed packets, soothing random pattern of scattered tiny seeds in the background, and soft, harmonious color palette create an easily understood and beautiful visual metaphor supporting the tagline "Watch your future grow."

0–6 Rubin's vase.

In his 1915 doctoral thesis, Danish psychologist Edgar Rubin presented a detailed description of the visual figure-ground relationship. This diagram illustrates a set of ambiguous or bi-stable (reversing) two-dimensional forms and is now well known as Rubin's Vase (or Rubin's Face, if you prefer).

psychological and social patterns of looking/seeing, critical theory, and media history for those in more specialized fields of study.

Images support text by adding a separate dimension of their own (rather than by merely repeating what the words say) and providing a richer, more nuanced understanding. But here's the catch: images are far more open to multiple interpretations than the written word because they are inherently more ambiguous. The same image can say very different things depending on context.

For instance, some people will describe the figure known as Rubin's vase as a picture of two faces, while others will see only the vase. Both are there in plain sight, but a viewer's take depends on what their brain registers first. Yet if the image is captioned, "This is a vase," those words will short-circuit any other interpretation. Pairing images with text affects the impact of both; the goal is to strengthen and clarify the overall message.

The images in this book are pulled from a wide variety of media, eras, and visual styles, and are meant to illustrate nuanced strategies for evaluation and selection. They were chosen not only for their usefulness in explaining a point but also because each is compelling, interesting, and beautiful in some way. In other words, they are good images. A good image can be a diagram, photo, scribble, illustration, or old master painting. The principles of visual grammar provide flexible evaluation criteria as opposed to a list of boxes to tick; they

This is the last picture that Van Gogh painted
before he killed himself.

0–7 *Ways of Seeing*, author John Berger, 1972.

Words are powerful; images are powerful; combine the two, and the meaning of each shifts irrevocably. Without the caption, viewers would likely pick up on the dark and somber mood of the painting, but to know that this was Vincent Willem van Gogh's final artwork before he ended his life invites other, grimmer interpretations (perhaps accurate, and perhaps not; only van Gogh would be able to say). To paraphrase Sigmund Freud, sometimes a crow is just a crow.

are a universal tool kit to aid in sorting out the best possible selections from a spectrum of image options.

Authors in nondesign-adjacent fields sometimes feel out of their element when considering how to use images to enhance their text. It can be difficult to know how to start the process, what criteria to use in evaluating images, and how to combine and sequence images for maximum impact. It's important to remember that we are surrounded from a young age with the visual language of images, but most of us have not had formal training in how they function and so feel underqualified to work with them at all. Authors familiar with the principles of visual grammar can use their personal sense of style, expertise in their subject matter, and knowledge of how best to reach their audience to choose images that will communicate effectively and well.

Rules for visual style are not always clear-cut; they remain open to experimentation and individual preference. There is never a

NO STANDING
ANYTIME
THIS IS IT
THIS IS IT
26 NYC
26 NYC
PANKO

← 0–8 2x4, New York City Marathon Nike campaign, 2009.

A New York City design firm imagined this project as a love story about New York and the runners who opt to live in a city where every day feels like a marathon. The imagery combines elements of layered street posters papered over each other and "legit" movie posters as well as graffiti and bright pops of color to match the familiar gritty feel of running (and living) a marathon in New York's streets.

→ 0–9 Centers for Disease Control (CDC), 1963.

This poster featured the CDC's national symbol of public health, the "Wellbee," encouraging citizens to receive the new oral polio vaccine. The cheery little honeybee character feels friendly and benign. It's also an apt choice of mascot given that both a bee and shot sting, but the oral vaccine does not. Most critically, it lightens the anxiety around the topic and allows the important health message to be taken in.

single strategy for image use that can be considered the correct and only solution; unlike tallying a column of numbers to arrive at the definitive answer, there are often multiple good solutions for marrying images with text. Through an understanding of the factors involved in making image choices, the reader will develop a process for the most dynamic communication combining words and pictures.

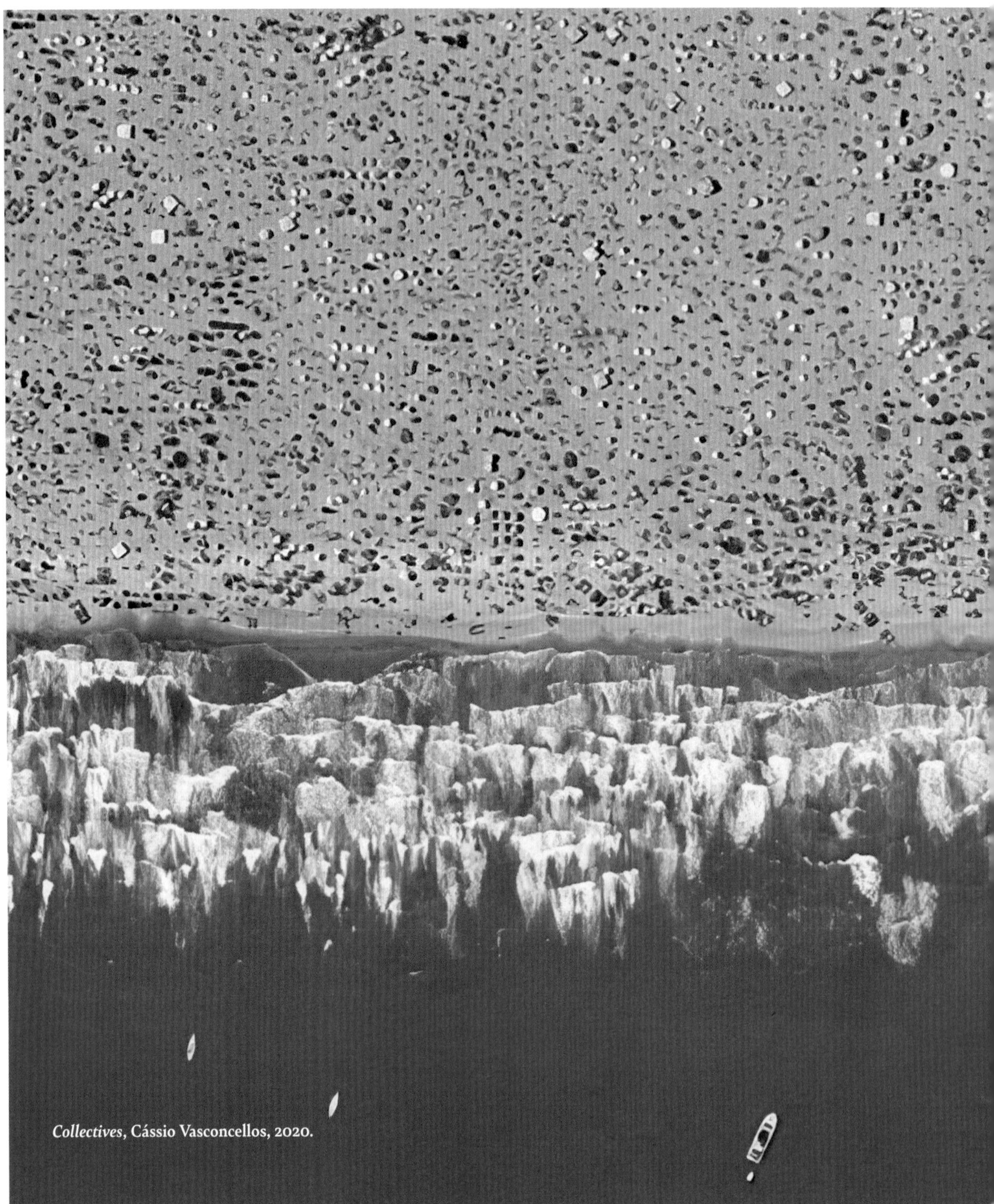

Collectives, Cássio Vasconcellos, 2020.

I Basics of Visual Grammar

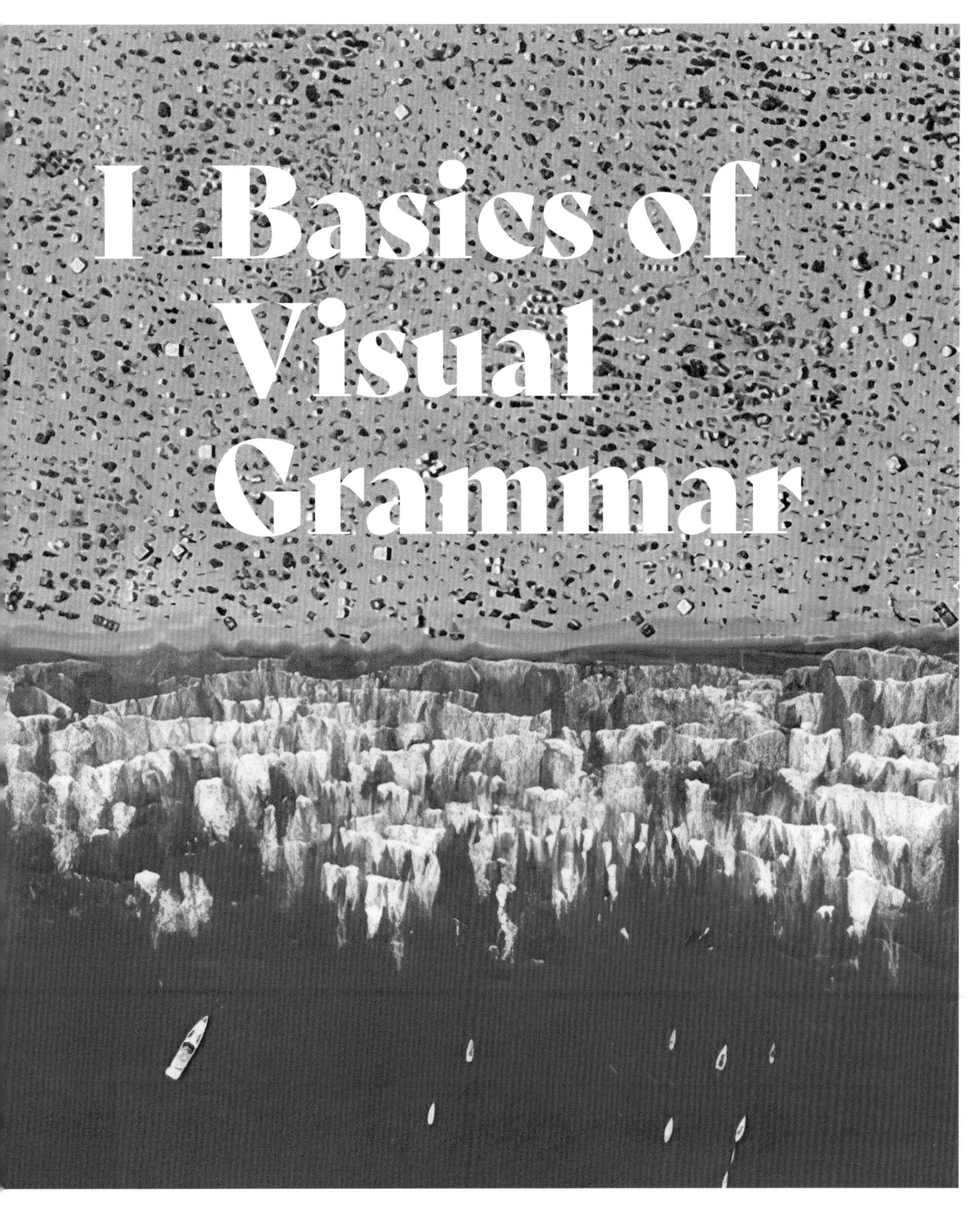

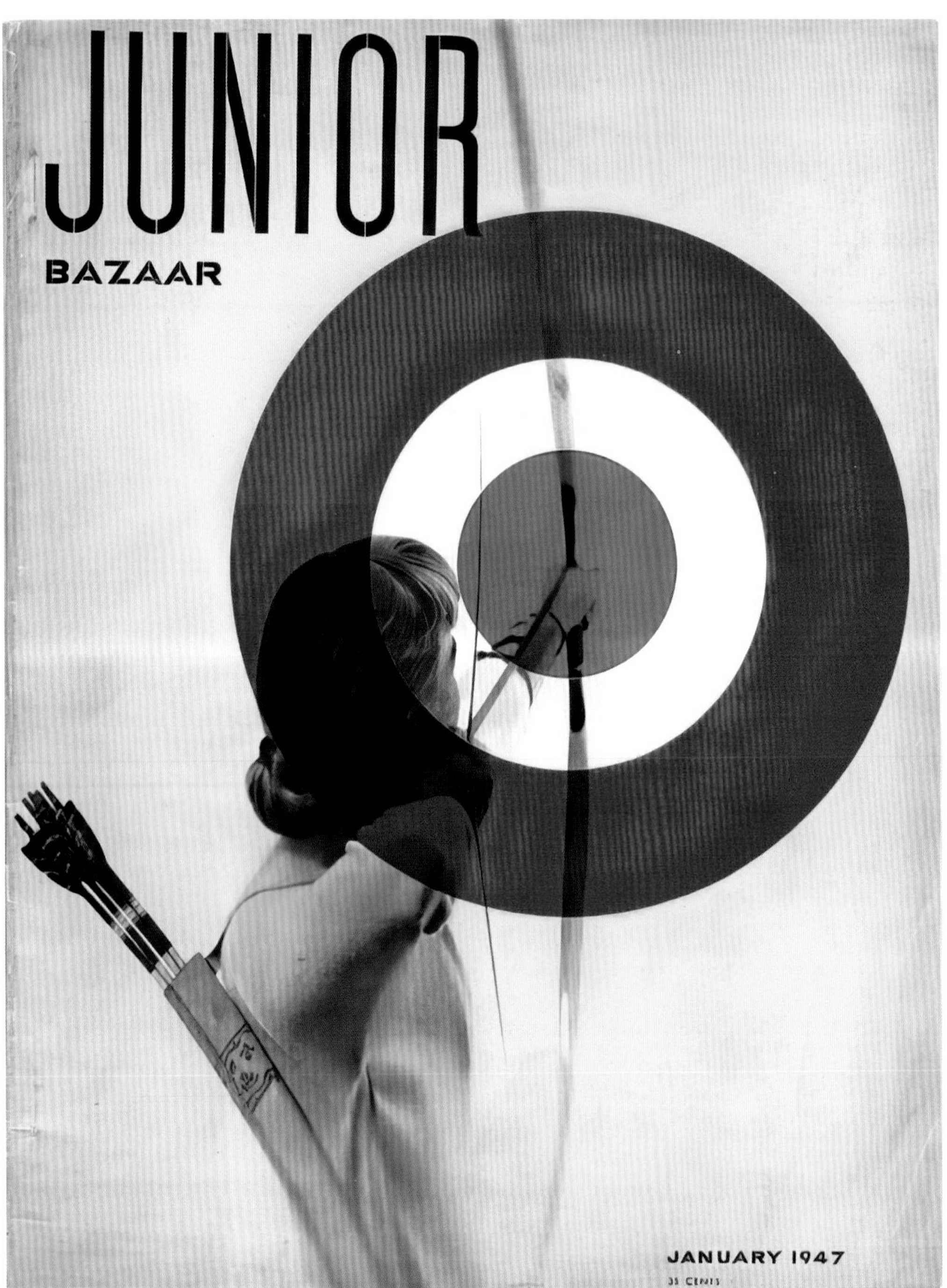
JUNIOR
BAZAAR
JANUARY 1947

01

What Is Visual Grammar?

1–1 *Junior Bazaar*, designers Alexey Brodovich and Lillian Bassman, 1947.

There is so much intelligent design in this deceptively simple image; the black-and-white photo overlaid on a bright geometric background is a neat fusion of the real with the abstract. The image of an archer is a strong metaphor for goals, focus, and precision, and the positioning of the model's left hand within the bull's-eye implies she will be successful.

Graphic designers must consider several factors simultaneously when developing a solution to a problem. Who is this for? What do I want them to know? What is the best, clearest way to say it? How can I say it in my authentic, individual voice? Increasingly, as authors incorporate images within their written texts, they need to deploy these same skills and thought processes to ensure that the images chosen enhance the material's intended message and deepen a reader's understanding. This chapter introduces an overview of how images work their magic within texts of all kinds. It also provides essential guidelines and goals for planning image use—the rules of visual grammar—that will be explained and unpacked in greater detail in the subsequent chapters.

This book defines the visual qualities of a "good" image—not as a value judgment or matter of opinion (tomato/tomahtoe) or level of taste, but as a set of criteria regarding image quality and inherent attributes, including style, content, color, and composition. The reader is urged to weigh the merits of a particular image in both formal

1–2 *Alice's Adventures in Wonderland*, by Lewis Carroll, illustrator John Tenniel, 1865.

Enjoyable on its own for the beautiful draftsmanship and sense of narrative, this illustration for a children's book slyly weaves in the politics of nineteenth-century London, a reward for adult readers astute enough to pick up the cues. The unicorn is widely believed to be a caricature of liberal British politician William Gladstone, while the lion represents conservative British politician Benjamin Disraeli. The two loathed each other; in fact, Disraeli referred to his opponent as "that unprincipled maniac."

terms and the more subtle emotive responses that it elicits from a viewer. Is this picture compelling/alluring? Do you care about it? What if we took it out? Would you miss it?

If that sounds like a tough call to make, it really isn't. Most people, even those without formal design training, have an instinct—a gut feeling—for what constitutes a "good" picture. Like the famous definition of pornography uttered in 1964 by US Supreme Court justice Potter Stewart, we know it when we see it. The good image moves us in some way; it makes something clear; it makes us stop and think; it exposes a hidden truth. It is, in some capacity, memorable. It is never generic. Oftentimes it is also unexpected, presenting us with a visual we didn't anticipate and that we enjoy even more for the pleasant surprise.

A set of images chosen with an underlying philosophy in mind will always communicate more forcefully than a group of images selected without a clear idea of how they will best support the text. The process is by no means an exact science, nor is there a right or wrong way to go about it. Some trial and error is always called for, but a successful conclusion—a set of images that enhances the written content of your work—is well worth the effort. As global

1–3 *Time* magazine, photographer David Burnett, 1984.

This image captures the complete and utter agony of US Olympic runner Mary Decker, who was poised to win the gold in the three-thousand-meter final in 1984 in Los Angeles when she collided with another runner, fell, and didn't finish the race. Her heartbreak is written large on her face and even her body language as she looks helplessly at the finish line she didn't cross. The raw human emotion of the moment captured in this perfectly timed shot makes the image unforgettable.

visual culture becomes increasingly image based, it's paramount for authors to supplement their texts with the sort of pictures that will delight readers and draw them in.

Design must attract, frame, and impart. Notice that the first part of that formula is attract. Only when a reader has been attracted can an author impart whatever information they hope the reader will take away. If you can't draw attention for the split second needed to make someone want to stick around and see what you have to say, you've lost them. Images provide this magnetic function, arousing curiosity and piquing interest, because visuals, as noted earlier, are taken in more rapidly than text, which must be read to be understood. Images evoke mood, feeling, and tone instantly and leave a

1–4 *Life* magazine, photographer Larry Burrows, 1965.

This image puts a viewer directly into the claustrophobic confines of an army helicopter with a dying pilot. The adrenaline and horror of the moment is plainly etched on the crew member's face at left. The photograph is a gut punch illustrating the fear and tragedy of combat, made all the more effective through journalistic black-and-white photography and a dramatic swirling composition. Notice how the wounded man's arms, the gunner's arm, and his weapon are all left-to-right downward-facing diagonals.

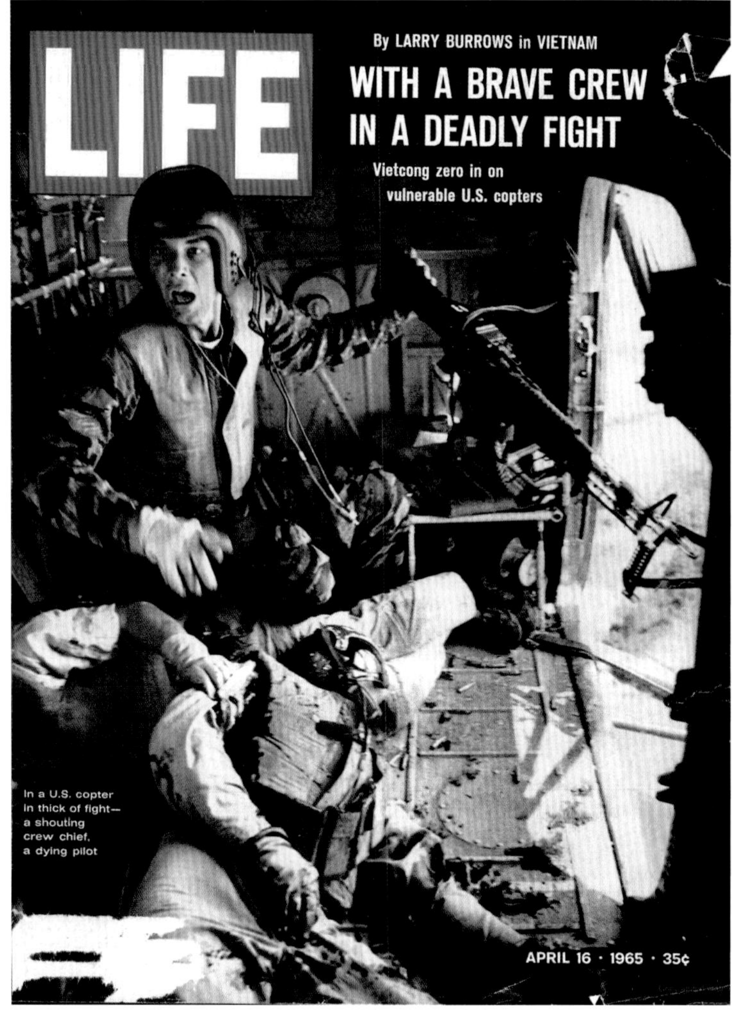

viewer hungry to know more. If your reader is a fish, images are the bait you use to reel them in.

LIFE
By LARRY BURROWS in VIETNAM
WITH A BRAVE CREW IN A DEADLY FIGHT
Vietcong zero in on vulnerable U.S. copters
In a U.S. copter in thick of fight— a shouting crew chief, a dying pilot
APRIL 16 · 1965 · 35¢

The high-wire act of combining different types of images successfully—illustrations, photos, charts, and graphs—becomes a far simpler activity when there is a well thought-out blueprint in place for their functionality, both individually and as they contribute to the larger narrative. It's best to begin the image selection

→ **1–5 *Irak+Ich*, designer Tarek Atrissi, 2012.**

The narrative oddness of this cover photo practically dares a reader to buy the magazine. Why is this older gentleman leaping and apparently shouting? What's with the stuffed animal in his left hand? Does he always dress like that when he strolls into the desert? Whimsical, mysterious images like this are bait that captures readers' curiosity and reels them in to read the text.

↘ **1–6 *Six Girls in Search of Shelter*, Stenberg Brothers, 1928.**

Vladimir and Georgii Stenberg were Russian avant-garde Soviet artists during the late 1920s, best known for their film poster designs. "Ours are eye-catching posters," Vladimir explained, "designed to shock. We deal with the material in a free manner . . . disregarding actual proportions . . . turning figures upside-down; in short, we employ everything that can make a busy passerby stop in their tracks." The bold but limited palette, abstract flat stripes, and rhythm of the repeated photographic faces and arms neatly illustrate this philosophy.

process with a direction—an idea of what you hope the images will contribute to your text. During the search process, don't be afraid to set off on detours if you feel inspired by an image that doesn't necessarily fit into your initial strategy. It's best to cast as wide a net as possible at first and try different image groupings before you narrow the choices down to your final selections.

Often, it's difficult to determine in advance how a particular image will function within a narrative or what a collection of pictures will say when viewed in total, but a few parameters and strategies will help narrow down the field to locate the optimal choices for any given text. Graphic designer Paul Rand wrote, "Readers of a report should be unaware of its 'design.' Rather, they should be enticed into reading it by interesting content, logical arrangement, and simple presentation. The printed page should appear natural and authoritative, avoiding gimmicks which might get in the way of its documentary character."

Why an image is good, suitable, or effective for its intended use, and *how* it communicates what it does, lie at the heart of understanding visual grammar. The examples in this book demonstrate a range of formal qualities contributing to their strong, memorable visual impact.

1–7 *The English Patient*, by Michael Ondaatje, designer Chip Kidd, 1992.

A book cover functions as a quick advertising poster for pages and pages of text. The imagery needs to be evocative and provide a clue to the content without trying to say everything (an impossibility, in any case). This pairing of a Cecil Beaton black-and-white photo and vivid strip of garden imagery captures many things with sensitivity: the North African desert setting of a key incident in the book, isolation of the mortally injured English patient himself, and the flashes of memory he relays to his nurse throughout the book.

1–8 *Orchanical Apparition*, Nathan Vieland, n.d.

"Exploded" diagrams are familiar to most of us, but they generally show mechanical objects or architecture. This diagram is anatomically accurate even as it takes a lighthearted approach (and mixes in some mechanical parts along with the whale's natural structure). The beauty lies in the surprise of seeing something organic rendered in the manner of a technical drawing. This image strategy—a play on the expected—can bring life to dry or complex topics without distracting from the seriousness of the text.

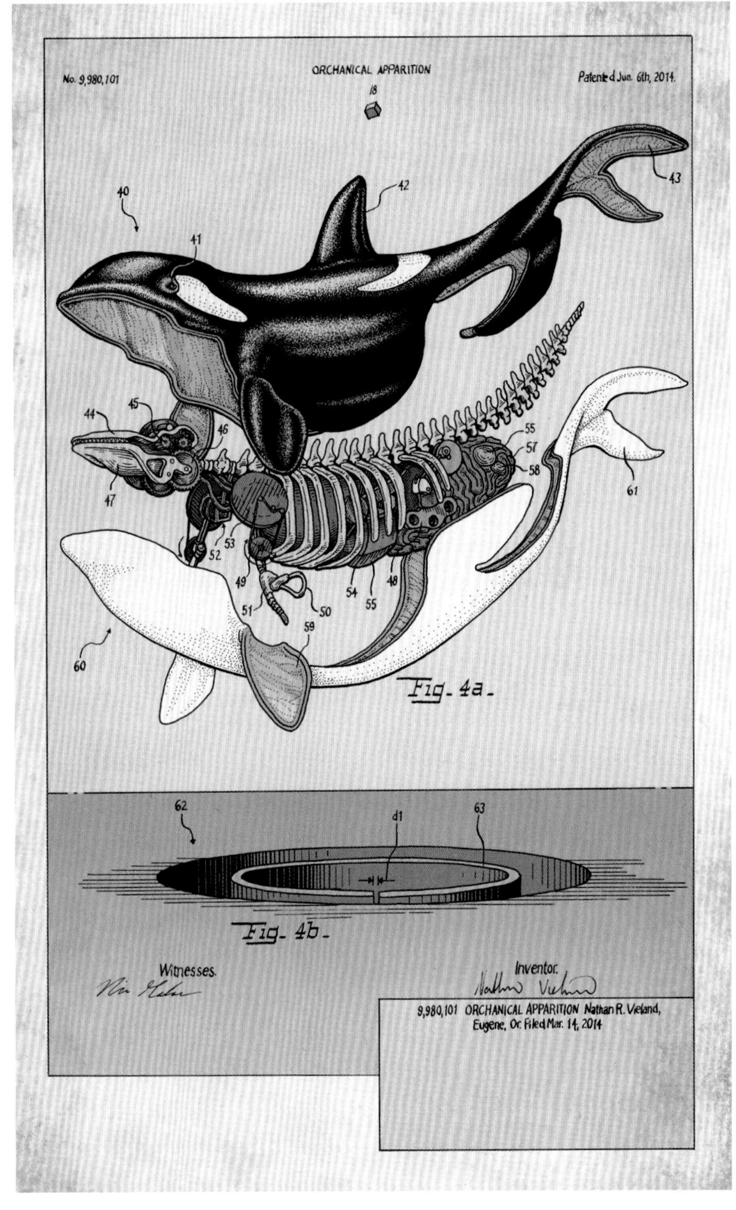

Baseline Rules of Visual Grammar

Images best support and enhance text when they:

1. Inform, delight, and intrigue

The most important role of images (after attracting the reader's attention) is to inform, delight, and intrigue. They inform by providing a visual corollary to what the author is writing about; they delight through aesthetic qualities that mirror the tone of the writing; and they intrigue by offering just enough mystery to pique the reader's curiosity and convince them to invest more time in the text. Well-chosen images are satisfying; they reward a viewer with something wonderful to look at alongside the text. They make the sheer mass of words less intimidating by supplying different entry points on the page, and offering a place for the eye to take a break and rest for a moment before diving back into gray columns of text.

2. Enhance understanding

Images expand an understanding of the written word by showing in order to tell. They assist comprehension via two main channels: getting between the lines, so to speak, by making visible what is not directly stated in words (mood, inferences, or how something feels), and/or clarifying what is directly stated (what something looks like or how it functions). Words are precise, but images are chameleons whose meaning shifts depending on the context. An image of colleagues sitting around a conference table says one thing when used alongside a text about the value of face-to-face meetings in office work, but something else when used within a text about the gender or racial dynamics of the workplace. The two separate contexts lead a reader to search for different things within the image. In the first, we might notice the degree of involvement in the conversation and how the workers appear to engage with each other. In the second, we may look to tally up the number of males versus females in this office or analyze the racial balance of the workers.

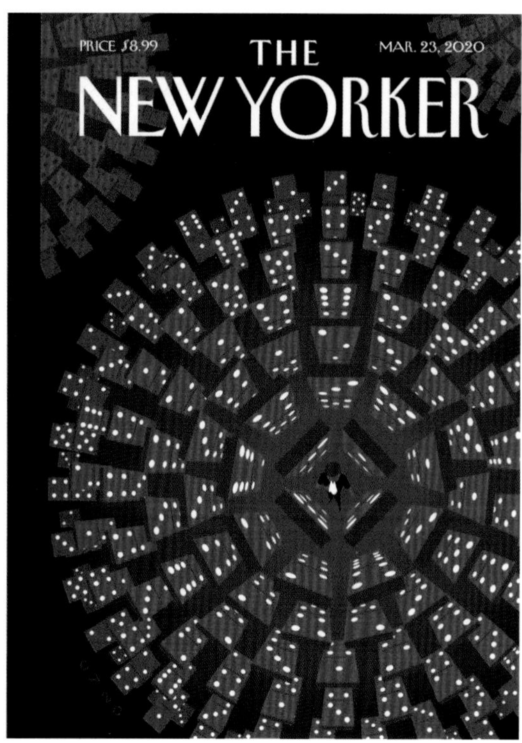

1–9 *New Yorker*, artist Christoph Niemann, 2011 and 2020.

In these March issue covers published almost nine years apart to the day, Niemann used objects with familiar associations to visualize upsetting current events. The 2011 nuclear disaster in Fukushima is evoked through atom-shaped cherry blossoms, a traditional symbol of spring and renewal in Japan. Both the isolation of the individual and danger to entire populations posed by COVID-19 at the beginning of the pandemic in 2020 is represented by the figure surrounded by easily toppled dominoes, with an added layer of meaning provided by the dominoes arranged to resemble a COVID virus.

3. Are specific and meaningful, curated and chosen with purpose

You can always tell when the person making your sandwich did it with love and care, or when they just slapped it together with a total lack of interest in the outcome. No one really enjoys that sandwich. Undertake the search for images with as much purposeful intent as you devoted to writing your text. Look for fresh visual examples. Images should not be generic (no one will care about them if so) but instead unique and meaningful on their own as well as suited to the specifics of the text. Allow your personal aesthetics to guide your choices, just as your writing reflects your unique voice and point of view.

With a clear strategy in mind, seek out pictures that fit your goals, and undertake the search with curiosity and an open mind as to what sort of images will best serve your purposes. Edit the options

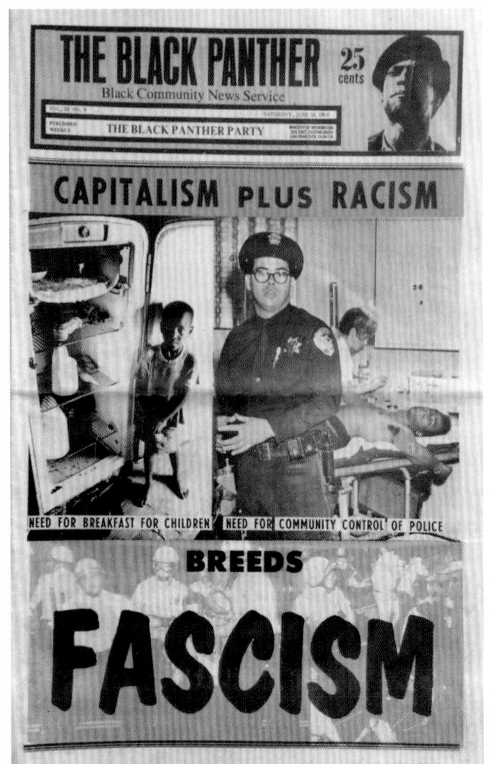
THE BLACK PANTHER
25 cents
Black Community News Service
THE BLACK PANTHER PARTY
CAPITALISM PLUS RACISM
NEED FOR BREAKFAST FOR CHILDREN
NEED FOR COMMUNITY CONTROL OF POLICE
BREEDS
FASCISM

1–10 *Black Panther*, designer Emory Douglas, 1969.

The official newspaper of the Black Panther Party was typically blunt and direct in its messaging, using its image-heavy pages to publicize the racial struggles of Black Americans and call for social justice. On this cover of *The Black Panther*, a pair of photos reinforces the provocative headline by contrasting a hungry Black child with a well-fed white police officer. In the background of the right-hand photo, the image of a Black patient being attended by a nurse suggests that the cop had something to do with the patient's injuries, without explicitly stating so.

down to the most suitable choices, sequence them with care and thought, and rest assured they will make a positive contribution to your publication.

4. Create a narrative arc in parallel with the text

Images should follow the text each step of the way, supporting the author's journey from point to point as they provide a visual narrative of their own. You can move along in a straight line or take the scenic route. In a paper or presentation of limited length, often the direct route works best (two or three well-curated images), but if you have the luxury of time and real estate, a more scenic route (several images with a wider range of visual content) will add color and flair to offer an enjoyable visual journey along the way. An image arc that develops and builds at the same pace and in the same manner as that of the written content (soothing or stirring, circular or linear, oblique or direct, fast-paced or leisurely) reinforces the structure of the overall piece to aid the reader's comprehension.

The first or opening image should have the visual impact of a movie poster summarizing key plot points of the film in a single image; subsequent images can illustrate corresponding text points or develop a parallel narrative of their own; and the last image should provide a sense of wrap-up or completion. For example, an author could choose to show images of a bud, flower, and fruit in various stages of ripeness and decay to accompany a story about aging. The reader will quickly understand the connection between images and text. The narrative about aging is better supported by the visual analogy instead of photos of specific people growing older, which would distract from the general topic by personalizing it. Rather than focusing on the aging process, a reader might wonder, Who are these people? Is this a story about them?

5. Support through composition, color, and mood

One of the most valuable contributions that images add to a text is their ability to express and reinforce the intangible, implied meaning within the written text. This is accomplished through nuances of composition and color (along with actual image content) that evoke and establish mood and emotive qualities mirroring those of the text.

Color plays a vital role in conveying mood—a fact supported by numerous scientific studies—and can be used to guide the overall feeling of a text in whatever direction the author wants. Context subtly shapes our perception of color; for instance, blue is positive when seen on a first-place ribbon, but a piece of meat with a blue tinge is likely spoiled. Wearing red has been shown to enhance performance in sports competitions; one study found that tae kwon do competitors wearing red outperformed those wearing blue. When used in website design, blue increases perceptions of quality and trustworthiness.

Composition, too, shapes the emotive impact of images, lending visual excitement or calmness, balance or lack of it, or a feeling of

1–11 Black Women Too, designer Zuleika Arroyo, 2021.

A limited color palette, generous white space, and inventive navigation system create a welcoming user experience for a website aimed at reducing violence against Black women. Positioning the figure at the heart of the solar system set up by the orbiting blue navigation dots implies that she is an important central figure.

random chaos or firm structure. Viewers don't stop to think about these factors; they don't need time to process visual information as with written text. This is part of the superpower of images: they hit right away, operating in an almost clandestine manner to make you feel first and think second. A reader's initial emotional response to the images within a text has a close relationship to their reaction to the text content. It hardly needs to be said that boring images don't often inspire anyone to start reading. Building in these considerations as part of the initial groundwork will develop a successful set of image strategy guidelines and steer the image research process.

6. Provide visual variety along with consistency

Think of the images you choose as a set. There should be an order and logic to their selection, making it clear to the viewer that these images describe individual aspects of a larger story. A simple but effective plan is to set some limits for your image search, such as this publication will be accompanied by (fill in the blank)—black-and-white street photos, full-color photo landscapes, botanical drawings,

1–12 *Cinémathèque Suisse*, designers Werner Jeker and Marcus Kutter, 1984.

A sense of mystery can be created quite easily with simple visual elements. This poster features just one black-and-white photo, minimal typography, and an imposing deep black void above the man's head. Is he rising or sinking, friend or foe? The repeated photo segments call to mind the interruption when film running through a projector accidentally skips—always a jarring moment for the audience. Come to think of it, does he look a bit sketchy?

or metaphoric illustrations. An overly ambitious or complicated image strategy can be difficult for the author to implement as well as hard for the reader to follow. By establishing some self-imposed ground rules to define the image quality and functionality, the author's task becomes narrower in scope but deeper in meaning, and more focused on what will bring the most additional value to their text. You can always adjust your search as needed.

An effective and interesting set of images features some variety within its consistency. It mixes up point of view, scale, balance, hierarchy, and other compositional qualities such that it doesn't feel repetitive, yet the images are clearly related to one another. Combine a long shot of greenhouses with a close-up of some of the flowers inside. Include a detail of an artisan's hands using woodworking tools along with a shot of the finished table.

When images are drawn from too many styles and sources, the main thing that gets communicated is haphazard chaos. If you decide to use photos, stick to that; don't throw in a random line drawing, unless your strategy is to use both photos and drawings together, and then you'll need to find a balanced number of each for the overall strategy to hold together. If you're using illustrations, don't mix up a variety of styles unless you do so purposefully and with confidence.

Defining Image Strategy

Authors should decide what their strategy and criteria for image selection will be before they begin to search for the images; while this may seem intimidating at first, it's merely a question of knowing your text and audience. In other words, the image selection process builds on your expertise in your field. A journalistic article can be supported by news photography or editorial cartoons, and neither is the "right" or "wrong" choice; it depends on the author's intention and the tone of the writing.

Images can either match or contrast the text; for instance, a serious message can be well served by humorous illustrations if they help get the point across. Within the basic image types of photography, illustration, and data visualization, each can have crossover functionality. For example, a photograph can be entirely documentary (I was here and took a photo of this) to support a journalistic text or digitally collaged into a photo illustration of something not possible in the real world (a man with a giraffe's head and neck), or it can be from the world of fine art with more abstract and ambiguous imagery.

1–13 ***Graphis*** **18, 1947.**

Form and function combine to create a compelling image. The razor-sharp calligrapher's pen point, seen at large scale, becomes a sculptural element as imposing as a skyscraper. The swirling handwritten flourishes and title bring a viewer back to the real-life miniscule scale of a pen—something familiar, to be held in the hand, that interacts with human movement as well as ink and paper to communicate ideas. You can almost hear the scratch of the nib traveling across paper.

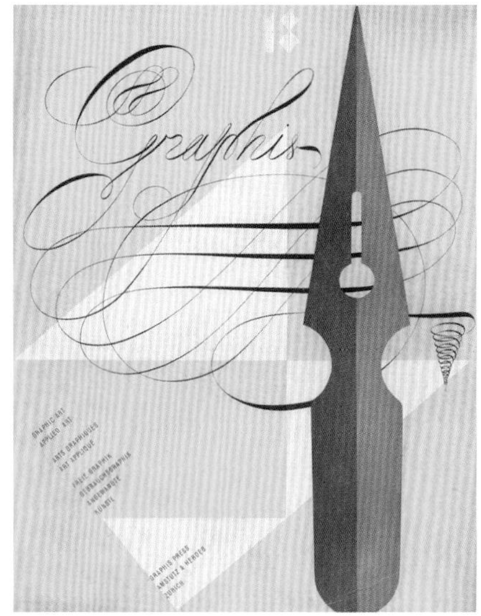

Analyzing text with an eye toward visual grammar ensures a satisfying relationship between image content, text content, and the overall effectiveness of communication. To get started, make a list of the key words that describe your text content along with its overall tone, mood, and feeling. Then ask yourself,

1. What is the purpose of my text?
2. What do I want to say?
3. Who is the audience?
4. What do I want them to know?
5. What will help the audience understand the text?

It's helpful to have an idea of how many images are needed as you define your image strategy. This can be a ballpark figure at first. There's no sense in spending days gathering hundreds of images if you have room in your publication for perhaps five total. With that said, always pull a wider selection than you think you'll need to allow room for serendipity and experimentation in your final choices and image pacing, but don't go crazy. If an image doesn't make you pause to consider it for more than a split second, move on. It didn't grab you. Remember, that is the image's job one: to attract.

02

Composition

2–1 From the series *Merchants in Motion*, photographer Loes Heerink, n.d.

There are so many elements of this composition to appreciate: the soothing neutral gray expanse of pavement framing the figure and burst of bright flowers; the repeated circular shapes, at different scales, of the flowers and the person's hat; the unexpected bird's-eye view. These are all formal visual considerations, but the outstretched right arm adds a secondary layer of narrative: the rider has been forced to walk the bike and perhaps struggle a bit with balancing the load, as evinced by the tight-knuckled grip on the handlebars.

Much of our initial response to images comes from a combination of compositional factors that play off one another. Asymmetrical images feel risky and even daring; symmetrical compositions feel safe and calm. A random structure within an image feels natural and spontaneous; perfect order feels mathematical, planned, and controlled. All of these factors help images increase comprehension of the writer's ideas.

Viewers respond subconsciously and organically to the composition of visual images without analyzing what they see. Image content is a separate consideration conveying some of the same messages that composition does. As an example, consider a photo of six puppies and a photo of six battleships. Imagine the puppies neatly spaced on a grid and shot from overhead, and a similar photo of the battleships arranged in formation. Both will convey order, but the puppies on a grid suggest triumph over energetic living forms while the battleships will mainly reinforce ideas about military regimentation and conformity.

2–2 "The Golden Mean (Fibonacci Sequence)," Jason Marshall, PhD dissertation, 2010.

The mathematical proportions of the golden mean (sometimes called the golden ratio) automatically feel "right" to a viewer, even if they aren't aware of it. This ratio is present in a variety of growth patterns in nature, from flowers to shells. The organic qualities of a composition conforming to the golden mean automatically make it seem familiar and comfortable.

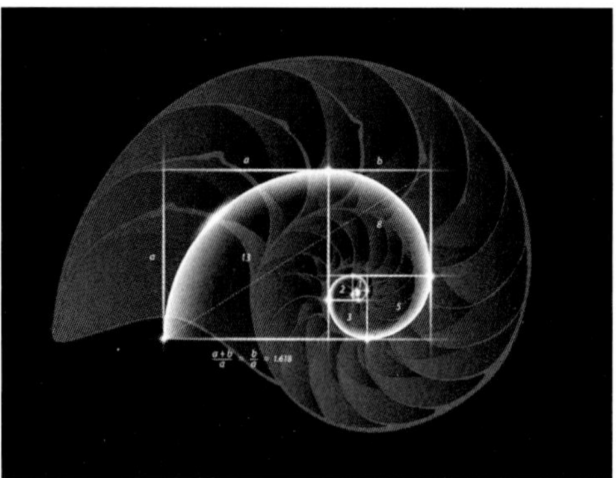

Many factors add up to pleasing compositions, but compelling images don't always conform to established rules. Guidelines set out in often-used principles are a good starting point for authors unfamiliar with the general standards of composition but should not be considered hard-and-fast rules to live by.

A well-known compositional ratio, the golden ratio or Fibonacci sequence, derives from principles dating back to the time of the ancient Greeks. Expressed as an equation, it is $\frac{a+b}{a} = \frac{a}{b} = \varphi$, with the Greek letter *phi* representing the golden ratio. In words, it is two elements whose ratio is the same as that of their sum to the larger of the two quantities. Numerically, it is 1.6180.

Images conforming to the golden ratio are inherently pleasing to the eye, in part because they follow proportions found in nature; the Fibonacci sequence can be seen in the growth patterns of plants (the seeds in a sunflower head develop in a Fibonacci sequence, for example) and chambered nautilus shells.

In a series of essays first published in the magazine *L'Esprit Nouveau* beginning in 1921, later issued as a collected edition titled *Toward a New Architecture* in 1927, Swiss modernist architect Le Corbusier described the principle as follows:

> Rhythms apparent to the eye and clear in their relations with one another. And these rhythms are at the very root of human activities. They resound in man by an organic inevitability, the same fine inevitability which causes the tracing out of the Golden Section by children, old men, savages and the learned.

The rule of thirds, first described by John Thomas Smith in 1797 in his book *Remarks on Rural Scenery,* is an adaptation of the golden ratio. It holds that an image of any proportion (rectangular or square) should be divided into nine equal parts by imaginary lines, two horizontal and two vertical, and that important elements within the composition should fall along these lines or their intersections. Many Renaissance paintings follow this rule. Adhering to the rule of thirds creates a more dynamic image by avoiding placement of the subject at dead center and offsetting the horizon so as not to cut the picture in half. For existing images that weren't initially composed following these guidelines, judicious cropping frequently can rebalance things to achieve a more exciting dynamic.

The composition of images seen in sequence can lead a narrative's rhythm and pacing in subtle or dramatic ways. A series of randomly composed images that gradually yields to more structured compositions communicates a sense of order building over time. Conversely, beginning a narrative with spare, calm images and ending up with fractured, busy ones suggests that things have, literally, fallen apart. The situation seems to grow more and more chaotic over time.

All images contain the following compositional factors to one degree or another:

- Scale: the size, location, or amount of one element in relation to another
- Hierarchy: the arrangement of elements in order of importance
- Balance: the distribution of the visual weight of objects, colors, texture, and space
- Positive space: the subject or areas of interest in an image
- Negative space: the background or area surrounding the subject
- Foreground: the area of the image closest to the viewer
- Background: the area of the image farthest away from the viewer
- Cropping or detail: cropping reframes the composition; detail pulls out a small piece of it for closer examination

→ **2–3 Swiss Auto Club, designer Joseph Müller-Brockmann, 1955.**

The dramatic difference in scale of the two main elements of this composition underscores the danger posed to the child by the speeding car. It appears monstrous; there's a terrible threat to the child, whose puny size makes him appear touchingly vulnerable like an insect, easily crushed. He is also looking away, not particularly attuned to the danger he's in, and has just started to run, although it already feels too late.

↘ **2–4** Scale depends on comparison for relevance; this feather horn beetle seen on its own in close-up could be imagined at any dimension, but the human fingertip allows a viewer to judge its actual size. Playing with the size of objects or creatures in images, either up or down from their expected scale, yields surprising and often delightful new information. In this case, without the extreme macro view, those amazing antennae might go unnoticed.

2–5 National Geographic Society, photographer Sumant Pinnamaneni, 2018.

Comparing the tiny oryx antelope at the lower left with the massive red mountains around it provides instant confirmation of the desert's vast size and emptiness as well as its ability to support life in limited quantity. The mountains seen alone would appear almost abstract, and it would be difficult to guess how large they are; the oryx brings the viewer back to solid ground in understanding the landscape.

Scale

The term *scale* is commonly used in a technical sense to refer to the specific size and resolution of an image, but it also refers to compositional qualities: the sizes of elements within the image, their relationship to one another, and the relationship of an image size to the page or reproduction size. Scale can convey contrast, drama, importance, or lack thereof (in the 1997 movie *Men in Black*, recall Will Smith's disappointment when he's issued a tiny little gun instead of a massive monster destroyer like Tommy Lee Jones's), or even a sense of balanced neutrality. Manipulating scale can also make the image's subject appear threatening or insignificant, depending on the author's intent.

A single image of a horseback rider on a vast plain, surrounded by Western landscape, suggests several meanings through the scale

← 2-6 **Image by T.O.K., 2019.**

The vastness of the grassy plain, sky, and distant buttes convey a peaceful, if lonely, feeling. There is an aspect of quietude and isolation as well as introspection—a cowhand alone with their horse and thoughts.

↙← 2-7 **Okeyphotos, n.d.**

The cowhands become secondary in this image focused on the horses. A viewer can practically hear the deafening hoofbeats and feel the swirling clouds of dust. This image is far more visceral than the previous one: louder, grittier, alive, and dynamic. It speaks to a different aspect of the horse wranglers' work.

↙ **2-8 Photographer Paul Szakacs / EyeEm, n.d.**

Everyone takes their shoes off at the end of the workday, including cowhands. This lineup of well-worn boots ends the image sequence with an aura of relaxation, tracing the narrative arc from quiet to action to respite. The somewhat battered condition of the boots hints at the difficulty of the job and communicates to a viewer that the rest was well-earned.

of its composition: the relative insignificance of humans in nature, a cowhand perhaps experiencing existential loneliness out in the wilderness, and the low ratio of humans to real estate in that location. The meaning that a viewer draws from the image depends on two aspects of its context: the text's content, of course, but also the image's relationship to other visual elements.

For example, adding two more smaller photos, one of a herd of horses and another showing a row of empty boots, generates a more complete image narrative. The horses are the day's work and the boots say quittin' time. By making these photos small compared to the establishing shot, the emphasis is on the cowhand. To use scale to switch it up, make the herd of horses the largest image and decrease the size of the other two photos. Now the visual narrative has shifted toward the animals; the cowhand seems less important, more of a minor detail in the bigger story, because the images representing them are now secondary.

The scale of an image's physical dimension on the page or screen determines its rank in the overall visual order, but the largest image is seen as the most important and needs to be the "best" image. Images used at smaller sizes are secondary in the hierarchy. Using complex images rich with detail at sizes too small to appreciate is a waste of space; if they cannot be properly seen or understood, the reader will just skip over them. By the same token, a large but uninteresting image poses a similar dilemma: Why is this bad picture so huge? Make sure the image's size in the publication does justice to its content.

Hierarchy

Hierarchy—a succinct way of saying "organize stuff from most to least important"—uses ordering and scale to communicate the most critical information first, with smaller or secondary points falling further down in the hierarchical order. This is true for both images and text; think of a text outline where the main headings represent the first level of hierarchy, and the subheadings represent information supporting the first (most important) content. Image hierarchy works in exactly the same way. A large image to start off with,

→ **2–9 *De 8 en Opbouw*, designers Paul Schuitema and Piet Zwart, 1936.**

A pleasing variety of scale in a composition can come from typographic elements as well as images. These magazine covers deploy vastly oversized numbers and type to complement and balance the photographic parts of the images. Notice how the number 8 at an exaggerated size carries as much visual weight as the human figures, and how the designers have used nearly identical compositions to create two different-feeling covers.

↘ **2–10 *Whistlejacket*, artist George Stubbs, 1762.**

An information hierarchy within images works much the same way as it does in text: the largest thing or most important point frequently comes first and dominates the conversation. Eighteenth-century paintings of horses typically showed them in context with other details—architecture, land, or servants—meant to convey their owner's wealth and status. This arresting composition cuts away all of that visual noise to say, Look at my magnificent horse.

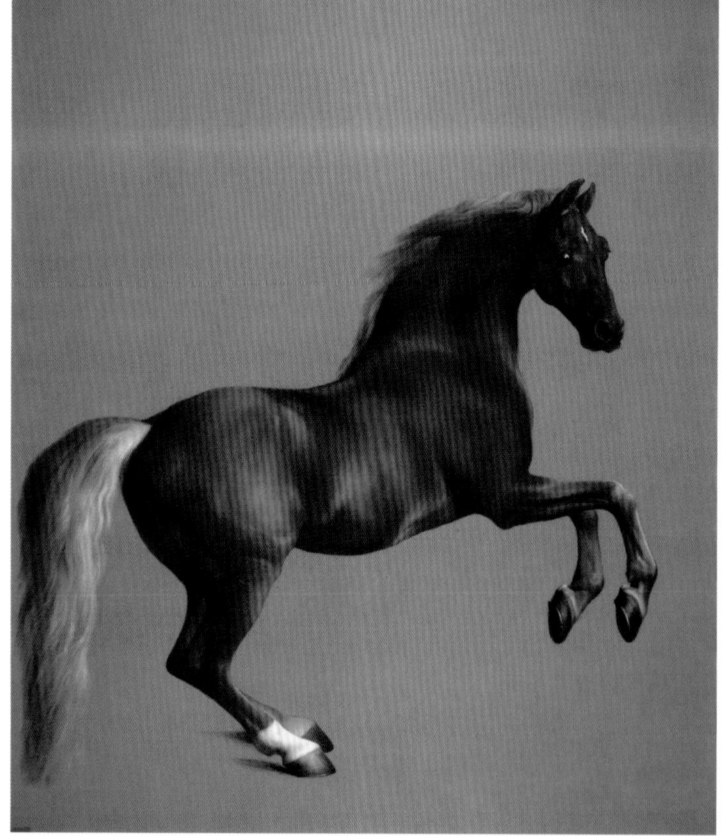

2–11 *NYC Break Dance*, photographer Boogie, 2006.

These break-dancers seem to be part of a stop-motion film—almost reading as a time-lapse image of a single person. The blurred motion from left to right tells us what they are doing, and the prominent cash bucket in foreground, perfectly still and in crisp focus, tells us what they hope to gain by doing it. The cropped (hence minimized) bystanders in the background tell us that an audience is there, but they are not the main subject of the photographer's narrative.

followed by a series of smaller ones, uses hierarchy and scale along with sequencing to orient the reader and lead them through the text.

Image hierarchies that parallel the text structure allow the visual and written content to support, not conflict with, one another. In a logical hierarchy, there are a number of ways to direct a reader's eye: color, contrast, size, and movement, among others. A strong image—one with dramatic content or rich color, for instance, shown at a large size—appearing early in a presentation or publication establishes an engaging dialogue with the viewer, who will be intrigued to keep following the narrative. Subsequent images can be slightly less dramatic now that you have the reader's attention.

Hierarchy isn't necessarily determined by the physical size of images alone. Image placement can create suspense through a narrative, building to a dramatic conclusion. For example, a hunt for a lost artifact can use images of the archaeologists, terrain, and

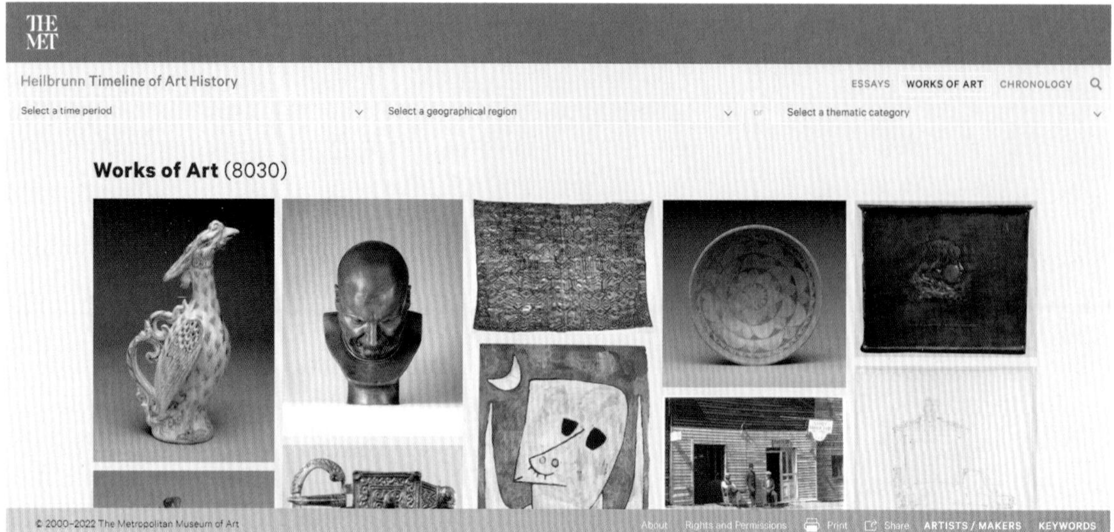

↑ 2-12 Metropolitan Museum, website, 2021.

The Metropolitan Museum's time line allows for entirely visual browsing. The initial page is constructed as a long vertical scroll; hovering over any image will bring up its title, and clicking it brings up a full information page. This streamlined approach doesn't clutter up the splash page with text for each work of art, allowing the viewer to scroll through quickly until the desired object is located. Search functions allow for pinpointing specific works, of course, but for someone who is just browsing by look, this image strategy works well.

→ **2-13** Zeroing in on the object alone makes it the only object in the visual hierarchy and strips away the extraneous distracting information of all the other artworks.

2–14 Arngren, website, 2022.

The haphazard sizes and scale of the images, along with a confusing mix of silhouettes and rectangular photos arranged without much attention to a grid structure, makes this site extremely hard to navigate. It feels like someone shouting at the top of their lungs. (The jarring bright color choices for type aren't helping either.)

historical background throughout before concluding with a shot of the artifact, found. It can be a large image or small and jewellike, but it gains most of its significance from its placement at the top of the imaginary image ladder that the reader just climbed to see it.

Along with size, image position is a simple way to establish hierarchy. Most viewers start scanning a page or screen at its upper-left corner and move toward upper right; studies have shown that this left-to-right eye movement appears to be more neurological than cultural, and holds true for readers in languages that read right to left or up and down. Readers perceive the top half of a page or screen as more important than the lower half; a large image placed at the top of the page exerts a magnetic pull on a reader's eye and is pretty much guaranteed to get looked at first.

Marketing research has demonstrated that for magazine covers, which feature a standardized hierarchy of logo-image-headline-cover lines, a face (and this can be anything from a photo of a person making direct eye contact with the camera to a crudely drawn smiley face) is the most important element when it comes to attracting a reader's attention.

There is also a hierarchy of information *within* images, with similar principles of visual engagement. A portrait photographer can choose to shoot a subject in their workplace, for instance, keeping an even camera focus on the person as well as the environment to provide visual detail about the subject's career. The hierarchy within this image? The subject is the first level, and the surroundings are the second level, supplying information that adds to our knowledge of the subject but is not the primary reason for taking the photo. Or that same photographer can opt for a shallow depth of field to keep the attention on the subject by blurring the background information to mute it, offering only one level of hierarchy.

When image-text hierarchies are fully integrated with each other, the resulting synergy brings text to life. The largest images should accompany an author's key points to highlight and call attention to them. Smaller images or marginalia will read as parenthetical asides, helpful as background information or additional clarification.

Consider the role of each image as you sort for sequence and relative size throughout a document. How much work do you need a particular image to do to further your reader's understanding of the text? Prominent size or placement will convey that an image needs more attention than other, smaller images appearing in the same document.

Balance

A composition is balanced when the elements within it achieve equilibrium. A group of small elements will balance a single, larger one; a small, brightly colored element balances a larger one of neutral coloration. Balance can be symmetrical or asymmetrical, with elements appearing at regular intervals or randomly distributed. Symmetry around a central axis, vertical or horizontal, is referred to as bilateral symmetry. Radial symmetry, also a form of symmetrical balance, arranges elements equally around a central focal point, like the petals of a daisy. Asymmetrical balance within an image feels less formal and contains more visual movement than symmetrical balance as the eye scans back and forth to weigh the varying elements' relationship to one another.

2–15 Photographer Rob Tringali, 2014.

Derek Jeter's active pose forms a strong diagonal within the composition. He is the central element, with his head breaking the curve of the stadium seating at the top, and his feet starting to take off from the straight edge of the field at the bottom. Notice how the background elements provide a sense of perspective as well as leading the eye to the ballplayer, who has just hit a home run in his last game ever, at the bottom of the ninth inning, in a tied five-five game with a runner on second. It was a historical moment, and the image does it full justice.

The visual balance within an image implies stability or lack thereof; balanced images feel calm and settled, and unbalanced ones suggest precariousness. As bilaterally symmetrical creatures (our bodies are identical on either side of a vertical axis), humans have an innate uneasiness with a lack of balance—it leads to falls, injuries, or a loss of control—and our brains flag this on a subconscious level when presented with an unbalanced composition. Balance or its absence can be a subtle way to reinforce text content. Do you want your reader to feel secure, or is there a benefit in using images to emphasize something with disturbing implications in your topic—such as a political development, alarming medical discovery, or social injustice?

As with hierarchy, there is balance in how an author chooses to distribute images throughout a presentation or publication,

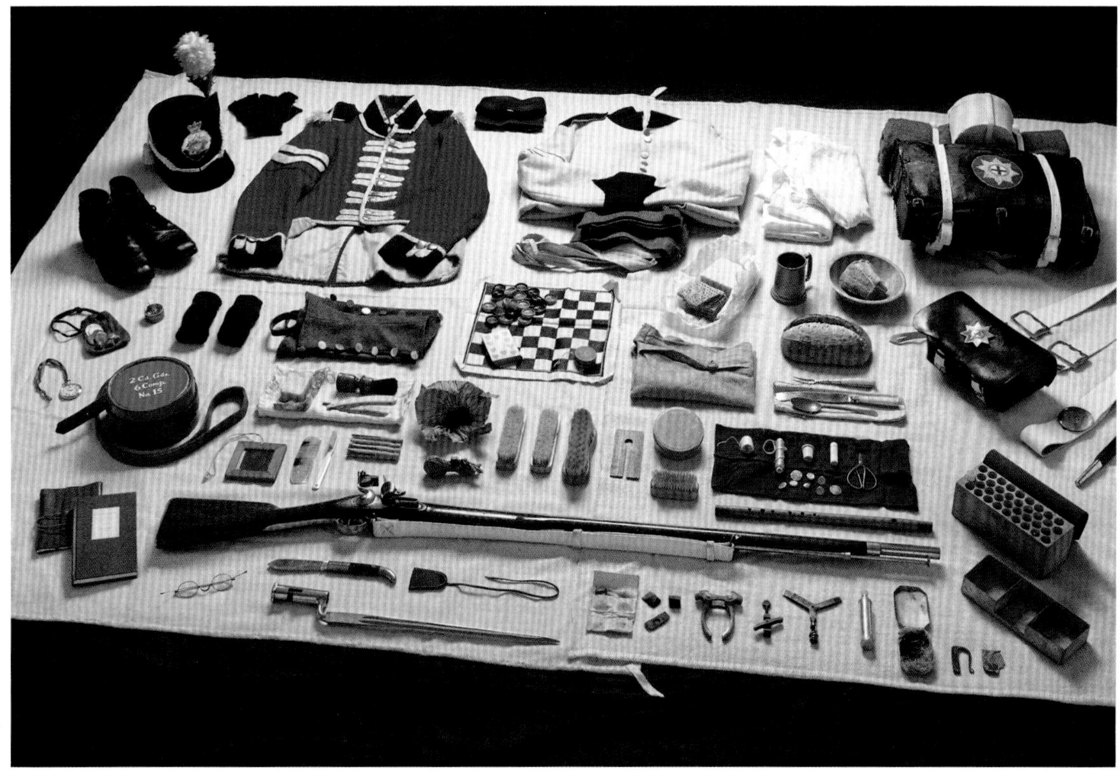

↖ **2–16** ***Greg Hunt and Dylan Rieder*, photographer Anthony Acosta, 2008.**

Expressed as an equation, this image would be: 2 × empty space + 1 × active space = perfectly balanced image; it divides up into horizontal thirds. The narrowest strip at the bottom of the photo is also visually busiest; it's where all the action is happening. The large expanse of green wall serves as respite to the flowing motion and activity below; it's a place where a viewer's eye has an opportunity to take a break.

← **2–17 Photographer Mike Krautter, n.d.**

Sometimes visual balance is achieved by placing one element a little off-kilter. The glass at the far right, whose rim juts over the edge of the concrete and interrupts its straight trajectory, provides a focal point midway between the glasses, their beautiful shadows, and the dancing blue water of the swimming pool. It also feels a bit precarious, peeking over the edge.

↑ **2–18** ***Private Soldier, Battle of Waterloo, 1815*, photographer Thom Atkinson, n.d.**

In his series *Inventory*, Atkinson laid out and cataloged all the possessions of single soldiers from various time periods in history. An image like this could easily feel jumbled or messy, but the meticulous attention paid to balancing groups of small objects with larger ones provides a soothing sense of order and balance, allowing a viewer to appreciate each item at leisure.

regardless of image content. The principle remains the same: multiple small images on the left-hand page will balance a single, larger one appearing on the right; a single red initial character balances a forceful black-and-white photo in a slide presentation, its bright color allowing it to hold its own despite the small proportion of real estate it occupies on the screen. A large, heavy element can be brought into balance by a group of smaller elements to add equal visual weight, or deliberately moved to one side of the image or the other to tip the scales. Imagine a perfect circle perfectly centered in a composition; it balances all by itself. Move that circle to the top of the page, and it becomes a perilously positioned boulder waiting to fall. Move it to the bottom, and it's a grounding anchor weight.

Positive and Negative Space

Negative space—the voids or unoccupied areas around the main elements of an image, often in the background—holds as much visual weight and is equally as crucial as the positive spaces occupied by objects or people. It may feel open and expansive (a wide blue sky), or oppressive and frightening (a large area of deepest black shadow). It can suggest isolation and loneliness, and evoke the unknown such as a frightening abyss or some sort of hidden dangers best avoided.

Yet negative space doesn't always have negative connotations; it also summons feelings of relief and respite by functioning as a blank canvas or untouched area of freedom and possibility, establishing a feeling of meditative solitude and peace. The Japanese design concept of *notan* holds that light and dark need each other for balance. (Shadows couldn't exist without light, after all.) Negative space provides an area for the eye to rest, particularly if other areas of the image are visually busy or crowded. Moreover, it directs a viewer's gaze toward the positive space; the phrase "nature abhors a vacuum" applies, as our brains quickly register areas of nothing and something in the visual world. After ascertaining that there is, in fact, nothing to see here, we move on to examine what else we might find.

2–19 *Tod Swank / the Push*, photographer J. Grant Brittain, n.d.

Diagonals lend a feeling of movement and life to compositions. In this example, the skateboarder is leaning directly toward the smallest point of the isosceles triangle formed by the sunlit area, with his shadow leading the way into the deep black negative space at the right. The image has a disturbing metaphoric quality. Is he hurtling into a void of no return? Or is he just a guy skateboarding into a dark shadow on a bright day?

← 2–20 ***Things Organized Neatly*, photographer Austin Radcliffe, 2016.**

Balance is a vitally important component of this portrait, but the play of positive and negative space also performs a starring role in its appeal. Artist Olafur Eliasson stands in front of his work, *Universal Diagram*, forming a strong black vertical down the middle of the image. A series of five concentric rings of glass orbs puts his head at the center of an intricate pattern system formed by the mirrored and matte black surfaces of the orbs. The image's contrast of busy versus still makes for a lively composition.

↗ **2–21 *Politiken*, 2008.**

The columns of gray text on this page offer a perfect opportunity to leave a light bulb–shaped area blank, forming an image out of pure white negative space. The lines of text forming the screw base of the light bulb are a playful touch reinforcing the visual metaphor and the literal appearance of the object.

↗→ **2–22 *Guardian*, 2008.**

Newspapers, with their densely typeset pages, provide designers with opportunity to create images out of negative space. The *Guardian*'s use of a four-column-wide photo that is mostly empty space powerfully reinforces the headline about British politician Tony Blair's defeat, isolating him in a sea of darkness, looking out as if to find an escape.

2

En mageløs rejse i tankens mangfoldighed

Inside the life of a child prodigy

What cocaine says about you

theguardian

After eight years in power Tony Blair hears a new word: Defeat

Labour rebels leave terror plan in shreds and question PM's future

For most authors, positive versus negative space within accompanying imagery will serve as a compositional tool supporting mood or inference rather than a direct correlation to texts. A vast negative space around a politician in a photo, as seen in figure 2–22, suggests different associations that will play out according to the context: Is there a lack of support for Tony Blair (no one came out to hear his speech), or does he have a singular vision, notable enough to stand alone in a crowded field of politicians?

Foreground and Background

Simply put, the foreground of an image refers to the parts that appear to be closest to the viewer, and the background is everything that seems farther away. A flat pattern such as a checkerboard seen straight on has neither foreground nor background since the image lacks relative depth. An image with a deep depth of field (the distance between the nearest and farthest objects that are in sharp focus) still has foreground/background relationships. Objects falling outside the sharp focus occupy the wonderfully named zone known as the circle of confusion; that is, they are no longer acceptably sharp enough to read clearly.

2–23 Photographer J. Grant Brittain, n.d.

The midtone gray background serves as a neutral stage as well as an effective framing device, allowing the focus of attention to center on the skateboarder in the foreground. The skateboarder's body angle and facial expression indicate that a fall is likely to happen in the next split second. Placing him in the foreground puts us right in the predicament with him, allowing a visceral connection between subject and viewer.

The relationship between the foreground and background communicates relative importance through a hierarchy of size and position. An out-of-focus object in the foreground of the image suggests that it is not the main subject, despite its placement and size, and the viewer will concentrate on the background elements instead. This sort of composition can be deliberately jarring, as if the out-of-focus object suddenly popped in and surprised the photographer. Conversely, an out-of-focus background places the visual emphasis on the foreground by fading away into a blur of color and shape rather than permitting specific objects to be seen clearly.

It isn't necessary for authors to take a formal, rigorous approach to visual analyses of the foreground and background when considering images; an awareness of how these compositional factors are at play and what will be suggested when pairing the images with text is sufficient. What's in focus in the image is an easy guideline; no matter where it's located, foreground or background, the eye is drawn to

→ **2–24 Portrait of Xanthe Elbrick, photographer Matthew Sussman, n.d.**

The softly blurred neon sign and arches behind the subject's head supply just enough background to be interesting but not intrusive. Her placement in the foreground establishes that she is the main attraction of the photo while the background location, a city entertainment district, adds contextual hints to her identity as a professional actress.

↘ **2–25 *Goan to the Dogs*, photographer Dougie Wallace, 2020.**

Never have two sweet pups at the beach looked so completely diabolical. Dramatic lighting and a composition placing them inches away from the camera lens allow them to loom large and menacing in the foreground. The small human figure in the background, framed by the dogs' scheming faces, feels insignificant—as if the human race has finally been overthrown and is just trudging back to their crate, defeated. I wouldn't trust the dog at right for a nanosecond.

the sharpest element. To diminish the impact of something, keep it in the background of what you're showing. To highlight it, find an image that brings it forward. Or choose an image with equal weight in the foreground and background to suggest that everything shown is equally significant.

Cropping and Detail

Thanks to smartphone cameras, most of us know how to edit a photo by cropping it to remove extraneous elements around its edges and zero in on the main area of interest. Unnecessary elements in an image are distracting. They dilute the impact by giving a viewer too many things to see that have nothing to do with the image's subject in the first place. For example, a photo that accidentally captures too much of the ceiling will benefit from cropping out enough of it to refocus the eye on the main subject. Photographers of fast-moving action—sports, street life, or journalism—often don't have time to frame a photo perfectly before pressing the shutter. To keep focus on the main action and amplify the photo's overall impact, unwanted elements creeping in from the edges need to be cropped out. Sensitive cropping frequently improves a composition.

Changing an image's orientation from horizontal to vertical or vice versa through cropping can be unwieldy and should not be the first order of business; if you need a horizontal format, it's best to find a horizontal image. A vertical forced to fit into a horizontal space will lose most of its image area since only a tiny sliver will fit in the wider space. A horizontal image trying to become vertical faces the same dilemma.

It's worth noting that fine art images (including photography) should never be cropped except to zero in on a detail, which will be noted in a caption. If an image is particularly complex but your text is discussing a specific item within it, it helps the reader to show both the entire image and then an enlarged detail, as seen in figure 2–27. The artist's larger message about the indifference of humanity to the suffering of others and danger of overarching aspiration is pinpointed through a small detail that's easy to overlook yet has a devastating impact once a viewer sees it. As another example, imagine a cluttered crime scene photo paired with a zoomed-in inset of the critical clue—a dropped earring or faint tire track—that allows the viewer not only to see the entire environment but the small, telling detail within it too.

Even if you have already obtained permission to reproduce an image, also request permission from the copyright owner before

2–26 *Animal Kingdom*, photographer Randal Ford, 2019.

A part can stand in effectively for the whole, allowing a reader to feel clever for solving a visual puzzle. This eye could only belong to an elephant, though a similar shot of its ear, tail, or trunk (of course—and more obvious) would also do the trick. Choose a similarly unambiguous detail when using this image strategy to be sure your message is understood as intended. The elephant's foot could be potentially mistaken for a rhino's or hippo's, and so is a less successful option.

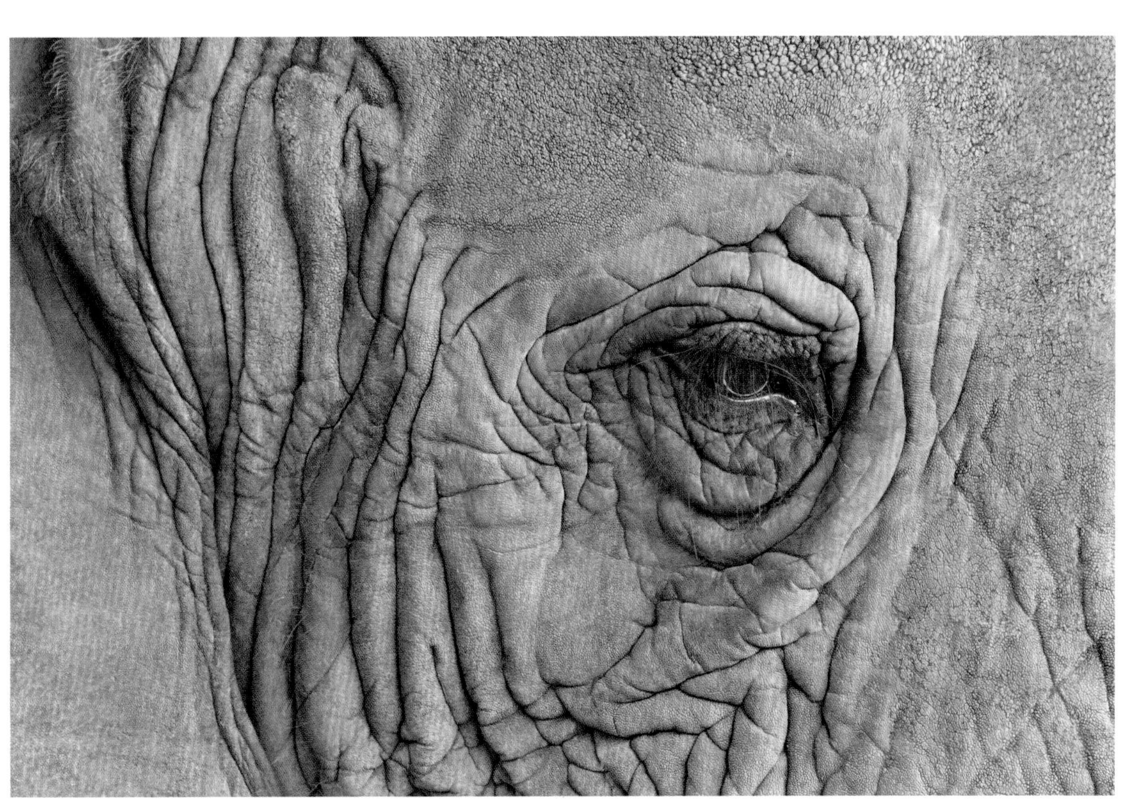

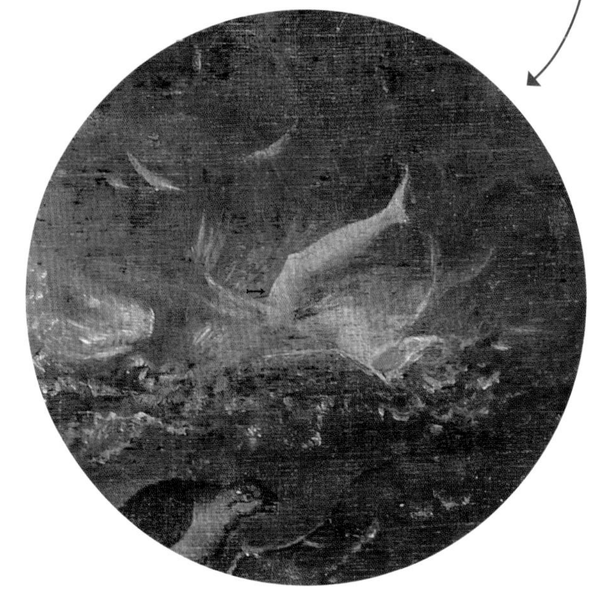

2–27 *Landscape with the Fall of Icarus*, Pieter Bruegel the Elder, 1555.

Oftentimes an author needs to draw attention to a detail within a complicated image. In this painting of seemingly unremarkable everyday life, at first glance it's easy to miss Icarus as he plunges to his watery grave. Showing the detail on its own and omitting the entire painting would not be enough to help a viewer understand the context. A wise strategy displays the image in full, indicates where the detail is found, and then pulls it out and enlarges it for a closer look.

cropping, as it alters the work in a way that the creator has a right to accept or reject. Altering images without permission is copyright infringement and may subject you to legal action.

Under US law, in certain circumstances called fair use, permission is not required to reproduce or alter images. The principles of fair use are: purpose and character of the use, including whether the use is of a commercial nature or for nonprofit educational purposes; nature of the copyrighted work; amount and substantiality of the portion used in relation to the copyrighted work as a whole; and effect of the use on the potential market for or value of the copyrighted work. Be sure you understand copyright law in your jurisdiction before making any changes to images.

Here's a checklist of questions to ask yourself when considering compositional factors during the image selection process:

- Is the tone of my text bold or subtle, emphatic or calm?
- How can I use balance, scale, and positive/negative space to best express this tone visually?
- What is the best hierarchy for my range of images—that is, which is the main, and which are secondary?
- Would a specific detail of a larger image be more useful than the whole thing?

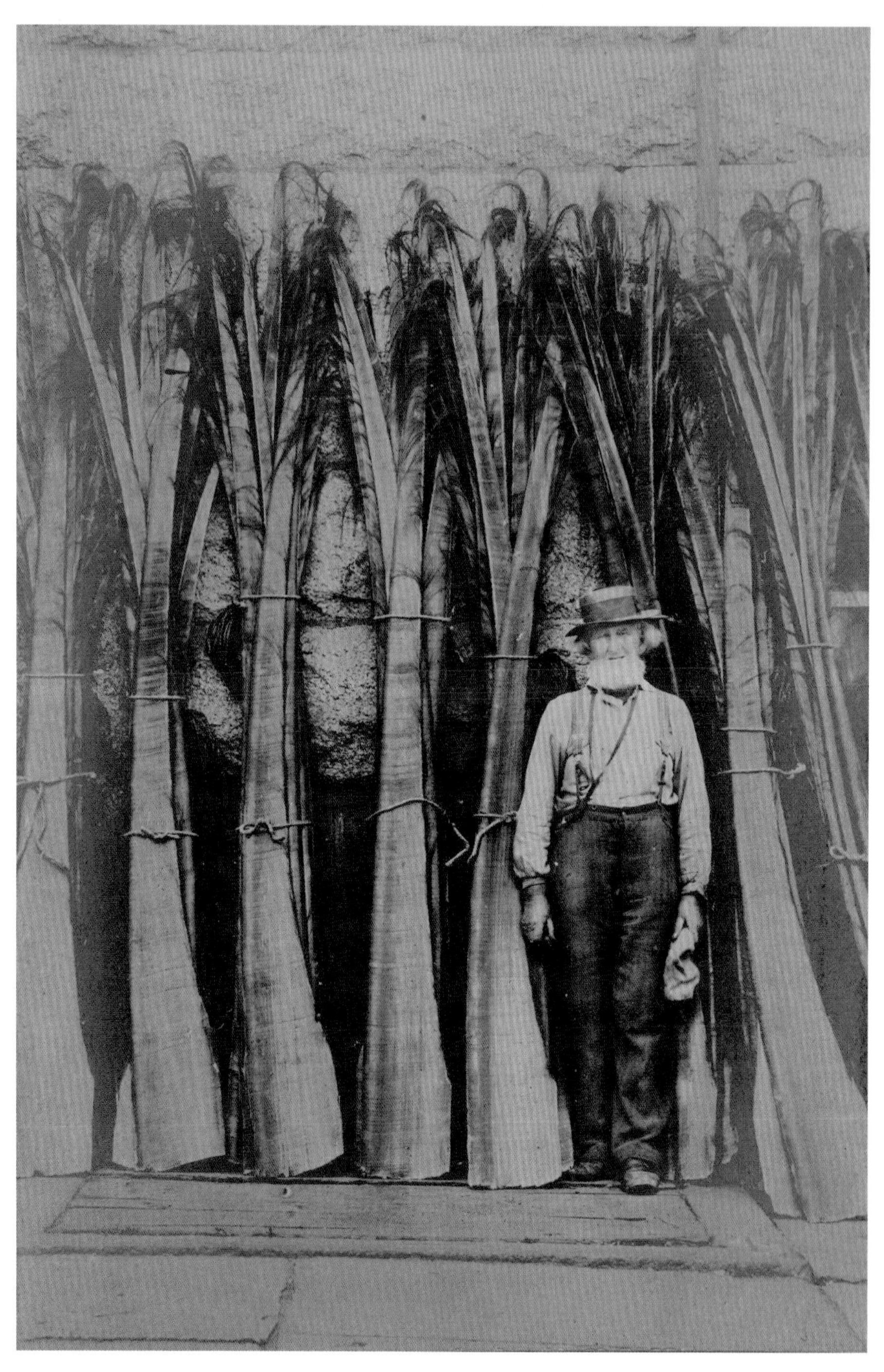

03

Active Surfaces

3–1 Photo album, New Bedford Whaling Community, ca. 1893.

The visual pattern provided by the regular verticals of the feathery whale baleen in the background is only slightly interrupted by the figure of a man—a different sort of vertical—sporting an abundant and feathery beard. There's a delight to this kind of image, where a series of similar things is interrupted by another thing that shares some of the same qualities and also has a key point of divergence: the baleen is quite dead, and the man is very much alive.

While most people would say that their eyes move smoothly over passages of text in a steady, linear flow while reading, this is not the case at all. Studies demonstrate that readers' eyes remain relatively stable at a fixed location and then make a ballistic jump called a saccade to the next viewing location (either forward or backward in the text).

The eye also moves in multiple saccades as it follows the rhythm, sense of movement, repetition and pattern, and point of view found in an image. Images allow a reader's brain to take a break from processing language (which happens in a number of brain regions: the temporal and frontal lobes, and the angular and supramarginal gyrus) and switch to absorbing pictorial information (using the visual cortex) instead.

Activity within visual compositions—the relative busyness or quietude of images—greatly influences the way in which the image is perceived. The image's internal visual rhythm affects the reader's emotional response to the words, subtly but significantly.

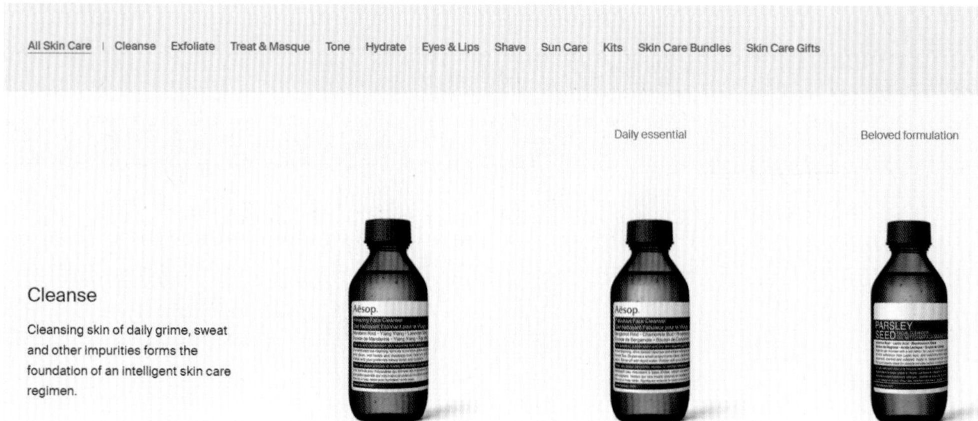

← **3–2 *Queen*, artist Audrey Flack, 1976.**

There's so much to enjoy in this rich composition, apart from formal elements such as the repeated circles used throughout. The sheer variety of objects hard and soft, ephemeral and enduring, makes for an image where the eye lingers to take in all the possibilities. Differences in scale and surface—a large velvet-petaled rose, small glass jars, and a wooden chess queen—add to the overall feeling of abundant variety.

↑ **3–3 Aēsop, 2022.**

Consistency in the appearance of the objects and the color palette produces a calm-feeling website. All the product labels are black, gray, and white, and the background is made up of three shades of neutral. Eliminating variety in color and scale is an effective way to evoke a quiet mood since the viewer's eye is not encouraged to jump around; the stillness of the image elicits a stillness of mind as well.

Regular, linear movement within an image such as a symmetrical pattern, or train tracks leading directly to the horizon, establishes direction and order. The reader subconsciously notes the image structure and, just as subconsciously, relates it to the structure of the text. A calm grid of elements on the splash screen of a website sets the tone for a quiet business—a spa or bookstore—while a splash screen showing a grid of lively animations matches the energy of a sports franchise or concert venue. Lively patterns practically jitter in place while large fields of muted color have a statelier presence.

Movement can be generated by the sight line in a photo; a reader will automatically follow the gaze of a person in the image. In daily life, anyone stopped in the middle of a sidewalk looking skyward will soon be joined by a curious crowd eager to see for themselves what's going on up there. We follow such cues when they occur in images too. When a photo of someone looking off camera to the right is placed on a right-hand page or to the right of a screen, it will direct the reader's gaze off the margin. The same image placed on the left-hand side of the spread steers the reader into the text on the facing page or the center of the screen. A circular composition of the main image elements—such as a group of medical personnel

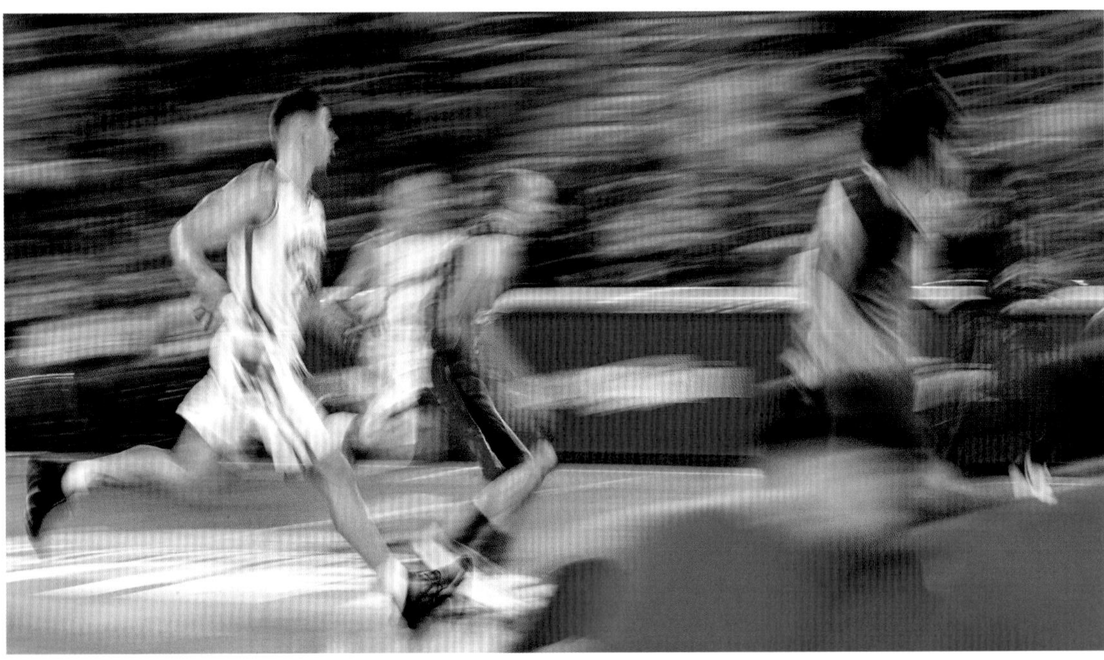

← **3-4 Ascent / PKS Media Inc., n.d.**

Golf is an almost-meditative activity that encourages appreciation of its beautifully landscaped surroundings. It's also not a team sport: the focus is on individual performance, not group effort. This image captures all of those key qualities.

↙ **3-5 Photographer Simonkr, n.d.**

Basketball is, visually speaking, the opposite of golf. The contrast of this photo with fig. 3-4 highlights all the differences between the two sports without needing further explanation. In fact, this caption is almost unnecessary.

bending over an operating table, with all of their attention fixed on their patient—encourages the eye to circumnavigate the picture without making an exit.

Authors should keep their text's degree of activity in mind as they search for images. For instance, within the larger topic of sports, differences in the speed of the games can factor into intelligent image choices. Golf, a hushed and sedate undertaking played on outdoor courses during daylight hours, moves slowly and quietly. Pro basketball, a fast-and-furious endeavor, takes place in brightly lit indoor gyms echoing with the shouts of the players, the sound of their footfalls, the bouncing and rebounding ball thwacking off the backboards, and the raucous cheers of fans. For a text comparing the two sports (though I can't imagine a reason for such a text to exist), it would make sense to shoot the golf images along the lines of majestic peaceful landscapes and the basketball pictures as busy compositions, possibly making use of motion blur, to highlight the innate contrast between the activities. Seen in tandem, as in figures 3-4 and 3-5, the images deliver all a viewer needs to understand the essential nature of both sports.

Rhythm

In a composition, rhythm generates a visual tempo that leads the viewer's eye around the image. It can be created by patterns, relationships between shape and color, and through the repetition of visual elements. Just as in music, visual rhythms have a lively menu of possible variations; they can be regular and repetitive, irregular and random, or geometric or organic. They can build and change in a progression or repeat regularly and infinitely; think of a jazz drummer's spontaneous improvisations versus the identical beats of a digital drum track. Alternating squares on a chessboard have a prescribed, potentially endless rhythm, while a printed wallpaper of vines and flowers may follow a natural rhythm based on the sprawl of real plants in real gardens, or a mannered rhythm composed of repetitive patterns and shapes.

Visual rhythm falls into three main categories:

- Regular: repeated elements in an evenly spaced arrangement
- Flowing: repeating organic shapes or irregular repetition of repeating elements
- Progressive: a repeating sequence wherein the elements change each time they are repeated

A regular rhythm can involve changes to its elements, if the change is the same each time. For instance, a stack of two blocks, then another stack of four blocks, and then another with six still represents a regular rhythm. The progression is orderly and predictable.

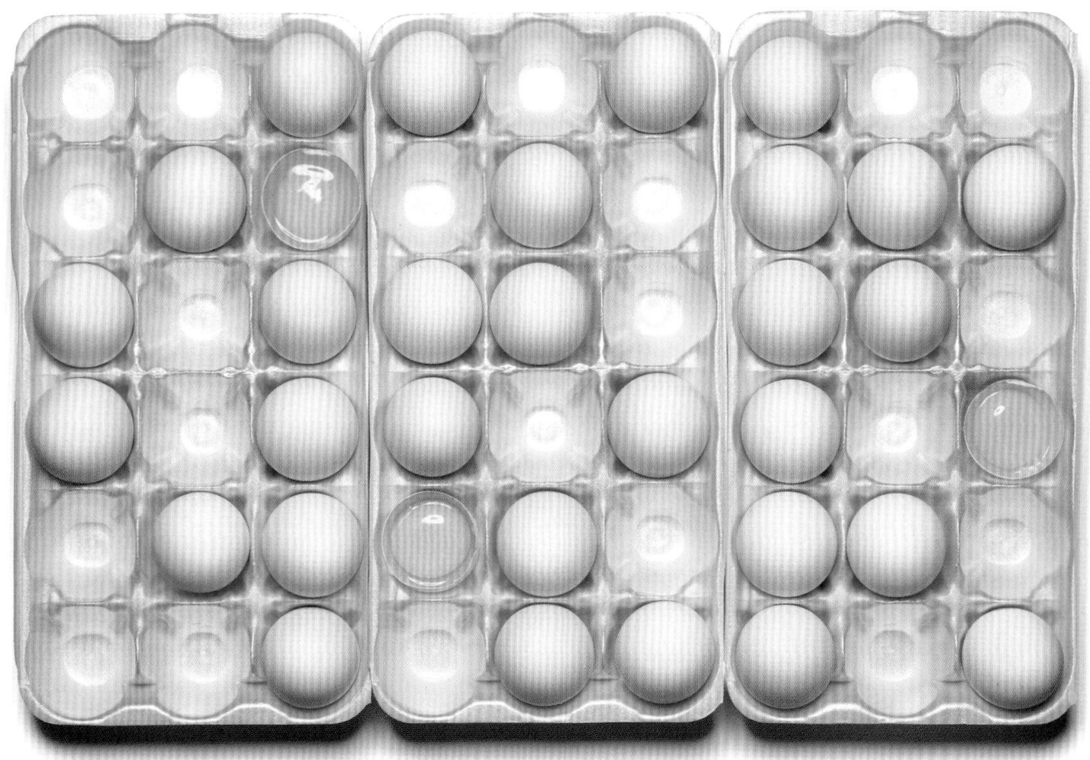

←← 3-6 Marimekko, designer Maija Isola, 1964.

Two separate kinds of patterning make up this large-scale asymmetrical design. The bold red and red-pink flowers read as alternating horizontal bands of bright color, while the black centers form a more randomized, staccato pattern. The overall effect is loose, spontaneous, and joyful without a hint of regimentation.

← 3-7 Photographer Levi Brown, n.d.

Humble dish sponges, with their two-sided textures, make up three separate pattern systems within a unified larger pattern. Take your pick: Do you prefer vertical stripes of alternating colors, or diagonal stripes of matched blue or green sides, or a mortar-like grid of deliciously wavy white negative space? All are there for your viewing pleasure.

↑ 3-8 Client, photographer Levi Brown, n.d.

What is more gridded and regular (and visually bland) than a carton of eggs? By removing some eggs to leave empty space and filling just three spaces with bright yellow yolks, the photographer banished monotony from this shot. The pops of bright color function like Morse code, quickly directing the eye in a few pulses around the image in a staccato rhythm.

PANTONE® White	PANTONE® White	PANTONE® White	PANTONE® White	PANTONE® White	PANTONE® White	PANTONE® White	PANTONE® White	PANTONE® White
PANTONE® White	PANTONE® White	PANTONE® White	PANTONE® White	PANTONE® White	PANTONE® White	PANTONE® White	PANTONE® White	PANTONE® White
PANTONE® White	PANTONE® White	PANTONE® White	PANTONE® White	PANTONE® White	PANTONE® White	PANTONE® White	PANTONE® White	PANTONE® White
PANTONE® White	PANTONE® White	PANTONE® White	PANTONE® White	PANTONE® White	PANTONE® White	PANTONE® White	PANTONE® White	PANTONE® White
PANTONE® White	PANTONE® White	PANTONE® White	PANTONE® White	PANTONE® White	PANTONE® White	PANTONE® White	PANTONE® White	PANTONE® White
PANTONE® White	PANTONE® White	PANTONE® White	PANTONE® White	PANTONE® White	PANTONE® White	PANTONE® White	PANTONE® White	PANTONE® White
PANTONE® White	PANTONE® White	PANTONE® White	PANTONE® White	PANTONE® White	PANTONE® White	PANTONE® White	PANTONE® White	PANTONE® White
PANTONE® White	PANTONE® White	PANTONE® White	PANTONE® White	PANTONE® White	PANTONE® White	ADVERTISING is 1% Black	PANTONE® White	PANTONE® White
PANTONE® White	PANTONE® White	PANTONE® White	PANTONE® White	PANTONE® White	PANTONE® White	PANTONE® White	PANTONE® White	PANTONE® White
PANTONE® White	PANTONE® White	PANTONE® White	PANTONE® White	PANTONE® White	PANTONE® White	PANTONE® White	PANTONE® White	PANTONE® White

TO FIND OUT HOW TO MAKE YOUR AGENCY MORE DIVERSE, CALL 318-449-1720. **SPECTRUM SPEAKERS PROGRAM**

← 3-9 *Advertising Is 1% Black*, designer Phil Mimaki, 2016.

The designer set up a meticulous grid of identical white color chips and swapped in a single black swatch to communicate a dismal fact: at the time, only 1 percent of advertising professionals were Black. While the pattern itself is unbroken, the black swatch, although part of the larger system, stands out as a lone entity—outnumbered and without others like it.

→ 3-10 *The Biology of Dragonflies*, 1917.

The horizontal dragonfly wings supply a visual counterpoint to their slender abdomens, creating a rhythm that leads the eye effortlessly through the image. The difference in size of the various species allowed the designer to fit them neatly into a rectangular composition, with its edges defined by the insects' linear bodies. Their delicate legs breaking out of the rectangle serve as a reminder that they are made of organic matter, not Euclidean geometry.

→ 3-11 *Het Parool*, 2008.

A design system that follows a regular grid offers the option of great variety within the structure and order. Every image here is a square, from the main one to the small thumbnails at left; even the landscape-format photos form square units with the type beneath them. The layout feels lively because of the changes in size, scale, and point of view of the photos.

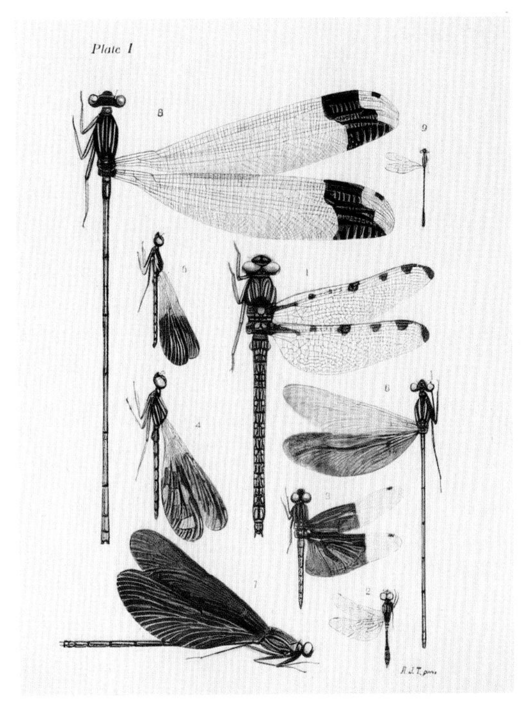

ZONDAG
15 MEI

Vrij, Onverveerd

Het Parool

Voorpagina | AMSTERDAM | Nederland | Wereld | Kunst & Media | Sport | Columns & Opinie

Nieuws

Vredesactivist Mient Jan Faber (81) overleden

Basketbalclub Apollo Amsterdam verliest licentie door problemen met financiering

Eredivisieseizoen ten einde: Willem II degradeert, Haller topscorer

Jason Bhugwandass verkozen tot Amsterdammer van het jaar 2021

Goals Openda voorkomen winst Ajax in seizoensafsluiter

Live | Finland en Zweden willen toetreden tot Navo

D66: rectificatie en schadevergoeding in MeToo-zaak

Examenleerlingen zijn ondanks zomers weer aan het blokken

Opinie

'Herdenkingsrituelen zijn nodig om corona te verwerken'

HAN LIPS
KIJKT TV

Het Songfestival hoeft geen kleinkunst te zijn, volgend jaar Snollebollekes?

Van Grinsven-Admiraal veegde de vloer aan met de columnist

3-12 ***New York Times*****, photographer Ramsay de Give, 2021.**

Shot from a low angle behind the participants, this image captures each person at a different joyful moment. The even spacing of the figures across the photo lends a sense of regular rhythm while their arms, in different positions relative to their bodies (outstretched, rising, fully raised, or relaxed) convey the energy and exuberance of a lively dance.

A flowing rhythm is often seen in the natural world, such as the placement of leaves on a vine or spots on a leopard. Flowing rhythms imply an organic sense of movement and growth. In a progressive rhythm, each element appears once and then changes slightly for each subsequent instance. Progression can be orderly but not necessarily predictable.

Progressive rhythms are also found in nature; the Fibonacci sequence mentioned earlier is one example.

A static image has no rhythm; it communicates stillness by minimizing the viewer's eye movements. In figure 3-13, the eye settles on the lone figure at the beach and does not move around. Add other people, as in figure 3-14, and the image gains a visual rhythm. The viewer's gaze will rove around the image to connect the dots, perceiving the relative distances and relationships between the positions of the subjects as a rhythmic pattern.

→ 3–13 Photographer Eye/Em, 2017.

All of a viewer's focus is drawn to the lone static figure in this composition. The eye settles upon him and remains there, searching for more information.

↓ 3–14 Photographer Robin Knight, n.d.

This image's composition is as dynamic as a rocket launch sequence. The eye travels from left to right, from seated to crouching to leaping figure, and keeps going toward the empty space at the right where the jumper will regain contact with planet Earth.

3–15 Photographer Matthew Sussman, n.d.

Patterns are most interesting if there's a single spot where the pattern breaks. The aerial view of a pool, with its regularly spaced tiles and neat pairs of lounges, would be far less compelling without the couple at left providing a sudden interruption of the visual rhythm. The people appear all the more organic and alive in comparison to the other elements in this geometric, gridded composition.

For authors, rhythm in images can serve as a tool to match—or contrast—the energy level and tone of the text as well as carry along the narrative progression. A regular rhythm feels calming; the orderly row of lounge chairs and grids of tiles in figure 3–15 convey a sense of peaceful relaxation.

Rhythms can show narrative progression over time, like a time-lapse animation when set up over several images, as seen in figures 3–17 to 3–20. The visual progression of raw ingredients to finished pasta allows a reader to understand the recipe preparation from start to finish.

Another related strategy creates rhythm through the number and placement of images in a document rather than the rhythm within the images themselves. For example, in an essay about

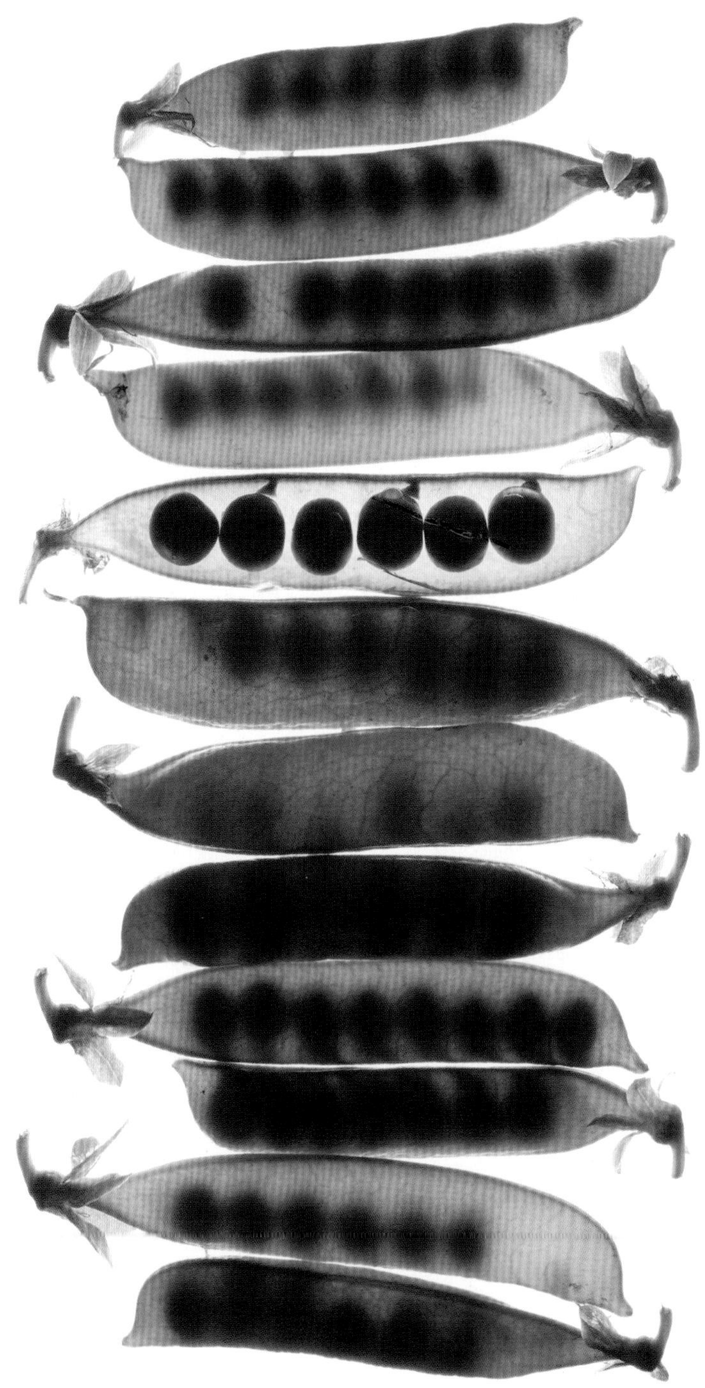

3–16 Photographer Levi Brown, n.d.

The different numbers and sizes of peas lend visual variety to a series of organic forms; each pod feels like a distinct individual thanks to careful lighting highlighting the varying degrees of opacity. The contrast of sharp-edged peas in the partly opened pod fifth from the top and the soft, blurry shapes of the peas still tucked inside whole pods adds a second sort of variety to this image.

3-17, 3-18, 3-19, and 3-20 Photographer Alexandra Rowley, 2010.

A sequence of images can demonstrate specifics in addition to communicating intangible things. The adult and child's hands working together speak of tender relationships, time spent sharing an instructional activity, and the joys of a delicious meal to come. Note how the child is mixing the dough on their own (easy), the adult helps with rolling it through the pasta machine (medium difficulty) and the adult alone handles the sharp knife (grownups only) in the final step. A feeling of caring love comes across in these seemingly straightforward step-by-step images, adding human interest and boosting the overall narrative value of the sequence.

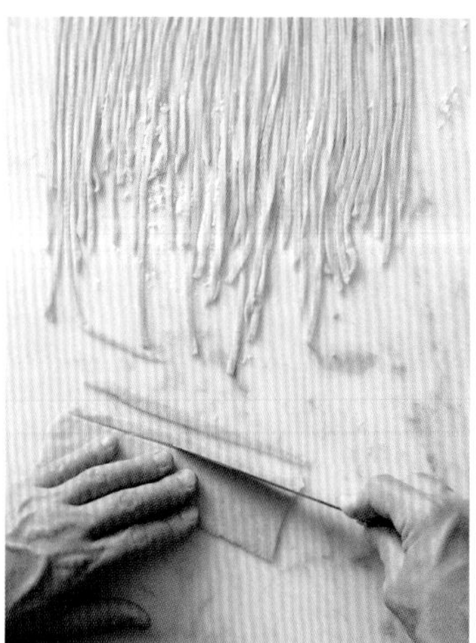

gardening, a photo of a seed packet could appear near the bottom of the first page, followed on a subsequent spread by a seedling growing to about half the page height, ending with a blooming flower at full-page height. The regularly repeated yet related images mimic the growth process of the flower, adding visual relevance not by repeating the text but instead by illustrating an answer to an implied question—"*What happens if I plant this seed?*"—in a rhythm of sequential images.

3–21 ***Through the Looking-Glass and What Alice Found There,*** **by Lewis Carroll, illustrator John Tenniel, 1871.**

The main sense of movement in this drawing comes from Alice's flying hair and dress streaming behind her, and two sets of feet, hers and the Red Queen's, fluttering above the ground. Even in the nineteenth century, the visual language of illustrations and cartoons used horizontal lines in an image as signifiers of rapid motion. Here, those lines are deployed subtly but effectively in the background—adding to the breakneck feeling of this drawing and freezing the action in midair, much as a photograph would.

Movement

Behavioral and neuropsychological evidence suggests that viewing a photograph depicting motion activates the same neurons involved in the brain's perception of actual motion. Studies demonstrate a close correlation between imagined and actual movements, and neuroimaging scans show activation of the seven different overlapping brain regions engaged in the physical execution of movement.

More simply put, a picture of something in motion stimulates the cerebral cortex in the same way that the body in motion does, even though cognitively we know that (nonanimated) images on a page or screen cannot be moving. Images showing motion can be extremely evocative for the reader, recalling not only the sight of a dog racing through tall grass in the early morning, for example, but also the sound of the grass rustling and dog panting, and perhaps

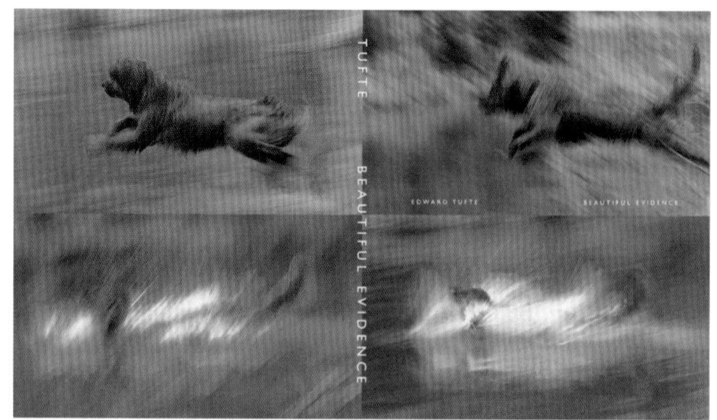

→ 3–22 ***Beautiful Evidence*, designer Edward Tufte, 2006.**

Here, motion blur created by using a slow camera shutter speed conveys so much information to a viewer: this is a happy dog, charging full-out toward the water and plunging in with apparent delight. Instead of freezing each moment in time using a high shutter speed, the blurred sequence of photos creates a cinematic feeling of spontaneity and exuberance. This dog is far too busy to stop and pose for a portrait.

↘ 3–23 ***Health*, photographer AB+DM Studio, 2021.**

High shutter speeds allow the camera to freeze motion in a way the human eye cannot, making images like this so joyful. Stopping the trajectory of gymnast Simone Biles in midair allows a viewer to fully appreciate the perfection of form and movement, energy and life, captured midleap. Paradoxically, a fully static image such as this suggests vigorous activity because our minds fill in the unseen parts of the sequence of launch, mid-air, and landing that we know are part of her jump.

→ 3–24 ***Densmore Shute Bending the Shaft*, photographer Harold Edgerton, 1938.**

When an action is happening too quickly for the human eye to register the individual stages in a sequence, multiple exposure images taken a few split seconds apart document the movement and make it visible as a sequential narrative. Such images lend a feeling of analysis and precision because the viewer doesn't have to imagine what came before or after any particular frame.

↘ 3–25 ***The Horse in Motion*, photographer Eadweard Muybridge, 1878.**

Muybridge's pioneering work captured each stage of motion for subjects such as racehorses galloping, women carrying buckets up and down stairs, men boxing, baboons strolling about, and hundreds more. The presentation shows the passage of time as well as the sequence of motion, paving the way for moving pictures and echoing the layout of comic strip panels—a familiar visual device that also divides up a narrative into small blocks of time.

3-26 *Ballet Folklorico*, photographer Michael Fletcher, 2007.

Motion blur shows that the dancer is spinning in a circular movement. Notice how the ghost of the foot near the floor conveys the full energy of a kick in comparison to its horizontal final position, while her other foot is planted solidly on the ground—the only stationary part of the image other than her head. Like a spinning top, her center axis remains still while the periphery rotates, which is crucial to maintaining balance and preventing dizziness while spinning.

even the feel of dewdrops flying through the air and striking the viewer's skin as the dog bounds past.

Photography has provided a way to "see" motion too fast for the human eye to register, or imply speed by showing a moving object as a blur, ever since the birth of the medium in the mid-nineteenth century. A photo of a moving subject shot at a high shutter speed captures the action in an artificial, almost scientific manner, suspending animation and freezing the motion in place. In 1877, photographer Eadweard Muybridge used multiple cameras to pinpoint the hooves of Sallie Gardner, California governor Leland Stanford's racehorse, at full gallop. Muybridge's innovative technique proved that a running horse does at one point have all four feet off the ground and is said to have decisively settled a barroom bet.

The photographer's groundbreaking work also paved the way for moving pictures. Each image represents a moment in the order in which it occurred, and each is static in the sense that it happened in a singular moment before things changed. Taken together, the flow of moments is a visual record of what we experience as the passage of time.

A longer blurred exposure shot with a slower shutter speed yields an image with a sense of motion as an ongoing phenomenon of both time and space, akin to how the eye (and our bodies) perceive motion in real life. Motion blur shows time as an ongoing linear phenomenon, with each distinct moment blending into the next. It's also a close representation of what happens to a person's vision during altered or dreaming states of mind and so can be implemented by authors as an expressive technique.

Authors can put images showing movement to good use by sequencing them throughout the text at different stages of the activity, almost like a film. Combining both stop-action and blurred motion shapes an active narrative with a static beginning, energetic middle, and static end. Stop action is useful for pinpointing the stages of complex movement in dance or sports but carries little tone or emotion; motion blur organically supports a wider variety of narratives.

3-27 *Let It Bleed*, designer Robert Brownjohn, 1969.

This iconic album cover for the Rolling Stones uses both sides of a record sleeve to relay a short narrative, with a repeated image altered in a two-step move from perfect order to chaos and destruction. On the front, we see a point in time before the party at the recording studio began, and the other side captures its messy aftermath.

Repetition

Like rhythm, repetition creates a sense of movement within an image. Repetition is the recurrence of a visual element (lines, patterns, shapes, or elephants) in either a single image or across a series of images. Repetition can be even or uneven, regular or irregular. It can radiate out from a single point (the petals framing the round yellow center of a daisy), or show a progression, graduation of scale, or shift in hierarchy as elements become smaller or larger, closer or farther apart, lighter or darker in tone.

The "rule of odds" holds that an image is more compelling if it features an odd number of subjects (three people in the image rather than four) based on the proposition that even numbers lack an obvious focal point to draw the viewer's attention while odd numbers feel more natural and expected. When a frame includes an even number of subjects, the brain automatically groups what it sees into pairs, which makes a composition look a bit dull. The rule of odds creates a focal point because the eye tends to wander to the middle of a group that is easily located in a set of three: the central object is seen as the main one, and the other two take on supporting roles.

3-28 Photographer J. Grant Brittain, n.d.

Similarly shaped elements appearing at different sizes in an image set up a measured rhythm of the space. Shooting this photo through the pipe in the foreground frames and emphasizes the subject skateboarding through the second pipe. It also allows a beautiful play of light and shadow, with the bright curve of the second pipe reinforcing the circular theme of the composition.

→ 3-29 *Arizona* 2, photographer Cássio Vasconcellos, 2011.

Repetition can lend a feeling of chaos, as in this overcrowded and static image. Smaller aircraft shoehorned into the spaces around the largest ones appear trapped and surrounded; while the image is lovely if viewed as a rhythmic, asymmetrical pattern, it also feels claustrophobic and anxiety producing. These grounded planes are not going anywhere soon.

→→ 3-30 *Biologia Centrali-Americana*, 1889.

With apologies to arachnophobes, this image displays a wide assortment of spiders within a repetitive visual arrangement. It immediately communicates quite a bit of information: the creatures come in many sizes and shapes; they hold their legs at different angles relative to their bodies; and they can be hairy or smooth. Here, a dozen specimens demonstrate this at a glance.

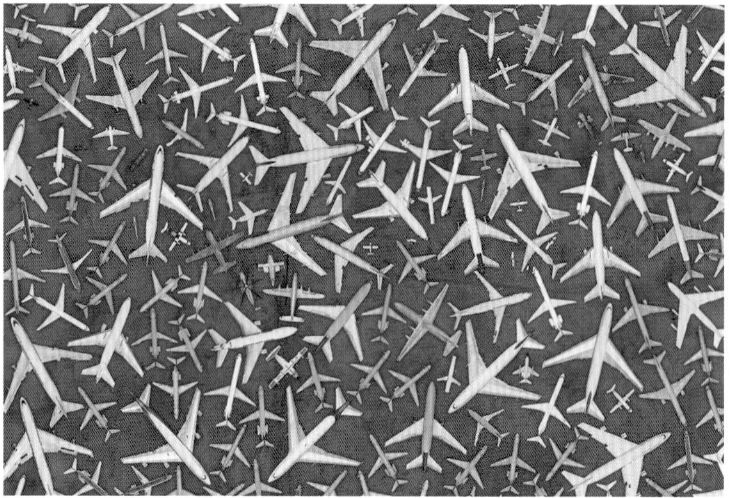

Authors can use repetitive images to show sameness or variety; imagine a photo of sixty red roses or the same photo showing every shade of rose available. Artist Andy Warhol's multiple screen prints of Jackie Kennedy and Marilyn Monroe varied the colors in each, presenting the viewer's eye with the opportunity to rove around the canvases.

For a series of publications or presentations over time, sticking with the same subject matter within the imagery and letting it evolve organically can become a sort of visual signature for an author. Claude Monet's waterlilies and haystacks were the constant subjects of several paintings but always appeared different depending on the time of day and the light that fell on them; their repetitiveness didn't become predictable or tiresome. A speaker who relays information over and over using the same words is a crashing bore; a speaker who reiterates points for emphasis and uses different examples each time will hold an audience's attention as well as impart a message effectively.

A single repeated visual device, used in conjunction with disparate images, will tie them together. For instance, keeping a selection of different images the same size and placing an identical frame around each leads a reader to view them as a connected set rather than isolated objects.

Biol. Centr. Am. Arachnida Araneidea Tab. 11.

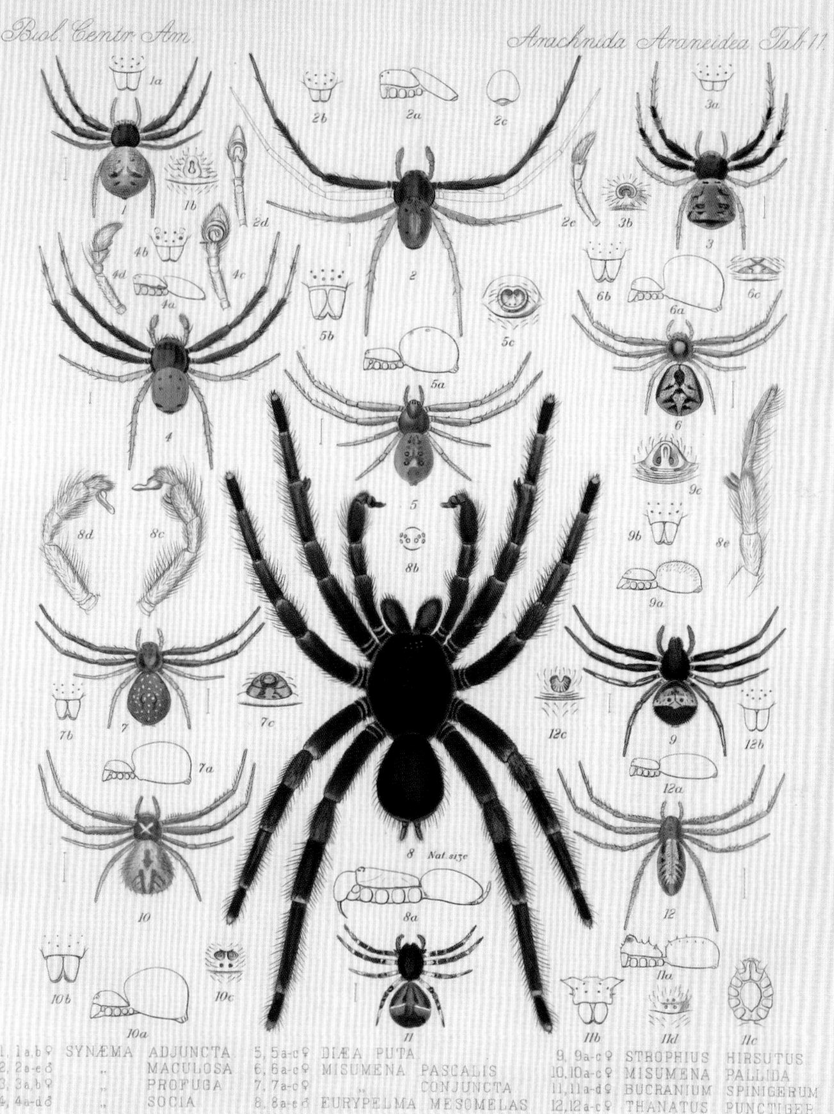

1, 1a,b ♀ SYNÆMA ADJUNCTA
2, 2a-e ♂ „ MACULOSA
3, 3a,b ♀ „ PROFUGA
4, 4a-d ♂ „ SOCIA
5, 5a-c ♀ DIÆA PUTA
6, 6a-c ♀ MISUMENA PASCALIS
7, 7a-c ♀ „ CONJUNCTA
8, 8a-e ♂ EURYPELMA MESOMELAS
9, 9a-c ♀ STROPHIUS HIRSUTUS
10, 10a-c ♀ MISUMENA PALLIDA
11, 11a-d ♀ BUCRANIUM SPINIGERUM
12, 12a-c ♀ THANATUS PUNCTIGER

A.T. Hollick del. Cambridge Engraving Company

ANTI

Point of View

An image's point of view bears tremendous effect on its impact, often adding the element of surprise to its narrative content. Sometimes a direct text benefits from a little whimsy in the accompanying images, and unexpected points of view will serve the purpose nicely. A photo of a cornfield taken from ground level is nothing like an aerial shot of the same acreage.

Point of view can be evocative of emotion, time, and place, and can show the familiar in an unexpected way: making something shot in close-up from below seem huge and monumental even if it's just a pebble on a beach; minimizing a herd of elephants seen from above; or capturing an Olympic ski jumper's view of the world in midair. Photos taken by young children that show people and surroundings from a kid's vantage point—close to the ground, always

↙ 3–31 Vans, photographer Anthony Acosta, 2010.

The bird's-eye view emphasizes the time-stopping moment when the figure hovers at the top of the ramp just before the plunge down. A worm's-eye view, looking from the bottom up, would convey nearly the same emotion, but because the skateboarder's face would be visible, it would allow a more personal connection to them. It would also feel dangerous, as in, I'm here at the bottom of this bowl and I'm about to get run over by that person up there.

↘ 3–32 Photographer Adam Hillman, 2017.

Zooming in close to focus on small objects lends them a monumentality and gravity they don't often possess in real life. Crayons, trivial playthings for children, seem important in this image. Blocks of city buildings, military medals, and even pointed weaponry come to mind. The crayon can be as mighty as the sword.

looking up—remind adults of what it looked and felt like to be small in a big world—a part of life all adults have experienced but few think about directly.

A text about gun violence in cities feels markedly more personal if the images' point of view is looking directly at a gun pointed at the camera. The danger seems real and present, not statistical and abstract. A horse is a hairy mane and two ears framing a landscape from the rider's perspective—a more intimate world than the familiar sight of a horse and rider racing across the distant horizon in a Western movie.

The end scenes of the final episode of the HBO TV series *The Sopranos* are shot from main character Tony Soprano's point of view as he sits in a diner, to devastating effect (a great illustration of the element of surprise for the viewer). At each point in the scene, the viewer sees what Tony sees except for moments when the camera cuts away to show the door of the diner as people enter and leave.

3-33 *Moving Cattle by Horseback*, photographer v.Horn, n.d.

Here the point of view puts a viewer in the saddle, rather than on the sidelines as an observer.

3–34 *Collectives*, photographer Cássio Vasconcellos, 2008–19.

Conversely, shooting large things such as landscapes from an aerial point of view strips them of their immersive quality, reducing them to color, pattern, and rhythm, and making them appear small. In this image, an observer might see fabric at first glance or a tiled mosaic rather than square miles of meadow intercut with roads seeming as insignificant as threads.

Images with unexpected vantage points add a lively tone throughout a text. A cornfield, shot from a plane, loses its individuality and becomes a fractional part of the checkerboard pattern of the landscape; if the photographer lies on the ground and points the camera upward, the corn becomes a dense frame of majestic stalks against the sky. Which type of image suits your narrative best? Decide whether you prefer a straightforward approach or a little more drama, and keep the visual point of view in mind during image searches.

Ask yourself these questions regarding the level of activity in images:

- Would lively images or quieter ones complement my text best?
- Is there a structural parallel between the text and visual?
- Would an unexpected point of view or unusual vantage point benefit my text content?

04

Color

4–1 Neon Rose #2, Victor Moscoso, 1967.

Chromostereopsis is a visual illusion of vibration caused when certain color combinations, particularly red-blue or red-green, are placed next to each other. Thanks to this effect, the waves surrounding the central figure appear to pulsate with energy—perfect for a gig poster during the psychedelic 1960s.

The use of color in design is a mix of art, science, and emotion. Color is not a physical entity but rather a sensation caused by light of varied wavelengths registered by the optic nerves and processed in the brain of the viewer. As every cell in a human body reacts to light, color affects us physically as well as mentally and emotionally.

According to the Institute for Color Research, humans make an unconscious judgment about an environment, person, or item within ninety seconds of initial viewing, and between 62 and 90 percent of that assessment is due to color alone. In fact, color is one of the most important cues that we use to recognize objects. Author Oliver Sacks described this case of a painter, called Jonathan I., who developed a rare condition called achromatopsia after an auto accident. Unlike types of color blindness where people can see most colors (except red/green, for example), his world looked like watching a black-and-white movie.

> Mr. I. could hardly bear the changed appearances of people ("like animated gray statues") any more than he could bear his own changed appearance in the mirror: he shunned social intercourse and found sexual intercourse impossible. He saw people's flesh, his wife's flesh, his own flesh, as an abhorrent gray; "flesh-colored" now appeared "rat-colored" to him. This was so even when he closed his eyes, for his preternaturally vivid ("eidetic") visual imagery was preserved but now without color, and forced on him images, forced him to "see" but see internally with the wrongness of his achromatopsia. He found foods disgusting in their grayish, dead appearance and had to close his eyes to eat. But this did not help very much, for the mental image of a tomato was as black as its appearance. . . . The "wrongness" of everything was disturbing, even disgusting, and applied to every circumstance of daily life. Thus, unable to rectify even the inner image, the idea, of various foods, he turned increasingly to black and white foods—to black olives and white rice, black coffee, and yogurt. These at least appeared relatively normal, whereas most foods, normally colored, now appeared horribly abnormal.

Many companies have made a color their own as a signature; think of UPS's rich brown trucks and uniforms, McDonald's golden arches, or Coca-Cola's bright red packaging. Color can become a shorthand for "organic" in food packaging—almost always shades of green and tan—or "chic" in high-end cosmetic packaging—often stark black or white, as opposed to the colorful packaging of drugstore makeup that communicates a more accessible, playful message and lower price point too.

In an era of widespread globalization, it's critical to know how the language of color works for a given audience. World cultures have differing associations with specific colors. For instance, white is the color of mourning in some Asian cultures, particularly in China and Korea, while in the West, white symbolizes purity and is a traditional choice for wedding gowns.

Color can be used to indicate a specific period by using tones derived from pigments available during a particular era. During the

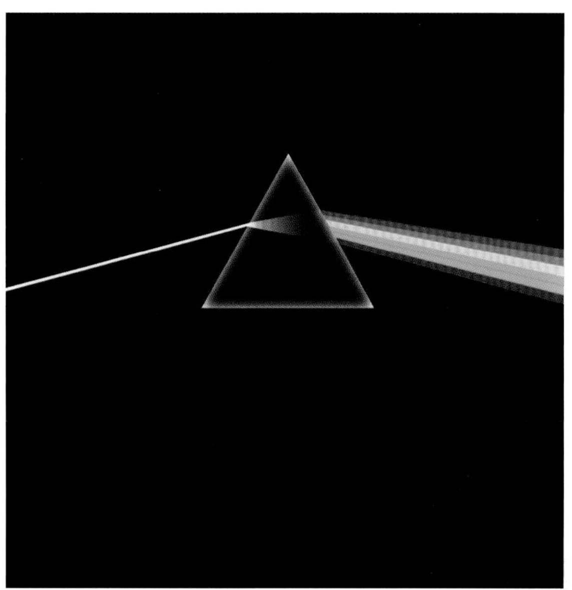

4–2 Pink Floyd Music Ltd., designers Hipgnosis, 1973.

This illustration of the invisible (and almost unbelievable) truth that white light is made up of pure, gorgeous color can also be interpreted symbolically as the transformation of the ordinary into brilliance, among other readings. Human eyes can't see colors beyond either end of the spectrum (ultraviolet and infrared), but bees, birds, and other animals can, relying on the additional visual information to find food and mates.

first half of the nineteenth century, early Victorian houses were painted in three-color palettes of rust, fawn, maroon, black, and brown derived from natural pigments. By 1870, paint was mass-produced, sold in resealable cans, and available in a wider range of colors thanks to new synthetic pigments. Rose, peach, terra-cotta, and olive as well as deeper, more saturated colors such as dark green and deep red in three-, four-, or even five-color combinations became common choices for exteriors. The 1950s in the United States were perky hits of seafoam green, pale pink, and lemon yellow; the 1970s were a feast of avocado, rust, and harvest gold; and the 1980s were a blur of magenta clashing with black and turquoise, with some punk rock plaid thrown in for good measure.

Fortunately, it isn't necessary to know all the voluminous information on color to use it wisely. By understanding basic color-related properties and terms, a user can make well-informed image choices that use color's power to evoke emotional reactions, mental associations, cultural references, and specific times and places. As legendary *Vogue* editor Diana Vreeland said, "Pink is the navy blue of India." What is considered festive or frivolous in some cultures is business forward to others.

This chapter covers these key principles:

- Basic color theory: primary/secondary/tertiary/complementary
- Perceptual phenomena
- Emotional response
- Symbolism of color across cultures
- Color use by decade

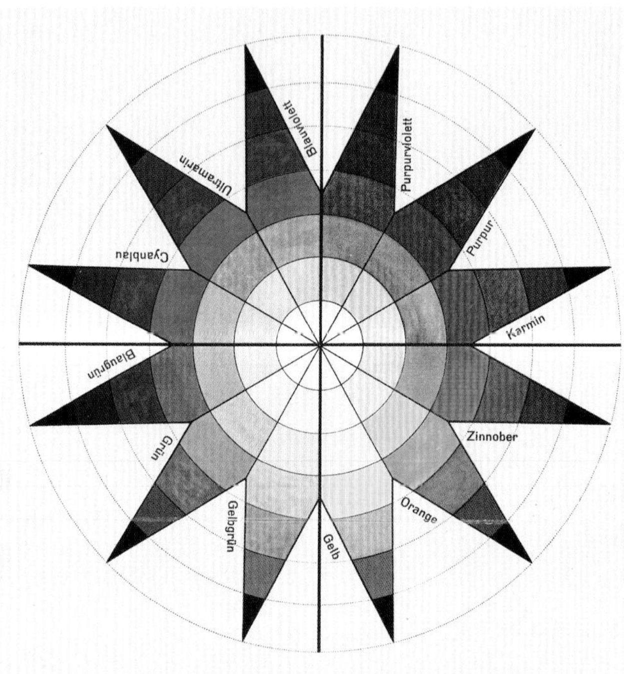

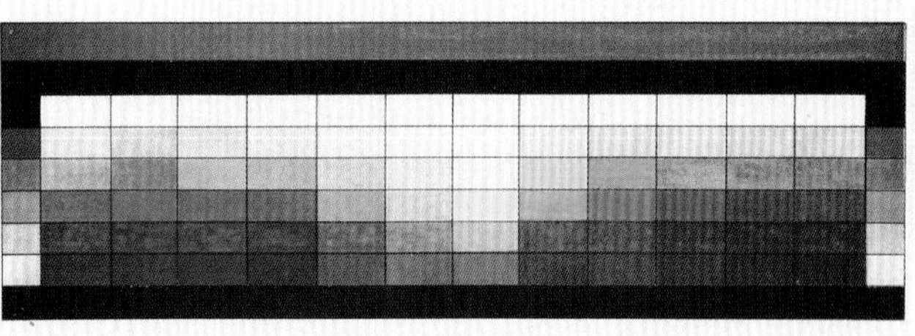

4–3 Johannes Itten, 1921.

Contrast this precise color star with Paul Klee's homemade version (figure 4–4). It feels "correct," but lacks emotion or individuality; it seems almost anonymous. Sometimes heart is not necessary. For pure information, this sort of image does the trick. It feels trustworthy; the drawing's mechanical exactitude lends an air of authority. It is, in fact, authoritative. Itten was one of the masters of Bauhaus color theory.

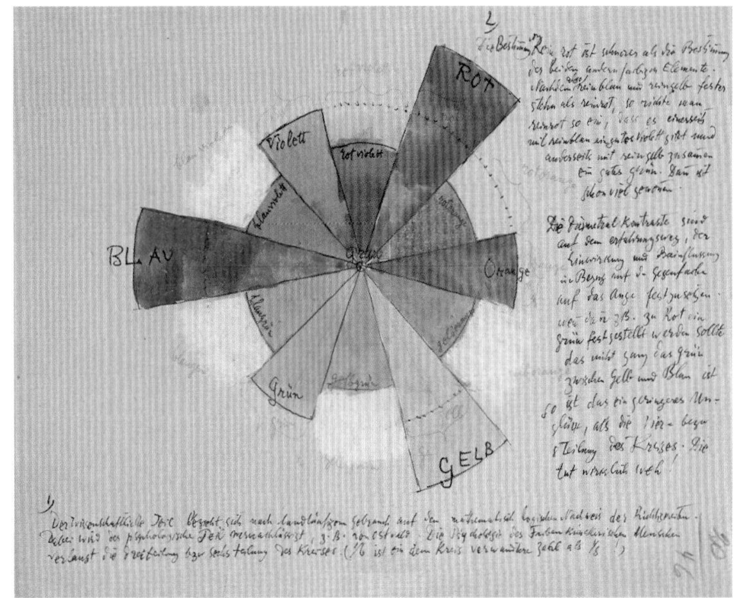

4-4 *Notebooks*, Paul Klee, 1921–31.

Klee, a consummate colorist, documented ten years of Bauhaus lectures in his detailed notebooks. His hand-painted rendering of the color wheel—the basic visual device showing the relationships of primary, secondary, and complementary colors—accompanied by his handwritten notes is far more charming than a basic computer-generated diagram while providing the same information.

Basic Color Theory

The twelve-step color wheel arranges colors according to their order in the spectrum of visible light and shows the relationship between colors.

- **Primary colors:** red, yellow, and blue cannot be mixed from any other colors
- **Secondary colors:** orange, green, and purple are made by combining two primary colors
- **Tertiary:** red-orange, orange-yellow, yellow-green, green-blue, blue-purple, and purple red are the steps between the secondary colors on the wheel

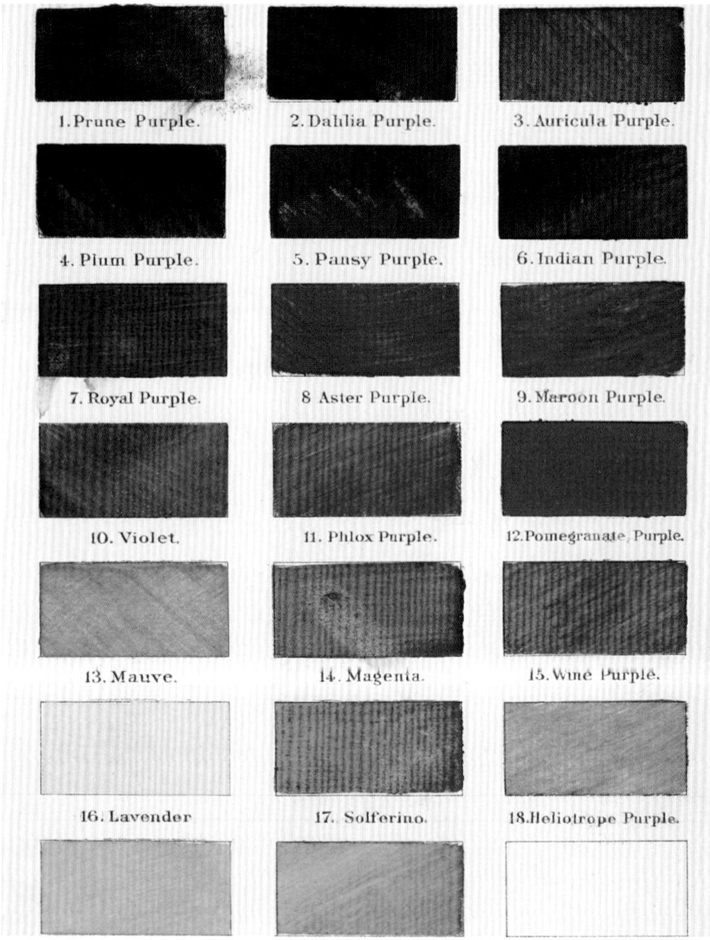

4–5 *A Nomenclature of Colors for Naturalists and Compendium of Useful Knowledge for Ornithologists*, Robert Ridgway, 1886.

Sometimes a little color can go a long way. Introducing small hits of a bright shade into an otherwise subdued range of similar colors creates a striking effect without disrupting the sense of order. Any of the brightest shades in this example taken from a nineteenth-century bird guide (numbers seven to fifteen) will pop when used sparingly with the darkest colors at the top of the palette or when paired with the most muted shades at bottom.

- **Complementary colors:** appear opposite each other on the color wheel and set each other off with sharp contrast
- **Warm colors:** Red, orange, and yellow
- **Cool colors:** Blue, green, and purple

There are six color relationships:

1. **Monochromatic (single color).** Uses just one color and shades or tints of it. Feeling: calm and orderly.

2. **Complementary (two colors).** Colors directly opposite each other on the color wheel are said to be complementary (red and green, purple and yellow, or orange and blue). Complementary colors have the most contrast. Feeling: Exciting and a sense of vibration.

3. **Split complementary (three colors).** One main color plus two more spaced one step away from that color's complement (blue plus red-orange and orange-yellow). Feeling: slightly toned-down excitement.

4. **Double complementary (four colors).** Two sets of complementary colors used together (orange + blue + purple + yellow). Feeling: clashing unless some colors are used in smaller quantities as accents rather than using all in equal measure.

5. **Analogous (two or more colors).** These combinations are formed by colors spaced equally from each other on the wheel. Feeling: pleasing and gentle.

6. **Triadic (three colors).** Any three colors spaced evenly around the wheel. The primary triad of red, yellow, and blue feels harsh, but triads made up of secondary or tertiary colors are easier on the eye.

→ 4-6 *Expresso*, 2008.

Contrasting shades of orange and violet oppose each other here to illustrate how sports support the economic growth of different countries to varying degrees. Tints of the main palette contribute a variety of additional colors without adding chaos. The layout designer used the colors to section off the different articles and create a unified page.

→→ 4-7 *New York Times*, photographer Kelly Marshall, prop stylist Paige Hicks, 2021.

Seemingly small choices based on color theory enliven even a simple photo of roasted carrots. Orange and blue are complements, displaying the greatest amount of visual contrast when used together. The vibrant orange carrots really pop against the turquoise plate, while the tablecloth contributes a layer of more subdued blue that fades into the background.

MACROECONOMIA

Exportações suportam crescimento no trimestre

A recuperação da economia mundial está a ajudar Portugal a **sair da crise**. Com a procura interna parada, o comércio externo é a solução

2625

13%

3ª

14%

3870.9 ESPANHA

1791.3 FRANÇA

1719.8 ALEMANHA

104.0 LETÓNIA

68.6 REPÚBLICA CHECA

59.9 RÚSSIA

55.5 COREIA DO SUL

53.0 BRASIL

E AINDA

ADMINISTRAÇÃO PÚBLICA

Jaime Silva dispensa 50 dirigentes

Hue is the name of a color as determined by its specific wavelength in a ray of white light. When the question is "What color is this?," its hue is the answer. The familiar order of the colors of the rainbow, red-orange-yellow-green-blue-indigo-violet, displays the spectrum of white light according to wavelength from longest (red) to shortest (violet). For precision's sake, a hue can be better described relative to the next hue on the color wheel; for example, a violet can be more accurately labeled red- or blue-violet.

Saturation/chroma refers to a color's intensity or richness, affected by the amount of white, black, or gray present within the color. A fully saturated color is vivid and clear; a desaturated color is dull and muted.

Brightness/value is the degree of darkness or lightness within a color, or its reflective quality or brilliance. Adding white increases the brightness to form a tint. Adding black decreases the brightness to form a shade.

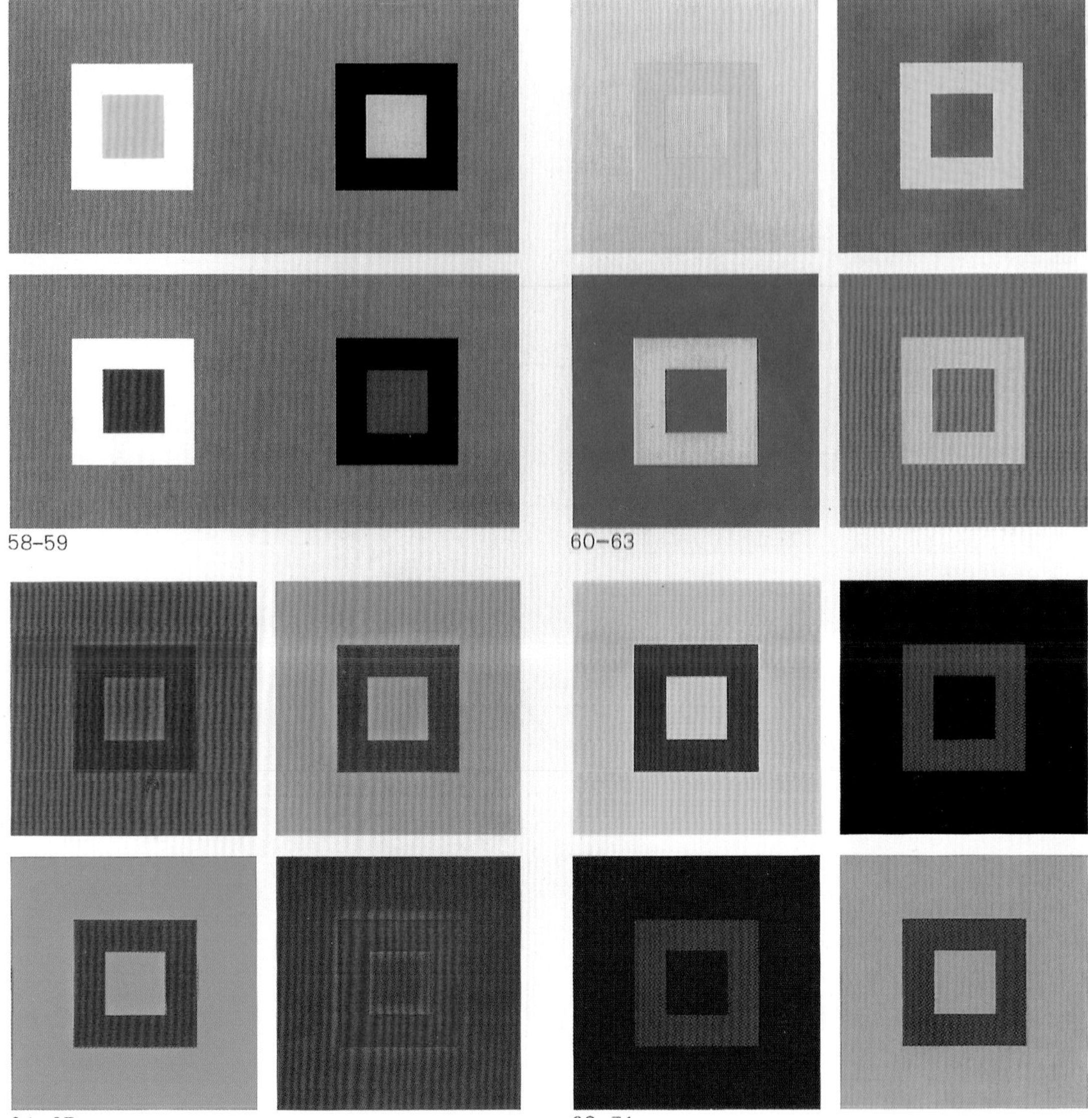

58–59

60–63

64–67

68–71

← 4-8 *The Art of Color*, **Johannes Itten, 1920.**

Color is surprisingly subjective; we assess individual shades by comparing them to the surrounding colors. This illustration shows how the inner outlined square (the same color in each set of four) appears vastly different when overlaid on different backgrounds, and how black and white (top left) placed directly next to a color change its perceived hue. Itten felt that the perception of color relied in part on the viewer's state of mind and personality.

→ 4-9 ***The Blue Flowers*, Peter Mendelsund, 2018.**

The artist pulls a sly trick with this cover. The book's title is *The Blue Flowers*, but what color is the flower/plume of smoke / masked face? Viewers don't even notice the reversal at first. We read the word *blue*, subconsciously take in the cobalt blue sky, and it all makes perfect sense until we stop and think about it. The approach perfectly matches the text, which overflows with puns, wordplay, off-color jokes, and overall zaniness.

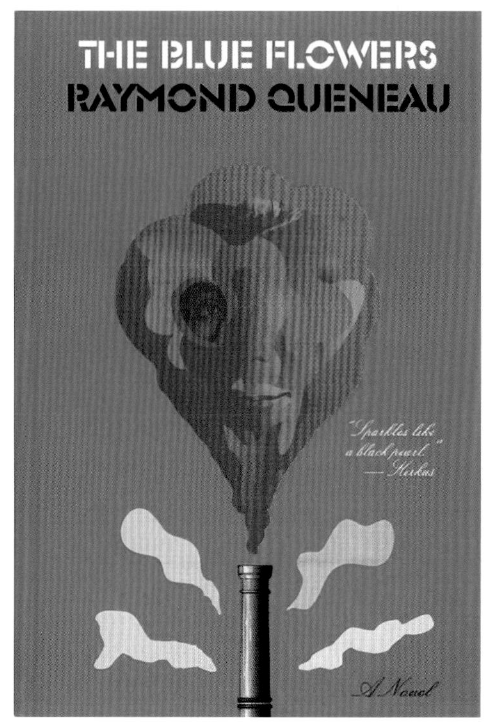

Perceptual Phenomena

Our eyes see colors not only because of the frequency of light waves; we also judge them in relation to other colors nearby. A color is perceived to be brighter, for example, if it is surrounded by a complementary color or lighter if the background color is darker. A color seems to vibrate when placed against a field of its complement.

Color is always subjective; every human sees colors slightly differently, and colors change in different lighting conditions. Moreover, they have positive and negative associations that vary by individual preference ("I hate orange!") as well as culture. As color theorist Josef Albers observed, "If one says 'Red' (the name of a color) and there are 50 people listening, it can be expected that there will be 50 reds in their minds. And one can be sure that all these reds will be very different." Red can mean excitement, power, and passion;

↑ **4–10 *Plastic Soup*, photographer Phoebe Rudomino, 2011.**

Simply increasing the shade (the amount of black added to a color) will shift the mood of an image completely. The ombré of lightest red fishing nets at the surface gives a real feeling of depth as it darkens to black at the bottom of the photo. What starts out bright and sunny morphs into a dark void, where no detail exists to clue a viewer in to what might be lurking there.

→ ↗ **4–11 Photographer Kate Mathis, food stylist Frances Boswell, prop stylist Pamela Duncan Silver, 2018.**

This image uses just three main colors: neutral grays and whites punctuated by various shades of orange, evoking a breakfast off to a gentle start. The ruddy orange-brown of the espresso plus the softer, brighter tones of honeycomb and tangerine keep the accent color all in one family so as not to disturb the early morning quiet.

it can evoke anger, violence, and immoral behavior too (think of protagonist Hester Prynne in the novel *The Scarlet Letter*.) Apart from specific political references, much of a viewer's reaction to color comes from the context in which it's used.

The light at noon on a bright summer's day bleaches out color while noon light on an overcast day in autumn reveals saturated, jewellike hues. Additionally, different creatures see different wavelengths; humans cannot perceive colors in the infrared or ultraviolet spectrums, but many insects, birds, and other animals can. In fact, their survival depends on it. Reindeer rely on ultraviolet light to distinguish edible lichens from the vast expanses of white snow, and butterflies use it to identify their preferred flowers as well as potential mates.

Emotional Response

Color is closely tied to emotion. Matching the prevailing emotion of a text to the overall color within images communicates on a potent yet subtle level, and images can be chosen to evoke feelings of passion, neutrality, tranquility, and even political stances based on their prevailing hues.

Cool colors evoke a calming response; warm ones lend a feeling of excitement and urgency. Brights communicate happiness; muted tones are somber. In the Western Hemisphere, red alerts us to danger or tells us to halt, while blue is soothing, making it a highly popular color in the branding of banks by suggesting a rational and levelheaded handling of a customer's financial assets. Colors cause a literal temperature response in our bodies; warm colors make our pulse rates increase, while cool colors calm us down; there's a reason that hospital interiors tend to feature restful shades of pale blue and green. People inhabiting a room painted a warm yellow will feel comfortable with a lower thermostat setting, but when the same room is painted powder blue, the inhabitants turn up the heat.

Authors can use the emotional power of color to their advantage in a variety of ways. Images bursting with bright, warm colors

→ 4-12 Jerry Seinfeld fans at the Colossal Stage, San Francisco, photographer Biz Herman, 2017.

Red signifies many different emotions across different cultures—passion, rage, and lust, among others—but here it carries a feeling of joy and heat. Color makes the jubilant crowd at a comedy show, set against a darkening sky behind them, seem all the more vital and alive, united by the bright monochromatic red that washes over them all.

Feyenoord-Ajax
Peter Bosz:
'Ik ben heel
ambitieus,
altijd geweest'
54

Alex Klaasen
'Ik wist niet
eens wat
ontspanning
was'
PS van de Week

Meneer en mevrouw Hamersma
Op wijnreis naar Californië:
Druiven-Disney en
'winetertainment'
PS van de Week

Het Parool

Vrij, Onverveerd

€ 3,00
ZATERDAG
22 OKTOBER
2016
OPGERICHT IN 1940
76STE JAARGANG
NR 21 991

Drukte

Toestroom toeristen maakt stad minder sociaal

De impact van de groei van het toerisme reikt verder dan drukte en overlast: de sociale binding tussen de bewoners verdwijnt. Onderzoeker Carla Hoffschulte: 'Straks is dit geen levende stad meer.'
9

Barack Obama
Hoop en
verandering, maar
niet voor iedereen
6

Kukeleku
Alex ten Napel
portretteert
hennen
en hanen
PS van de Week

Roxeanne Hazes
'Ik heb
gelukkig
een goede
dronk'
22

Robert Vuijsje
'Zwarte Piet?
Het gaat om de
vraag of wij
accepteren
dat Nederland
is veranderd'
10

⟵ 4-13 *Het Parool*, 2008.

The colors used in this portrait of Barack Obama convey two main emotions: the yellow seems like heat directed toward him from an outside source, while the blue feels like Obama's typically cool and rational way of expressing himself. Together the colors capture both the external pressures of office and internal reserves of the former US president, communicating both in a subtle, intelligent manner.

⟶ 4-14 *Hartford Courant*, 2008.

Playing with a viewer's expectations can be a satisfying visual strategy. Like it or not, the color pink (especially when combined with elaborate patterns of curlicues and stars or flowers as seen here) often reads as soft, sweet, and feminine to viewers. It's possible to have the cake and eat it too, however; the page designer combined a stereotypically feminine color with a dangerous-looking triangular shape for the type. The sharp edge cuts through and counteracts all of that pink.

7:30pm

10·8

8pm

CELEBRITY SCENTS:

The Smell of Success

Why 20s Is No Golden Age

'Dolls' Lively As Ever

Long Wharf Show A Small Miracle

Poker Drawing Them In

generate a sense of excitement; the same images reproduced in black and white will be received in an entirely different way. For instance, a photo essay documenting a surgical procedure will feel far less overwhelming in black and white, lessening the impact of the gore. Photos of a carnival feel more like the vivid experience of being there when reproduced in color.

Consider food photography (and Sacks's poor patient suffering from achromatopsia); what looks gorgeous in full color is frequently unappealing in black and white. Chromolithography, introduced before the turn of the nineteenth century, was vivid and oversaturated, making food advertisements printed in magazines look garish and almost frightening. Not surprisingly, trade journals of the time favored black and white over lurid or unnatural color reproductions. By 1910, advances in two- and three-color printing technology helped, but the results still look artificial and unappetizing to a viewer today. Color may not be the first criteria that an author has in mind for the images they select, but it's a powerful one.

↦ 4–15 Freaksville Records, designers BrestBrestBrest, 2019.

The hushed shades in this album cover recall those of a hand-colored photo, where layers of transparent tints over a black-and-white print become muted and darker from the photo's gray midtones. The effect is soothing and calm, especially when confined mostly to a single shade as seen here, with a wealth of blues set off by the soft red at the bottom. The stark monochrome figure rising mysteriously from the sea is all the more jarring by comparison.

↘ 4–16 Designs for the Russian state airline Dobrolet, Aleksandr Rodchenko, 1923.

Not a color combination for the faint of heart, red and black set off by the white of a page or screen form an assertive duo. Often used in military contexts (or to evoke order and precision), this pairing telegraphs a no-nonsense sense of authority. The crisp black steadies the vibrant red, and together they convey strength and solidity along with a measure of excitement.

↦↦ 4–17 *Still Life*, photographer Max Aguilera-Hellweg, 1997.

In full color, this autopsy photo would be difficult for the average person to see without feeling squeamish, but in black and white it can be appreciated on other levels. The beautiful composition, intricacy of anatomy, intimacy of the medical personnel and human body, and rich range of tonalities transcend the gory reality, and instead present an artful and engaging image of mortality, physicality, and the temporal quality of life itself.

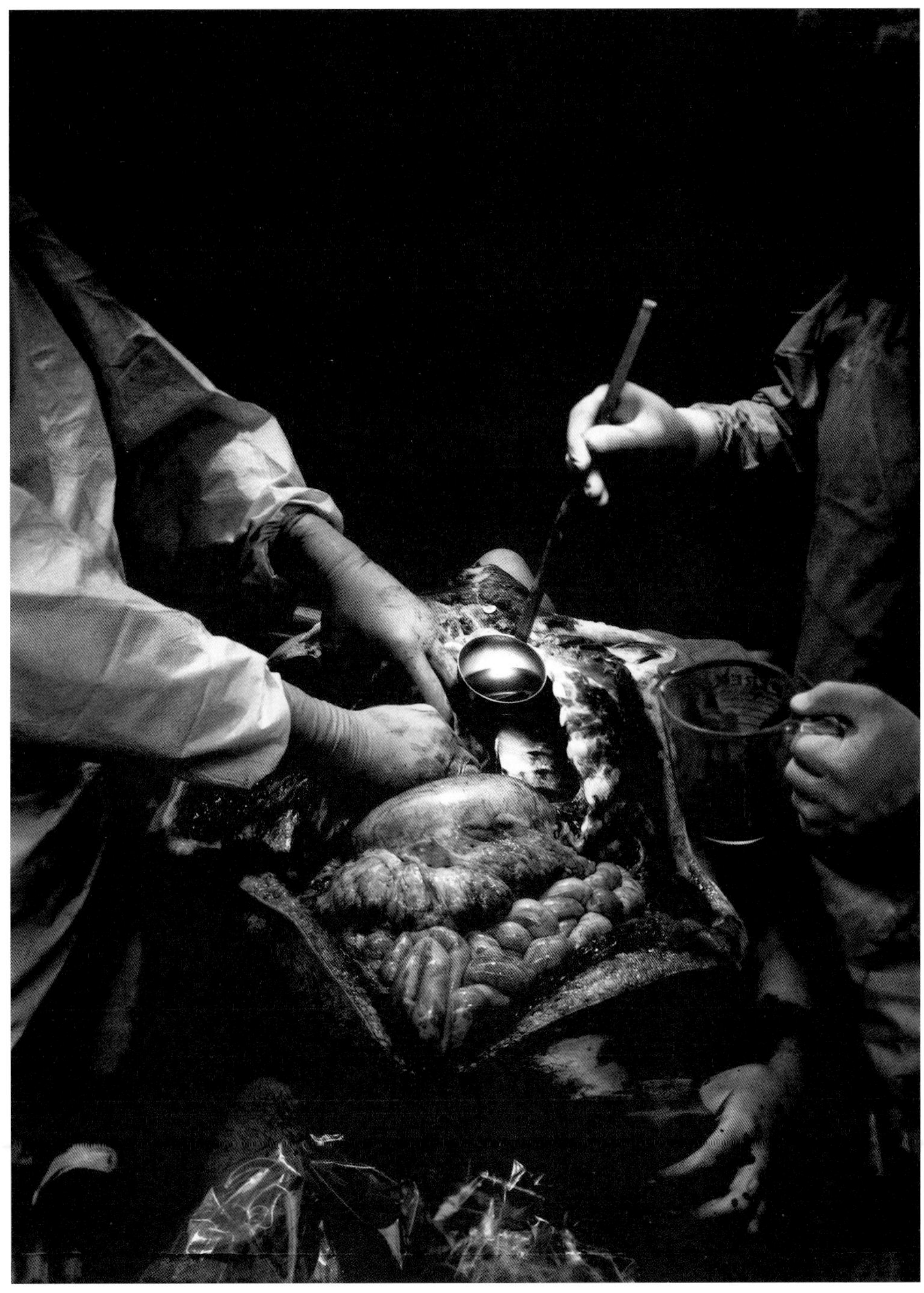

4–18 Coca-Cola, Haddon Sundblom, 1931.

During the Great Depression, Coca-Cola hired Sundblom to depict Santa Claus as a kindly figure as a way to boost Coke sales during the winter months. (Previously, Coke was considered a summer beverage.) Sundblom's neighbor, retired salesman Lou Prentice, was happy to model. The artist created a new Santa painting every year until 1964, always using the bright Coke red along with deep pine green, forever linking both the figure and color palette to the Christmas season.

THE SATURDAY EVENING POST
Drink
Coca-Cola
elicious and Refreshing
"MY HAT'S OFF to the pause that refreshes"
Old Santa, busiest man in the world, takes time out for *the pause that refreshes* with ice-cold Coca-Cola. He even knows how to be good to himself. And so he always comes up smiling. So can you. Wherever you go shopping, you find a cheerful soda fountain with ice-cold Coca-Cola ready.
The Coca-Cola Co., Atlanta, Ga.
LISTEN IN
Grantland Rice—Famous Sports Champions—Coca-Cola Orchestra. Every Wed. 10:30 p. m. Eastern Standard Time. Coast-to-Coast NBC Network.
OVER NINE MILLION A DAY . . . IT HAD TO BE GOOD TO GET WHERE IT IS

Symbolism of Color across Cultures

It's important to know the cultural associations of color for your intended audience. Because color triggers a subconscious emotional response, it's possible to make your viewer into either an immediate ally or instant opponent by using a color with a specific meaning within their culture. There are vernacular language links to color too; in English, you are said to be green with envy, but in German, envy is yellow (*gelb vor Neid sein*). Knowing your audience will spare you from introducing unintended political or cultural overtones via an image's color palette.

For many of us, red and green are the "official" Christmas colors, so much so that the combination is almost never used for other purposes. While the cheerful red berries and glossy green leaves of winter holly contributed to this association (which dates to the Roman winter solstice celebration Saturnalia), it was Coca-Cola advertising artist Haddon Sundblom who cemented the visual in 1931 by creating the definitive fat, jolly Santa in a crimson red robe with touches of forest green in the typography and background elements. Most colors, however, lack the power to function as such a specific form of shorthand, instead offering a range of connotations from positive to negative depending on cultural context.

● **Black** carries positive associations including elegance, formality, sophistication, and seriousness. On the flip side, it is often linked to death, the fearsome unknown, evil, and emptiness. From the United States to Europe to Japan, it has also come to be seen as the color of youth rebellion.

○ **White** conveys a sense of light and purity, hinting at innocence, cleanliness, and sacredness. Its less positive associations call up emptiness (a blank slate) or isolation. In some Asian countries, white is worn at funerals or is frowned on for married women because it brings unhappiness—yet a white flag is a worldwide symbol for a truce or surrender.

● **Gray** is universally seen as a neutral color, a positive indicator of nuance, balance, maturity, and wisdom. It can also feel gloomy, conveying a sense of cloudy bad weather, sadness, or the faded glory of old age. In some Native American cultures, gray is a color of friendship and honor.

● **Red** is a vivid hue, calling up dramatic imagery: sexual passion, flames, and blood along with heat, excitement, and great energy. It can also represent cruelty, aggression, anger (I saw red), or provocation (that statement was like a red flag to a bull). Across most of Asia, it's a happy color of prosperity worn at weddings, but in parts of Africa it indicates mourning or death.

● **Yellow** is the color of pure, warm sunshine, linked to feelings of radiance and bliss. Yet it's used as a cautionary color too, such as in traffic lights telling drivers to slow down, police tape around crime scenes, and hazard warning signs. In Japan, it signifies courage (in direct opposition to Western cultures associating yellow with cowardice). It connotes mourning in Egypt and Burma, and is an indicator of occupation for farmers and merchants in India.

● **Blue** brings to mind vast expanses of sea and sky. It carries a feeling of coolness and rationality, and is often associated with masculinity. A mildly depressed person is said to have the blues, and this hue can represent unwelcome coldness or distant feelings of apathy and despair as well. Worldwide, it is the most popular corporate color—look at all those bank logos.

● **Green** is the color of nature and growing things. As such, it stands for harmony and fertility, and can represent youth and inexperience. It's also the color of US money, symbolizing financial success or wealth. Its unhappier connotations include poison, corrosion, and envy, with the latter voiced in William Shakespeare's *Othello*: "O, beware, my lord, of jealousy; It is the green-eyed monster." It indicates sickness too; to be green around the gills is to feel nauseous. Green is frequently associated with Ireland; in Celtic cultures, the Green Man is a symbol of fertility and untamed nature.

● **Purple** is a color long associated with royalty (and more recently with the musician Prince, a nice play on words) thanks to its origins in 1500 BC as a rare and expensive dye obtained from a small mollusk found only in the Tyre region of the Mediterranean Sea. It took more than nine thousand mollusks to create just one gram of Tyrian purple. Since only wealthy rulers could afford to buy and wear the color, it became associated with the imperial classes of Rome, Egypt, and Persia, and the connection with royalty persists in many contemporary Western cultures. Purple conveys luxury, nobility, and mysticism along with the more negative states and emotions of cruelty and insanity. In Latin America and Thailand, it is associated with death and mourning, and in nineteenth-century Great Britain, lavender was a transitional color worn by mourners for three to six months after the first period of deep mourning (a year plus one day when the mourner dressed entirely in black).

● **Orange** calls up zesty bright citrus rinds and the blazing hues of fall foliage. It's an energetic, invigorating, active color but can also be considered unpleasantly loud or crude. Orange is linked to the Protestant movement in Northern Ireland and has strong political associations in the United Kingdom, while in the Netherlands orange is a symbolic representation of the country because the former republic became a monarchy under the House of Orange-Nassau in 1815. To the Dutch, orange says national unity; to the Northern Irish, it speaks to the division of their country. In India, orange is associated with Hinduism.

Color Use by Decade in North America

Just a few splashes of aqua, baby pink, and lemon yellow can function like a time machine rocketing a viewer straight back to the 1950s, but the specific associations these colors evoke depend largely on that person's age. If they were a teenager then, all the memories of that time (good, bad, and indifferent) are part and parcel of the reaction to this palette. Someone who wasn't born until the 2000s, however, will perhaps feel nostalgia fed by pop culture references but will have no personal experiences to draw on. The older person will have a more emotionally based response, while the younger one will react from a quite different perspective. Keeping the age demographic of your audience in mind will aid in determining how much to rely on color within images as a positioning element.

There's no way to standardize the more subtle associations of color because such a range of personal responses are possible; in other words, outside the "warm colors exciting / cool colors soothing" dictums that are generally true, sometimes it's not so easily categorizable. Does anything come to mind when you hear the phrase "grandma colors"? Probably so, although for each person it's different: it could be the distinct 1940s' color palette of your grandmother's house that she hasn't updated since the World War II era; or it could be what she wears, such as a range of gentle soft pastels or fondness for leopard print; or it might call to mind the bland color palette of the rooms of the senior living facility where she now resides.

1950s

4-19 and 4-20 Color combinations can be so distinctive that they serve as permanent bookmarks of time and place. Sweet pastel shades in clothing, fabrics, automobiles, and home furnishings were a hallmark of 1950s' America. These typical palettes evoke the optimistic, prosperous years following World War II, even without other visual cues such as tail fins or a dress with a full skirt and nipped waist.

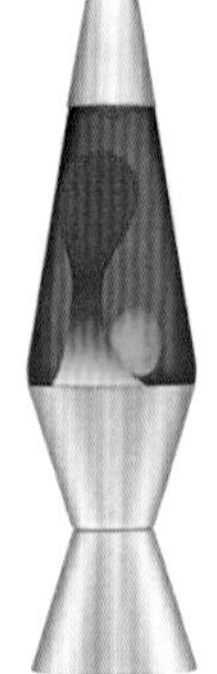

1960s

4-21 and 4-22 It's pretty simple to evoke the 1960s through colors: the soft tones of the 1950s became sharp and acidic. Harsh, jarring hues reflected an era of social upheaval and change. Life heated up, and the prevailing color palettes went along for the ride. There was no relaxing in soothing pastel-toned living rooms during the 1960s; the colors used for everything from clothing to home environments screamed go-go-go.

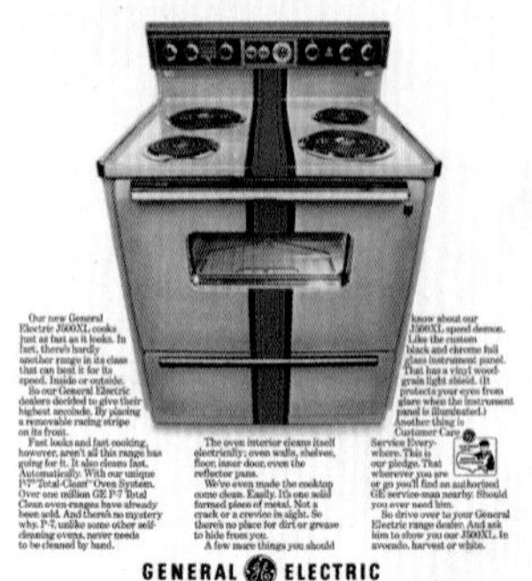

GE's new J500XL goes from 0 to 350 in 250 seconds.
GENERAL ELECTRIC

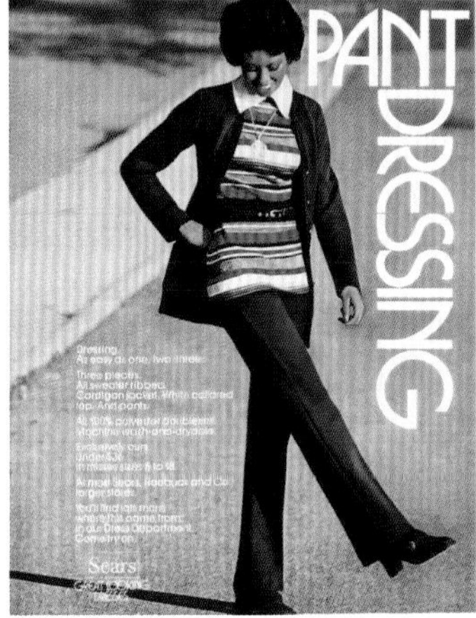

1970s

4-23 and 4-24 In the 1970s, colors pivoted away from the clear brights of the 1960s and took a deep dive into murky midtones of avocado, rust/orange, brown, and harvest gold. (Stripes and plaids had a heyday as well.) Images where these colors dominate transport a viewer squarely into a tumultuous era that both continued and refuted the social changes of the 1960s. Deep divisions within society were reflected in more somber color palettes that were more muddy as well as less innocent and joyful than in previous years.

1980s

4–25 and 4–26 The 1980s saw a return to vivid color palettes as a new social conservatism (and of course, a rebellious youth backlash against it) took hold during the Reagan-Thatcher years. Pop culture embraced decidedly loud, unconservative colors. This was the era of MTV and the internet, cable TV and the yuppie. Color palettes had all the brightness of the 1960s but none of the optimism, instead expressing what feels like anger and aggression.

Purposely evoking an era through the use of color is a simple goal; just be careful not to do it accidentally. Even if your favorite colors are avocado, rust, chocolate, and golden yellow, unless you intend to summon up the 1970s, shy away from images with predominating palettes so closely associated with time and history. Such easily identifiable color schemes bring a rush of cultural and even political associations directly in the door with them; 1960s' psychedelic colorways can usher in a mental connection to the upheaval and social turmoil of those years, such as the Vietnam War, civil rights, feminism, the pill, the sexual revolution, LSD, Woodstock, and so on—positive associations for some viewers, but negative for others. If these topics don't align with yours, alter the colors you're using. Often a slight shift is enough.

When considering the impact of color in the images you're using, keep these questions in mind:

- What is the mood of my text? What colors support this?
- What are the cultural associations with this color palette to be aware of and use accordingly?
- Do my image selections as a group feel harmonious with one another in terms of hue, brightness, and saturation?
- Do I need to evoke a specific historical period or place? How can I use color to support this goal?
- Does the color combination unintentionally evoke a well-known corporate palette?

The People's Republic of Brooklyn, photographer Sean Michael Pridgen, 2020.

II Strategies

RISE

PHILADELPHIA

05

How Images Support Text

5–1 *Rise*, designers Jonai Gibson-Selix and Andrea Hu, 2020.

The image and text support each other perfectly on this cover for a publication produced by a pair of University of the Arts graphic design students during the summer 2020 Black Lives Matter protests in Philadelphia. The four-character vertical title visually mirrors the woman with fist raised in protest. The title and figure become twin pillars of strength and power, reinforcing a call to action.

Text is precise and less open to individual interpretation than images that can be chameleons; their meaning shifts depending on the context as well as what the personality, culture, and life experience of the viewer brings to the encounter. Keep in mind that images have a degree of inherent ambiguity so they can be bent to an author's will, seeming to say what we need them to.

An awareness of this slippery aspect of imagery will ensure that your images are saying what you intend *and* will clearly communicate with your viewer. A collection of random and haphazard images is confusing and adds no meaning to the text—unless your text is purposefully random and the visuals are deliberately chosen to mirror the writing technique.

The categories of image use described below are not hard-and-fast or exclusive of one another. There can be a great deal of overlap; for instance, the same image of a vast forest fire can serve as proof that it happened while evoking emotions such as grief and horror, and generating shock and outrage. It isn't necessary for authors to

5–2 *Jumbo*, London Stereoscopic Company, 1890.

Was Jumbo really the largest elephant in the world, standing over 13' tall at the shoulder, as circus entrepreneur P. T. Barnum claimed? If his human companion pictured here is about 5'6" to 5'10" tall—the average height for an adult male in 1885—the beast appears to be easily twice that. As it turns out, Jumbo was about 10'6" feet tall—smaller than Barnum asserted, but still 20 percent bigger than the average height for elephants his age. So what does this picture actually reveal? Simply put, this is a tremendously large animal, record-breaking or not.

pin down exact categories when choosing images. The intention here is to provide broad guidelines on the different ways that images function and how authors can best deploy them. Understanding the mechanisms by which images convey meaning makes the selection process far simpler and more intuitive.

Images support text through many different channels, and authors should consider literal versus emotive qualities from the outset when deciding how best to use them. What are you trying to evoke or reinforce? Do you simply need to let your reader see visual proof (Jumbo was the largest elephant in the world), or is your goal to generate outrage and spark change, as seen in journalist Jacob Riis's *How the Other Half Lives*? Do you need to visually reinforce some strongly stated opinions or supply backup for factual statements? Is your goal to decorate the text, match its mood, or provide a parallel narrative? Images can help you do all of these things while serving as a source of delight for your reader as well.

Literal images (this is a Granny Smith apple; here is Beatle John Lennon as a child) are generally best for application in humanist, business, law, scientific, and public policy texts, and abstract/metaphoric images (this picture of a house at the bottom of a lake parallels the overall mood of this essay) for application in literature, poetry, and social science texts. As a useful rule of thumb, a reader should never be expected to puzzle over images, and distracting your reader from the text risks losing their continued engagement as well as confidence in your ideas. Well-chosen images have the opposite effect, drawing the reader deeper into the text and enhancing the communication of your subject matter. The following pages break down different functions that images serve and offer criteria for choosing images to best suit the needs of your text.

Here are the main ways that images support text:

- Explain
- Document or prove
- Illustrate assertions
- Get between the lines
- Evoke mood or feeling
- Decorate or make pretty
- Shock or outrage
- Enhance or emphasize

Explain

Images explain structural and spatial realities beautifully; think of a floor plan shown alongside photographs of a home's interiors. The diagram gives a viewer an overall sense of the entire house: how each room flows into the next, the location of the front door in relation to the kitchen, the relative sizes of the bedrooms, and so on. The interior shots provide intimate visuals of the furnishings, mood, and light. Together they give a more complete accounting of the space than either type of image on its own. To effectively support text, explanatory images should be unambiguous and to the point, not easily open to interpretations other than what the author intended.

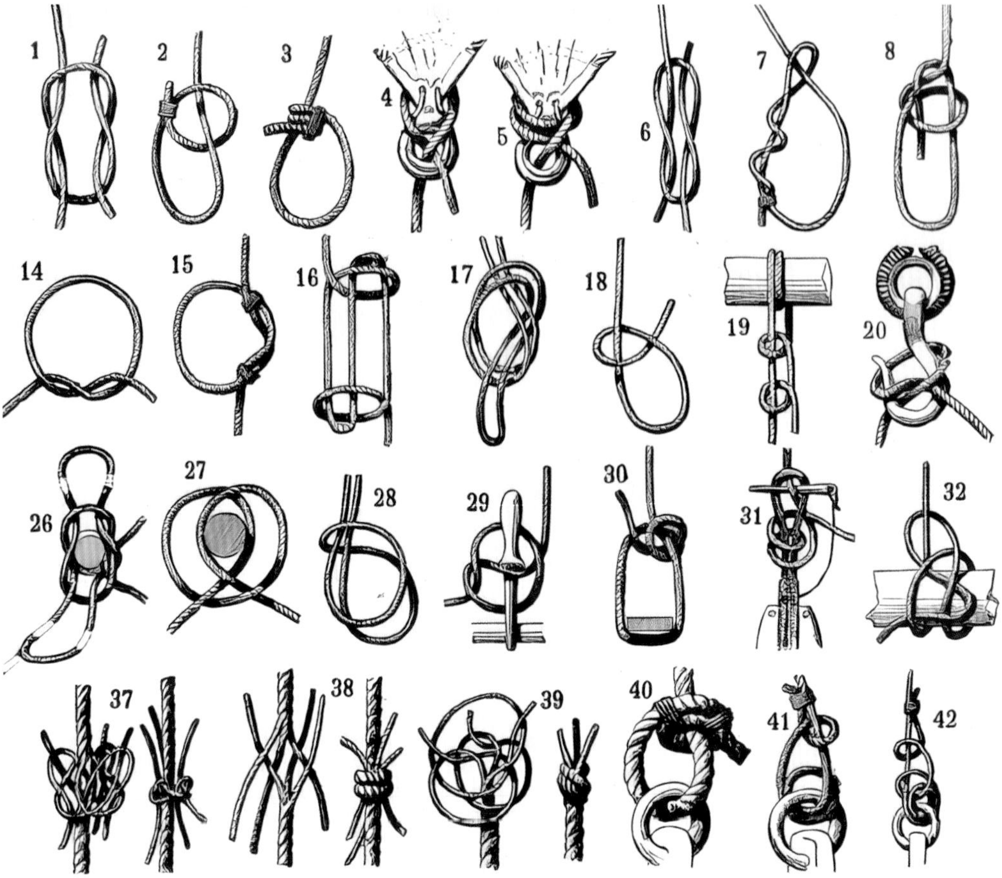

1 2 3 4 5 6 7 8
14 15 16 17 18 19 20
26 27 28 29 30 31 32
37 38 39 40 41 42

POINT 1
POINT 2
TRISTAN GOOLEY
THE NATURAL NAVIGATOR
S

← 5-3 ***Nautical Knot Diagram*, ca. 1800.**

How do you learn to tie a knot if you've never tried it before? The best way is to have someone demonstrate it, but lacking a sailor at hand to help out, a clear step-by-step guide like this one makes written directions comprehensible. Showing the over-and-under motions of the rope strands clarifies complicated instructions in a situation where words often get snarled up.

↙ 5-4 ***Atlas Obscura*, illustrator Chelsea Beck, 2017.**

Answering in words alone "Which way is north or south?" by aligning the points of a crescent moon with the horizon might be confusing to a reader, but this simple diagram illustrates the concept quickly and effortlessly. It supports the text as a learning aid, presenting the instruction in a straightforward way that's easy to retain.

↗ 5-5 ***New York Times*, photographer Glenn Hunt, June 6, 2020.**

Sometimes event organizers will talk up attendance after the fact, inflating the numbers to make their cause seem more popular than it actually was. This image of a Black Lives Matter protest in Australia, ten days after the murder of George Floyd at the hands of Minneapolis police officers, shows a viewer that a large portion of the public was no longer willing to ignore police violence against people of color.

Document or Prove

Visual journalism requires the same sort of careful observation—not merely looking—needed in written reportage. Anyone can say that a million people attended a rally or march, but a photo of a sparsely populated event tells the viewer something else entirely. It's one thing to state in words that of course, homelessness is hard on children and their parents, but visual documentation of the single room where a family of ten lives in a homeless shelter doesn't just tell, it *shows*. Together with the text, the images powerfully represent the harsh daily reality for nearly seventeen thousand homeless children in New York City.

Like most tired clichés, the old saw "A picture is worth a thousand words" grew from a fact. Visual proof of written assertions helps a skeptical reader decide to believe the author (or not). Going back to Jumbo the elephant, the mental picture of just how big he was will vary from one person to the next, but photographic evidence of Jumbo next to a man barely as tall as the creature's knee provides a definitive answer. In 1912, a steel eyeglass case and fifty-page speech that former US president Teddy Roosevelt was carrying in his jacket pocket stopped an assassin's bullet and saved his

← 5-6 *Karl Marx*, 1875.

This portrait of political philosopher and revolutionary Marx is so well-known that to use it alone reads as a disappointingly obvious choice. Used as a secondary smaller image along with an image of Marx in the Reading Room at the British Library, however, its meaning shifts to become supplementary rather than primary. By showing the environment where he worked as opposed to just the man, this pair of images provides context and atmosphere that a portrait alone can't convey.

↙ 5-7 *Paris Catacombs*, photographer DJTox, 2007.

It's one thing to read that six million Parisians are interred in the city's eighteenth-century catacombs, but visualizing that many bones (consider that every individual has over two hundred) is impossible for most people. An image of the tunnel walls formed from thousands of stacked femurs interspersed with skulls, however, makes the sheer number of the dead far more imaginable—especially when a viewer realizes this represents just a tiny percentage of the denizens of the necropolis.

↗ 5-8 *Buzz Aldrin on the Moon*, NASA, 1969.

There are people who believe the 1969 moon landing was a fake event shot in a photo studio (and frequently attribute it to filmmaker Stanley Kubrick as the photographer). To these folks, this image is as trivial as a fashion feature in a glossy magazine. For others, this is photographic proof documenting a singular moment of triumph for the United States. A hoax or a historic groundbreaking image? You decide.

life. A photo of the bloodstained speech with its bullet hole proves the incredible sequence of events that took place on that day long ago. Using images as proof is reassuring for viewers, allowing them to judge for themselves the plausibility of the author's statements. The sentence "The Paris catacombs hold the bones of six million people" remains somewhat abstract because it does not help the reader visualize the sheer quantity of the dead. Seeing an image of the vast subterranean passageways and chambers made of tightly packed skulls and femurs immediately gives a vivid sense of just how many citizens rest there.

Support Assertions

On occasion, images need to be literal and plainspoken—showing exactly what the author is writing about—to complement the text with precision. For example, consider a paper about various varieties of hybrid apples. The most useful images to aid the reader's comprehension would show each type of apple in close-up, and perhaps also sliced vertically in half, to demonstrate the variations and details of the varieties' different colors, shapes, and textures.

For this type of use, it's critical for the author to choose images with the highest degree of specificity and least possible ambiguity or potential for multiple interpretations. You are trying to explain, after all, not confuse. In a presentation about a certain building in a specific year, the images selected cannot vary from the dates under discussion (unless the author calls attention to that fact; "As we can see, by the following year shown here . . ."). If an image of the building in that year cannot be located, the author will have

5–9 Photographer Con Poulos, n.d.

Process photos paired with instructive text, such as recipes, add allure and immediacy. In these luscious food shots, a viewer can almost feel the cool, smooth dough as it flattens out from the pressure of the rolling pin against the marble surface. The pears and lemons in various stages of peeling, slicing, squeezing, and grating look juicy and fragrant—and delicious.

5–10 ***Historic Football*****, photographer Federico Tardito, 2019.**

Sports fans and players are always jubilant after a big victory, none more so than these men cheering the winning team. Here we see pure animal joy in an image accompanying factual reportage after a game of Calcio Fiorentino, a brutal and exhausting event combining rugby, football, and wrestling that originated in sixteenth-century Italy.

to change the text, skip using the image, or risk losing credibility should a reader decide to double-check the facts.

What if, in this scenario, a single picture exists and is available for use but it's of low quality (blurred, too dark, grainy, or out of focus)? Whether to use it or not depends on if it will lend authenticity, enhance understanding, or show something that the viewer cannot get from text alone. If not, it's best to leave it out; if you can't really tell what you're looking at, that image brings little to the party. We've all perhaps shared the disappointment of learning that the famous 1934 "surgeon's photo" of the Loch Ness monster turned out to be a hoax—just a photo of a toy submarine from a dime store, with a head and neck made from wood putty. We believed, and then felt cheated when the truth came out. Don't do that to your readers.

5–11 *Snowflakes*, photographer Wilson Bentley, 1885.

Prior to the advent of this kind of photography, humans could catch a fleeting glimpse of snowflakes before the tiny crystals melted away, but no one had ever seen their structures in such clear detail before. Images such as this make the world visible in a way our eyes can't quite manage and add a sense of wonder to our understanding of any text they accompany.

Make Visible

As outlined in the previous section, there are times when images need to be direct and concise, showing a reader precisely in pictures what the author is saying in words. For certain kinds of text, these images enhance understanding by providing a visual lexicon for the topic that leaves nothing to the reader's imagination. In other circumstances, however, inviting a reader to use a bit of imagination to draw a connection between the images and text can lead to a greater appreciation of both components.

Here we are discussing circumstances where the images need to get between the lines, so to speak—to be evocative, to lend the suggestion of something. In this case, a well-chosen image forms the equation 1 + 1 = 3. While the text and images are informative on their own,

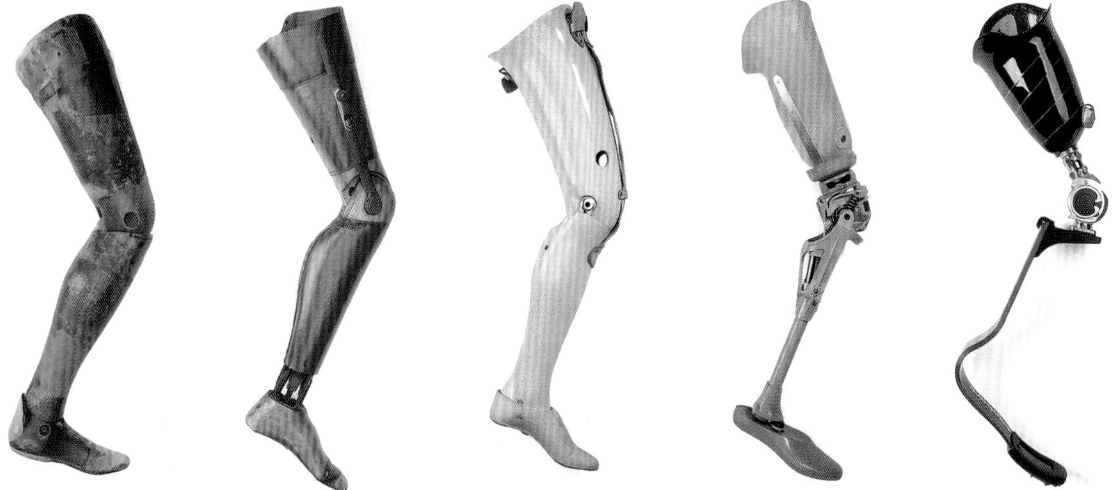

5–12 Time line of artificial above-knee prostheses, from left to right, 1894, ca. 1915, ca. 1930, 1978–81, and 2012.

Artificial limbs have come quite a ways from their humble beginnings as carved (and heavy!) wooden legs fitted with metal joints. The evolution of limb shape and material, read from left to right, demonstrates advancing technology over time. The progression of increasingly sophisticated artificial legs allows a reader to imagine their far greater functionality and ease of use for the amputee, adding a human dimension to a scientific image.

seen together their alchemy surpasses their individual usefulness. For obvious reasons, this approach is effective for literature, essays, poetry, memoirs, and fiction writing, but it can be powerful in journalism and documentary contexts as well. In a story about poverty, for instance, an image of the nearly empty refrigerator and cupboards in a kitchen says hunger without directly stating it. By showing, it tells.

In a 2012 TED talk, graphic designer Chip Kidd shared a beautiful and concise example learned from his Penn State professor Lanny Sommese. Show either a picture of an apple or the word *apple*, but do not under any circumstances show the picture and word together because "that is treating your audience like a moron, and they deserve better." Grammatical inaccuracy aside, that statement is powerful and well worth remembering. If your intended audience is reading your text, presumably they have some prior knowledge of the subject and are there because they're already interested. Author and grammarian E. B. White wrote, "No one can write decently who is distrustful of the reader's intelligence, or whose attitude is patronizing." The same is true for choosing images; don't insult your audience's intelligence.

Captions are the exception here, by the way; if you're working on that paper about varieties of apples, of course you would need a caption to specifically identify each image.

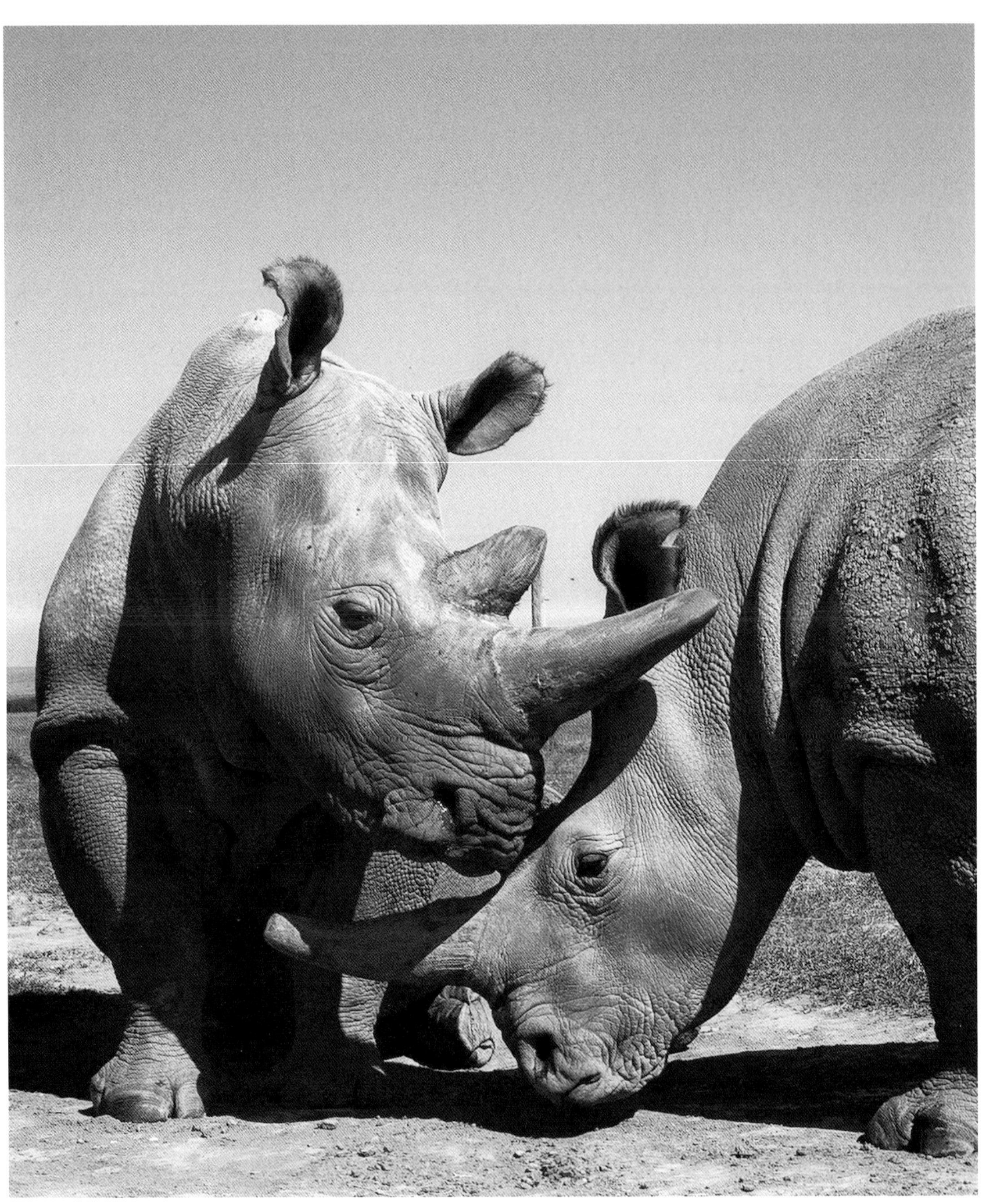

Evoke Mood or Feeling

5–13 *New York Times*, photographer Jack Davison, 2021.

These are the last two remaining white rhinos on earth, Najin and Fatu, both females. The image is powerful and poignant; its formal composition expresses the weight and mass of these monumental animals, yet also emphasizes their vulnerability. As the creatures gently nuzzle each other, a viewer can't help but think of the sad day ahead when one of the pair will die, leaving the other completely alone, soon to be followed by the extinction of the species.

In addition to getting between the lines of the text, images can be used to create or directly support a mood. For this type of usage, images don't need to illustrate the words with a direct one-to-one correlation; they need only to evoke a feeling mirroring the text's emotional range. Evocative images greatly enhance the literary content, placing a viewer into a time, place, and feeling that adds to the overall enjoyment of the text.

The criteria for selecting such images is not quite as clear-cut as choosing pictures that directly support the text, for obvious reasons. Individual human reactions to what we see in images varies tremendously; looking at the same photo, one person sees an image of a peaceful lake, while another sees a body of water that might contain hidden dangers or even the Loch Ness monster. Consider how an image could potentially be interpreted from a different point of view before committing to it. One person will see a statue of a proud Civil War general on his horse as a positive monument to bravery in wartime, while another will see the statue in a more negative light, as a legacy of a painful and difficult time in US history.

Decorate or Make Pretty

On occasion, images don't need to fulfill a deep meaning when paired with text; they can serve as pure eye candy. Most of us are familiar with the saying "Less is more," commonly attributed to Bauhaus architect Ludwig Mies van der Rohe (even though it was first uttered by Peter Behrens, Mies van der Rohe's boss at Berlin's AEG Turbine Factory during the early years of the twentieth century). Ah, but what about writer Oscar Wilde's witticism "Nothing succeeds like excess"? Fortunately when it comes to image selection, we don't have to choose one approach over the other; this is not a case of either-or but instead an instance of both-and. When the circumstances call for it, sometimes too much is just right. If the subject matter of a text is visually stunning—such as landscapes,

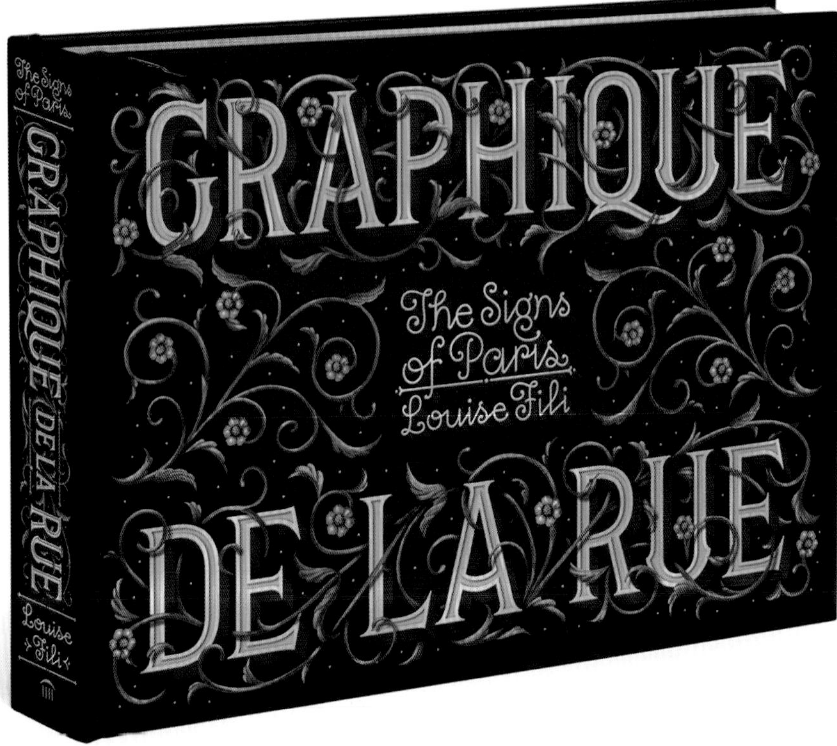

5–14 *Graphique de la Rue*, Louise Fili, 2015.

This book, one in a series documenting street signage in European cities, focuses on Paris. The lettering style of the title along with the carefully twining flowers and vines evoke the feel of that city's grand boulevards and graceful architecture, setting up a Parisian state of mind for a viewer before they even crack open the cover.

the decorative arts, exotic birds, or gemstones—use a quantity of images and at a large size.

The sweet spot is in the edit. Using many images requires care in selecting a group that provides an embarrassment of visual riches: wide-ranging in terms of color, composition, and content rather than presenting a repetitive succession that feels like more of the same. Seek to provide variety. For example, consider accompanying a text on nineteenth-century designer William Morris with as many selections of his wallpaper patterns as possible. To deepen a reader's appreciation of Morris's work along with his role in the overall arts

→ **5–15 Photographers Gentl + Hyers, n.d.**

Some pictures entice a reader along through the text by virtue of their sheer loveliness. Starting with a tumble of lush stone fruits practically guarantees an alluring photo. In this example, the lighting is reminiscent of an early summer morning, before the day has become too warm. The image feels ripe with possibilities (fruit salad for the beach? nap in the hammock with a good book?), bringing a languorous, expectant mood to the photo.

↘ **5–16 *Wall Street Journal*, illustrator Jessica Hische, 2010.**

Every late spring, like clockwork, publications produce "best of summer reading" lists. It's such a commonplace feature that art directors have almost run out of imaginative ways to illustrate it: books at poolside, books under a beach umbrella, books in a beach bag. . . . This approach feels particularly fresh and appealing because it incorporates the title into the pool's tiled floor, offering a simple twist on the predictable.

5–17 *Travel + Leisure*, photographer Mikkel Vang, 2014.

This pair of travel photos evokes time, location, and a beautiful vacation meal all at once. Everything we see is presented in an aspirational but not fussy way. Combining two photos creates a larger narrative made up from the details of each: the reader will assume without even thinking about it that the grilled fish was pulled from the ocean hours before.

and crafts movement, look for images with a range of colors and themes, and use them at a scale large enough to appreciate the fine detail.

It's worth noting here that this example overlaps with another category of image use—namely that of documenting and directly supporting text points. It's one thing for an author to state that Morris's wallpapers were beautiful; by showing them, the reader can appreciate them in real time. The same image can function in different ways depending on the context. It isn't necessary (or possible) to pinpoint just one role that an image can play.

Shock or Outrage

5–18 ***Kent State*****, photographer John Filo, 1970.**

Just two words allow most of us to conjure up this exact scene in our minds without the actual photo. Such searing images have earned their iconic status and carry a powerful, specific narrative that will never transcend their original meaning. They can't be repurposed unless it's a deliberate provocation or satire, which even then carries a high risk of making the author appear clueless or insensitive. Images like this can only and ever represent that one moment in time.

This image category overlaps with the function of images to document and prove, and additionally ventures into the area of evoking emotion or feelings. But why would an author want to shock or outrage a viewer? Think of it as adding emphasis, like a bold underscore, to text calling attention to injustice, war, poverty, illness, or corruption.

The image of fourteen-year-old Mary Ann Vecchio kneeling over the body of student Jeffrey Miller, gunned down by the National Guard during Vietnam War protests at Kent State University, is an indelible part of contemporary visual culture. The *Washington Post* called the photo "one of the most important images of the 20th century." Taken by student photographer John Filo, it captures Vecchio's raw grief and disbelief at the realization that the nation's

5–19 *New York Times*, photographer Fred Ramos, October 2021.

When durable physical objects—clothes, cars, or buildings—serve as evidence of terrible fates, the images of these once-ordinary items seem pitiful and horrifying simultaneously. This bloodstained outfit, worn by an unidentified body found in Mexico's Sonoran Desert, silently bears witness to a violent end. Learning that close to a hundred thousand other "disappeared" people met similar ends as unidentified corpses dressed in stiff, blood-covered rags, a reader feels revulsion and outrage.

5–20 *New York Times*, photographer Kevin Carter, March 26, 1993.

The South African–born photojournalist took this Pulitzer Prize–winning photo during a time of severe famine in Sudan. The patiently waiting vulture in the background all too vividly illustrates the child's potential fate. The image forces a viewer to acknowledge the immense human suffering caused by war and famine. It also caused a great deal of controversy; readers were outraged that Carter didn't try to help the little girl.

soldiers had just fired on its own children. The Kent State Pietà, as it's sometimes called, is one of those rare photos that fundamentally changed the way we see ourselves and the world around us." An unforgettable image such as this sears itself into a viewer's consciousness, ensuring the retention of the text's content in a permanent, meaningful way.

That said, such well-known images are off-limits for almost everything other than their original purpose. Just two words, *Kent State*, allows many of us to conjure up the exact scene in our minds without needing to see the actual photo. Images such as this have earned their iconic status and carry a powerful and specific narrative of their own that will never transcend the original meaning. They can't be repurposed unless it's a deliberate provocation or satire, which even then carries a high risk of making the author appear clueless or insensitive. Even if an author is writing about Vietnam protests, it's preferable to search for a less familiar but still powerful image—one that most viewers haven't yet seen.

Enhance or Emphasize

5–21 ***New York Times*****, photographer Ruth Fremson, 2013.**

For this family of ten sharing a single 520-square-foot room in a Brooklyn homeless shelter, privacy and storage space for possessions are nonexistent, children sleep two to a mattress, and a mop bucket serves as a toilet. The shelter is plagued by mice and roaches; black mold creeps up the walls. It's difficult to imagine small children living in this unhealthy and claustrophobic situation; to see it captured in a photo communicates the reality with brutal simplicity.

Authors can emphasize text points with images in other ways too. Here the 1 + 1 = 3 equation comes into play again. Saying that living in a family of twelve has challenges as well as joys, accompanied by a photo of a week's worth of laundry, makes it clear that some of the challenges involve tremendous amounts of housework. This of course can be assumed implicitly; it seems too obvious to say it in words. But a photo of the sheer volume of dirty clothes gives a visual shape and time dimension to the chore, triggering the reader's almost instant comprehension.

Illustrations can be particularly useful for stressing text points as they draw on a wide range of visual symbols and metaphors to make visible what is implicit in text in subtle (or not so subtle) ways. As an example, an illustration can emphasize the difficulty of talking

5–22 *8x8* magazine, illustrator Diego Patiño, 2019.

This drawing's exuberance, comic book style, and vibrant color perfectly capture the excitement of the most amazing penalty kick ever in women's soccer. The color, composition, and mood of the image convey a crazy, joyful sports moment, and enhance the text in a nonsubtle, hit-you-over-the-head, and totally appropriate way. When it's a good moment to shout, why not shout?

about sensitive topics by putting an elephant into a drawing room or shine a light on the bad behavior of banking executives by depicting them as spoiled children fighting over a piggy bank. Chapter 6, "Conceptual Strategies," describes this in more detail, but here we're talking about the value of relying on an image to make a text point visible without the text coming out and saying it directly.

Images used to enhance and emphasize can be bold or discreet. Texts calling for justice or social change can be supported by images with a higher visual reactivity quotient—those that are intended to evoke strong emotions in viewers. A presentation about a proposed new park would be enhanced by before and after photos as well as renderings of the space—images that allow the audience to imagine themselves enjoying the park instead of hurrying past a weed-strewn vacant lot.

Begin your image search with these questions in mind:

- What is the mood of my text, and what mood do I want to see in the images?
- What do I want the images to say?
- What function do I want the images to perform for my text—decorative, documentary, or something else?
- Which format will best achieve this—photographic or illustrative?

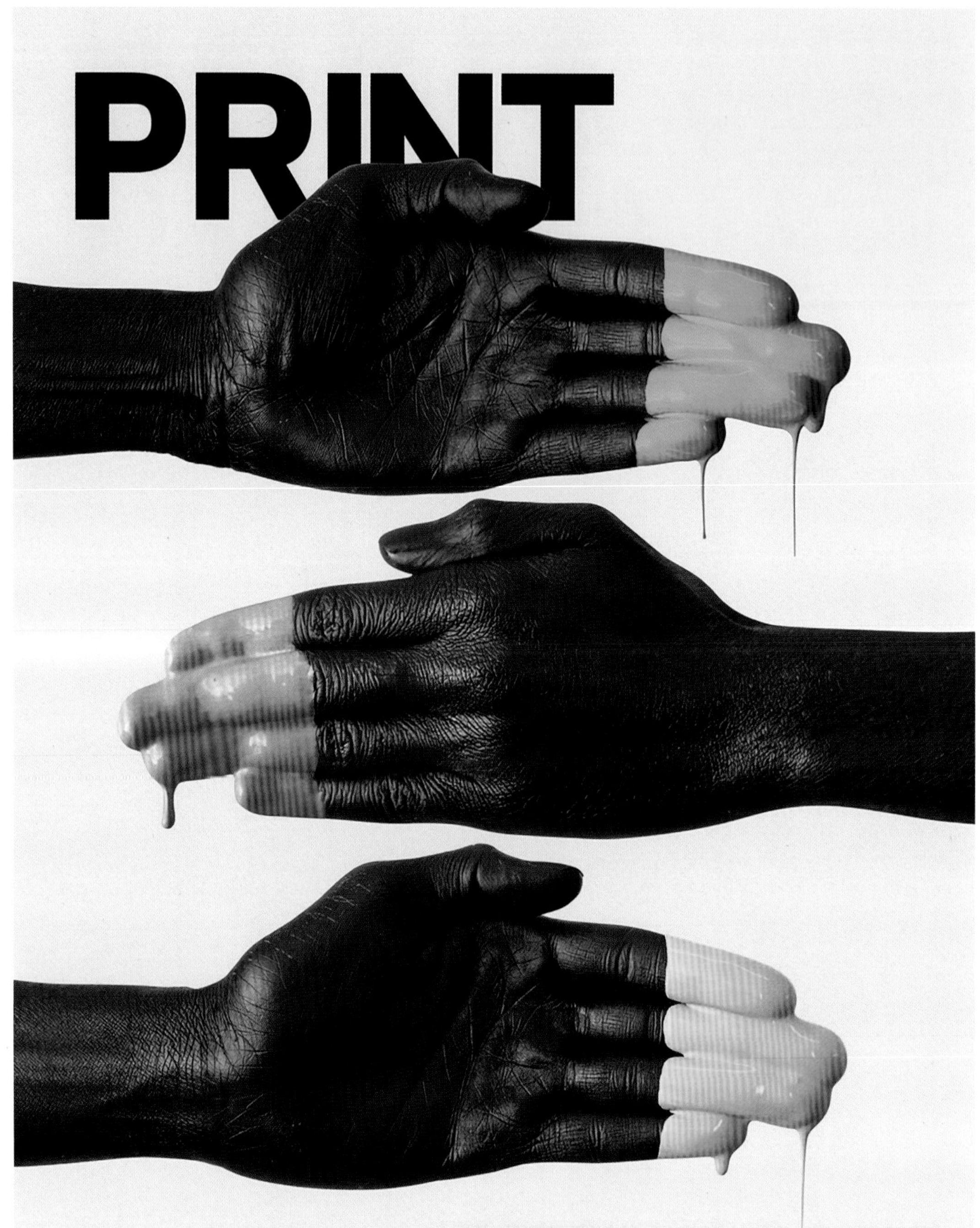
PRINT
THE NEW VISUAL ARTISTS 2015: 15 UNDER 30.

06

Conceptual Strategies

6–1 *Print*, designers Wael Morcos and Jonathan Key, 2015.

This magazine cover piques curiosity about the mystery of the black-inked hands dripping with bright paint. The designers have created an opportunity for a viewer to decipher a strong visual with a range of potential interpretations: Is this a statement about race, individuality, or creativity? They are all possibilities, but Morcos says, "While racial representation is undeniable in this image, the thinking was not about revealing or hiding the person's race. It was a way to illustrate the craft (the hand) when designing for print using CMYK colors." The initially ambiguous impact of the photo adds to its allure; a viewer is motivated to stay with it a bit.

Contemporary visual culture is image saturated. Social media users are exposed to more than 3.2 billion images and 720,000 hours of video shared daily. As a result, most of us are quite adept at understanding the nuances of visual content. Even if we aren't consciously aware of this mental skill, it's a natural adaptation to parsing the sheer number of images bombarding us daily through screens, news and social media, entertainment, and the built environment. Today's visually sophisticated audiences not only adapt quickly to new media experiences but also easily make the connection between text and a metaphoric or allegorical image choice.

The forward march of new visual technologies means a constant assimilation of such wonders as virtual reality and AI-generated art (not to mention holographic performances where some band members have been dead for years). Our acceptance and understanding of how images function in new technologies isn't always an instant process. An 1885 short film, *Arrival of a Train at La Ciotat*, by groundbreaking filmmakers Auguste and Louis Lumière, depicts a locomotive pulling into a station. Innocuous enough? Not in 1885. It's said that audiences reacted in terror, screaming and running to the back of the theater, on seeing a moving train seemingly coming straight at them.

In the centuries before a large percentage of populations were literate, complete stories were conveyed through images alone. Many of the narratives depicted in Renaissance paintings are drawn from the Bible or classical mythology. Viewers were already familiar with the tales and had no difficulty in deciphering the visual language of images on canvas. Paintings by Sandro Botticelli, Raphael, and Titian overflow with narrative symbols, allegories, metaphors, and iconographies that eloquently speak for themselves, independent of any text accompaniment. These narrative image techniques have retained all of their value over time.

Beyond the more direct image functions of explain–document–prove and other strategies discussed previously, there are conceptual tools for authors to use when pairing images with texts. Every author has an individual writing style built on their approach to the subject matter, an ear for language, and a personality that determines their ability to successfully connect with the intended audience. Familiar literary devices such as metaphor, synecdoche, allegory, and so on function the same way in imagery as they do in text, and these devices can be used to strengthen the visual narrative and aid in the reader's appreciation of the written word.

Devising abstract strategies for image use, as opposed to the overly simplistic "this is a text about a building and here's a photo of the building" approach, may seem daunting, but remember there will be several possibilities, with subtle distinctions between them. Is it 100 percent necessary for an author to classify an image under consideration as an icon or allegory, simile or metaphor? Of course not.

Define the differences between varying conceptual strategies, and decide which feels most appropriate for the text, to lay a few ground rules and provide a starting point for a productive image search. Even when an image marries well with the text's tone and content, other choices will work equally well but bring a different angle into play. Consider a few strategies and types of image before

6–2 *The Nightmare*, artist Henry Fuseli, 1781.

We don't "see" nightmares; we live out their terror in our sleep. This image of a nightmare (the word derives from an Old English term meaning a mythological demon or goblin who torments others with frightening dreams) visiting a tortured sleeper adds in the goblin as a symbol of what he represents. Using a tangible form to express a concept helps a reader visualize the narrative elements.

finalizing the decision, and allow intuition to weigh in. Often, if it feels right, it is the best choice; don't overthink it.

Here are the main conceptual strategies for image use:

- Symbolism
- Synechdoche
- Allegory
- Metaphor
- Analogy
- Iconography

6–3 NYC and Company, 2021.

Landmarks become widely understood symbols of cities and countries. Authors seeking to establish location without resorting to full-on cliché (Is that the Eiffel Tower? Oh, we must be in Paris!) might consider this approach, which mashes up that most iconic NYC symbol of all with simple road signs and fragments of city buildings across the five boroughs to create a recognizable but fresh version of the Statue of Liberty.

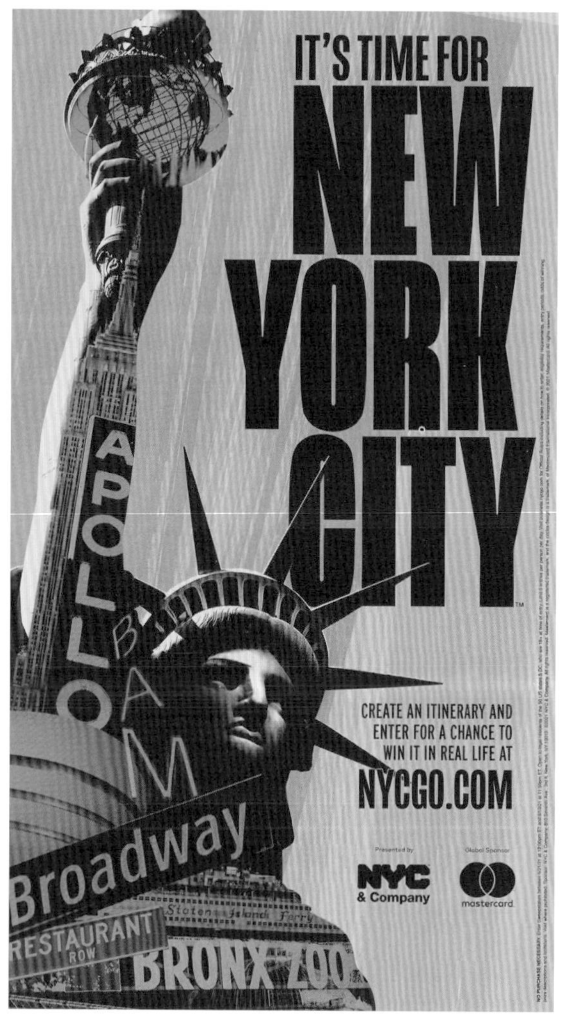

Symbolism

Symbolism uses one thing to stand for or suggest something else; it represents something beyond the literal meaning.

> **Example:** in Edgar Allen Poe's most famous poem, "The Raven," the persistent black bird is a symbol for loss, regret, mourning, and loneliness after the death of the narrator's wife.

6–4 American Institute of Graphic Artists, designer Paul Rand, 1982.

Rand arranged the four-letter acronym AIGA on a circle resembling a face, opening up an opportunity to slip in a visual pun. Despite the high level of abstraction, there is such a direct relationship that the eye as an *I* stands in perfectly well as both a human feature and letterform making up part of a corporate identity.

As a visual or literary technique, symbolism is fluid and heavily dependent on the context; fire, say, can symbolize passion or utter destruction. Symbols can be a flexible device used at an author's discretion as part of a personal iconography, assigning meaning specific to a situation and only that situation. Several of painter Frida Kahlo's self-portraits depict her with one or more of her spider monkeys, whom she loved for their mischievous, playful nature. Kahlo was deeply troubled by her inability to have children, and has said the pets featured in her paintings were representations of frustrated maternal feelings. In pre-Columbian Aztec society, monkeys are symbols of lust. We cannot know exactly what the artist intended the primates to stand for in her work; this example demonstrates the mutability of symbolism.

Even the most familiar symbols (a rose representing true love, for instance) do not communicate the same thing to different people, depending on the viewer's culture and life experience. While the fox is a symbol of sly cleverness across many cultures, and the jackass a symbol of stubborn stupidity, the goat has been seen as both a symbol of fertility and representative of Satan. Be aware of such predetermined associations when choosing symbolic imagery; don't risk bringing unintended meaning to image choices.

Is it possible to define universal symbols to communicate concepts and ideas? In a word, no. Images of familiar objects can take on appropriate symbolic meaning within the context of the text. Authors should not expect readers to undertake interpretative gymnastics to grasp the meaning of symbolic images. Instead, present readers with a visual language that corresponds to the text and is easily understood. Clarity in choosing symbolic images goes a long way.

Synecdoche

A synecdoche uses a part to stand in for the whole in a rhetorical manner.

> **Example:** the White House is frequently used as a representation of the entire government of the United States.

6–5 *White Glove: Michael Jackson*, photographer Tom Schierlitz, 2011.

An image of a trademark accessory is often enough to represent a celebrity: think of comedian Groucho Marx's ever-present cigar or singer-songwriter Madonna's 1990 cone-breast bustier. The single glove worn by Jackson during performances comes in a wide variety of colors and bedazzlement, but any one of them can represent an entertainer whose facial appearance changed frequently as the trademark glove stayed constant.

In the world of images, sometimes less is more. The power of synecdoche, a subtle communication technique that speaks volumes, creates an opportunity for a single detail or component of a larger element to serve as a jumping-off point for the reader's imagination. In this way synecdoche resembles symbolism, but it has a kind of sneaky aspect too: it can both celebrate and denigrate. A celebratory example might be a close-up image of a cabinet of first-place trophies that evokes the image of an accomplished athlete in the reader's mind. Conversely, an image of a broken plastic engagement ring says many things about the relationship—few of them positive.

Synecdoche often uses a smaller component of something to stand in for the bigger picture, but the technique also works in the opposite direction, where an entire thing stands in for a small component of itself. An image cannot use a random part of something and create synecdoche; there must be a widely understood specific meaning assigned to the part if the viewer is to comprehend. For instance, a red rubber nose seen on its own says "clown," while pots of makeup could refer to other professions—modeling or acting, not just clowning—and so are not specific enough to form a synecdoche. An effective visual synecdoche is one where the significance of the smaller part to the larger whole is obvious to the viewer, allowing them to draw the implied connection with ease.

Allegory

Allegory refers to a story, picture, or other piece of art that uses symbols to convey a hidden or ulterior meaning, typically a moral or political one.

Example: George Orwell's book *Animal Farm*.

An allegory has two components: its intended meaning and its vehicle—the text or image that conveys the meaning. In *Animal Farm*, for example, the sheep who disrupt meetings by bleating loudly to drown out opposing speakers represent the crowds swayed by Joseph Stalin's massive propaganda machine as he came to power in Russia. The sheep stifle dissent by making noise rather than engaging in discourse, just as Russian populations came to believe Stalin's simple slogans without questioning his underlying motives. The allegorical meaning here is: beware of propaganda. The sheep are the vehicle.

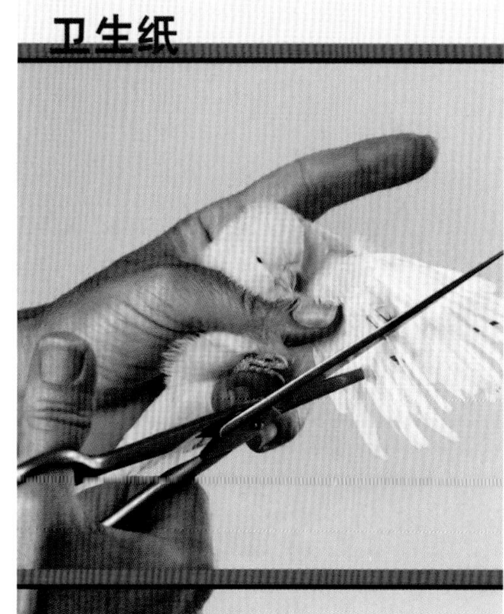

6–6 *Toilet Paper*, Maurizio Cattelan and Pierpaolo Ferrari, art director Micol Talso, 2012.

This image hits hard: a viewer instantly feels pity for the canary about to be cruelly deprived of flight. Having one's emotional or mental wings clipped by another person hurts immensely, and this photo uses a literal image to evoke feelings of helplessness and victimization along with empathy and sorrow. What's sadder (and more vulnerable) than a bird that can't fly?

← 6–7 ***New York Times Book Review*, illustrator Melinda Beck, 2019.**

The artwork for a review of *Kintu*, a novel by Ugandan writer Jennifer Nansubuga Makumbi, makes good use of the origin story represented by the Garden of Eden's tree of knowledge. This starting point uses powerful iconography to parallel the sweeping historical themes centered in the book's main character, nobleman Kintu Kidda, the origin of a cursed family tree. Kintu's mind (the tree) is tormented, and the serpent winding its way around the tree trunk speaks to Kintu's own suffering as well as the extended family simmering with resentments, rivalries, deceptions, and internal contradictions that is choking him.

↗ **6–8 *Self-Portrait with Death Playing the Fiddle*, artist Arnold Böcklin, 1872.**

There's nothing subtle about this painting's "hidden meaning," portrayed front and center. The narrative is closely tied to the Latin phrase memento mori (remember that you will die); even as mortals carry on with their lives, Death fiddles around in the background, patiently waiting for its moment to swoop in. Here, the allegorical skeleton representing Death plays a single-stringed violin—a clue that the artist's time is near.

Other well-known allegories are Aesop's fables, in which characters stand for abstract ideals summarized by a moral at the end. Allegories work perfectly well as complete narratives on their own while providing a second, hidden layer of instruction about behaviors and/or values. The fascinating thing about allegorical images is that in order for them to work as the author intends, the audience must engage from the outset, approaching what they see with the expectation that there is a hidden meaning, and a willingness to decipher it. For this reason, a reader must be willing to approach an allegory as a tale with a secondary meaning or else they will simply interpret it as a story about a selfish fox who wouldn't share some grapes.

All allegories rely on symbols to convey their underlying message, but the use of symbols in an image does not automatically make it an allegory. In an allegorical visual narrative, nearly every element symbolizes something else, or the image itself is standing in for a wider concept or historical event. Texts about politics, ethics, and religion often benefit from a partnership with allegorical images; political and editorial cartoons are especially useful to audiences that will quickly grasp the hidden meaning riding along in the allegory's vehicle.

Metaphor

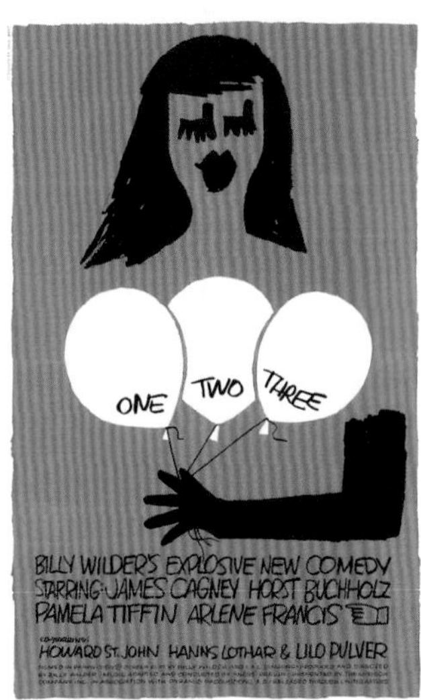

6–9 *One, Two, Three*, United Artists, designer Saul Bass, 1961.

Bass immediately captures the spirit of this political comedy by using balloons to represent breasts. The extra balloon is confounding at first (breasts come in pairs, after all), but helps define the film's screwball tone for the poster. Viewers could understand a further clever reference only after seeing the movie—the heroine meets her fiancé while blowing up balloons.

Metaphor compares two things to represent something else, particularly abstract ideas or concepts. A metaphor asserts that the two things are identical in some way rather than just similar.

Example: this new employee is a prize.

Is the employee literally a blue ribbon or silver-plated loving cup? Of course not. Unless it's meant sarcastically, a statement is being made about that person's high value to the company—a quality that would take many more words to explain literally. Saying they are a prize is a more interesting shortcut. Bringing two seemingly unrelated things into proximity with each other can be illuminating. Images function in this way too; use a visual metaphor to make a bridge between idea and text, and your reader will gladly venture across. Human thought—the mental activity we use to process and understand the world—is essentially metaphoric, making this strategy for image selection especially powerful. Metaphoric images are fine partners for literary texts, poetry, and dialogue. They add color, snap, and emphasis to make complex thoughts easier for the reader to visualize or relate to.

A key difference between a metaphor and allegory is that the allegory conveys a complete story, and a metaphor is more like a phrase or small figure of speech. Advertising often relies on metaphoric images since they are a complete and succinct shorthand, able to transmit an idea in a minimum of time. Metaphoric images ask the viewer to connect the dots; for instance, a 1969 ad for the Volkswagen Beetle didn't show the car at all, just a photo of the *Apollo 11* lunar module with the tagline "It's ugly, but it gets you there." The appropriateness of the metaphor (both the module and a Volkswagen are means of transportation, and while neither is particularly lovely to gaze on, both are reliable) is enhanced by the tie-in to the moon landing, and connects the Volkswagen brand to the feelings of success and pride many Americans shared on their country's achievement. A metaphor can establish a quick link to positive emotions, as this one does, or express negativity as well. "My boss is a monster!"

↦ 6–10 *Artificial Life after Frankenstein*, University of Pennsylvania Press, illustrator David Plunkert, 2020.

The artist creates a Frankenstein 2.0 feel by merging a human figure with wired electronics occupying a proportional space resembling a smartphone's dimensions. The image gives a viewer a look behind the scenes, literally, to see that the head is filled with a tangle of wires and circuits instead of human neurons. The snap-on, snap-off face tells us that under the surface, this life-form is artificial; with face in position, it would be hard to tell if the figure was human or robot.

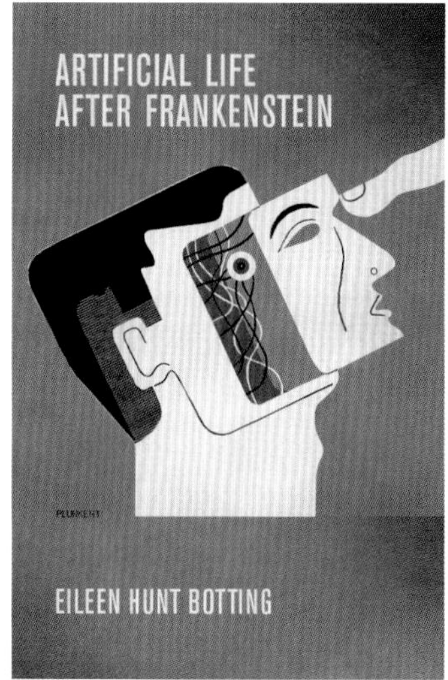

↗ ↦ 6–11 *The Voyeur*, Grove Press, designer Peter Mendelsund, 2018.

Once a person learns that they are being observed without permission, they typically feel violated, humiliated, and angry. Here, the figure of the voyeur looms large on the horizon, only partly hidden by blinds, minimizing everything else in the landscape. Depicting the voyeur in this monolithic manner addresses the power imbalance of spying and its reductive effect on its victims.

↦ 6–12 *Sunday Sketch (Brushgirl)*, artist Christoph Niemann, 2016.

Adding a few simple hand-painted limbs transforms an ordinary paintbrush. We're willing to see a girl with a swingy skirt because the visual correlation is so accurate: bristles = skirt and handle = shoulders read immediately. Using one object to stand in for something very different sets up a charming image strategy if the visual connection is as clear as it is here.

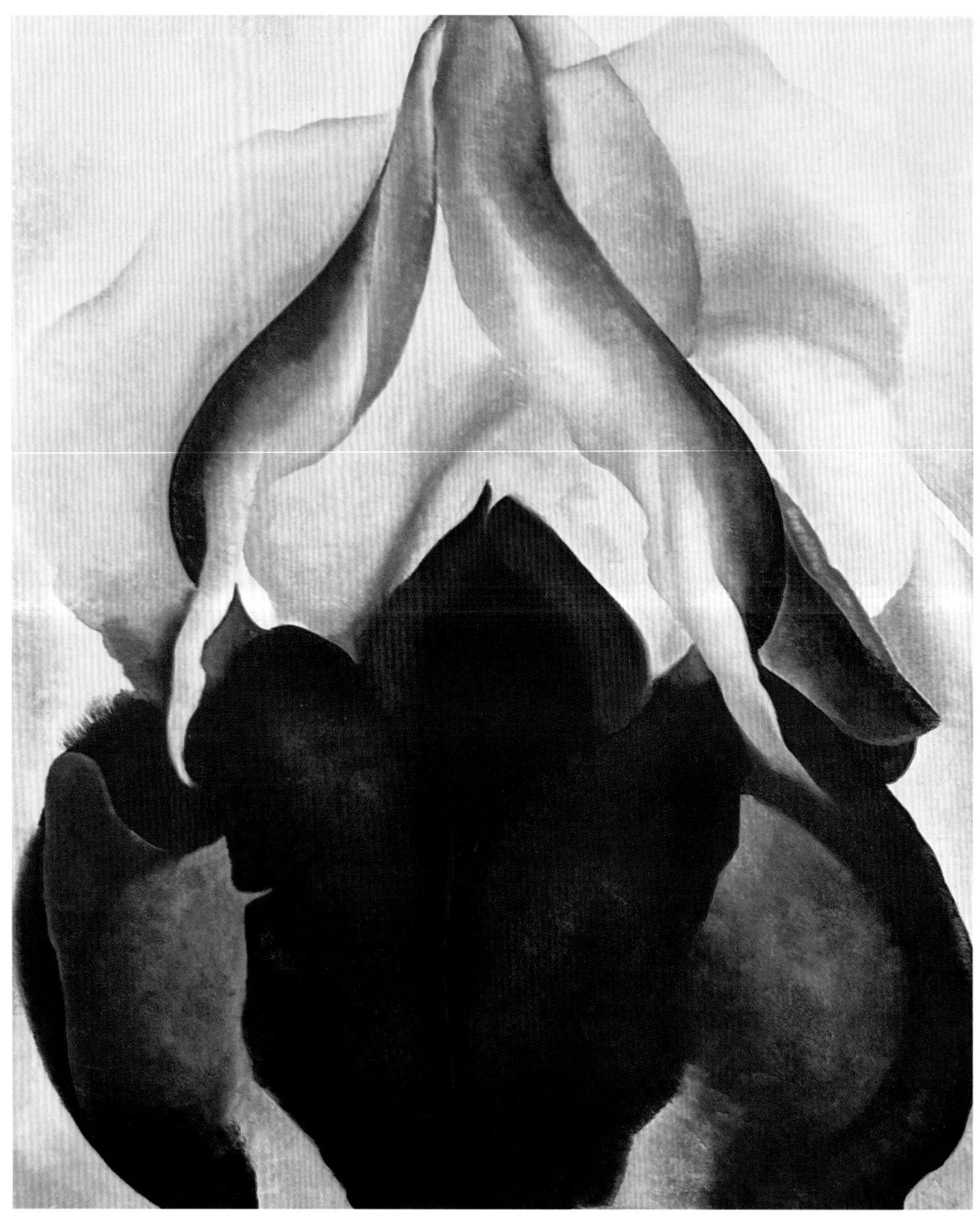

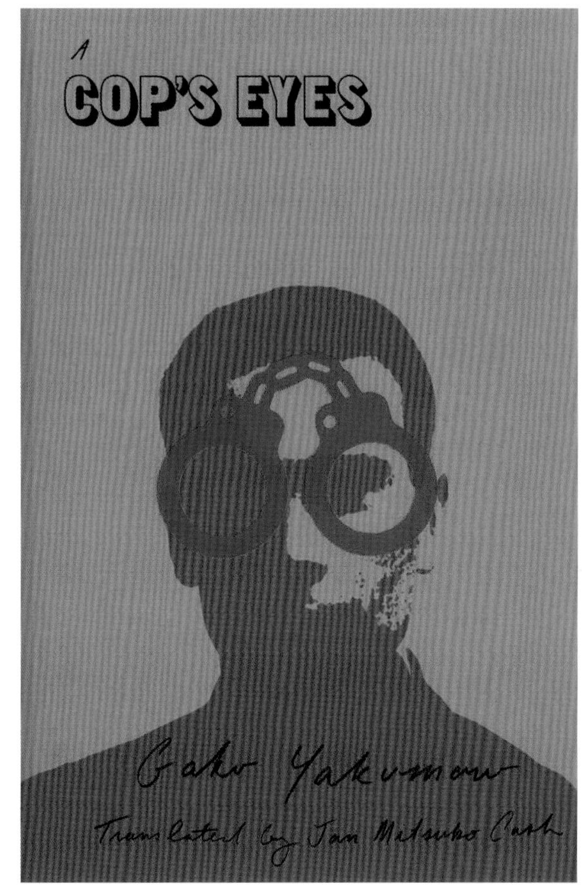

← **6–13** ***Black Iris*****, artist Georgia O'Keeffe, 1926.**

Finding a stand-in for images that might be considered too controversial (or in this example, pornographic) is a great strategy for texts where the actual subject is difficult to depict. O'Keeffe's giant, detailed paintings of flowers were considered shocking at the time because of their similarities to female human anatomy. Flowers are the sexual organs of plants, after all, so the visual parallel is undeniable. The approach is unassailable if you can find an appropriate visual pinch hitter.

→ **6–14** ***A Cop's Eyes*****, designer Peter Mendelsund, 2016.**

The background figure is anonymous, stylized to the point where it's difficult to even tell what gender it's meant to portray. The decisive placement of handcuffs immediately illustrates the book's title, letting a viewer know that those eyes belong to law enforcement. This pared-down visual analogy is direct and to the point; it tells just enough of what a reader needs to know before diving into the text.

Analogy

An analogy draws a similarity between things that are otherwise dissimilar.

> **Example:** a computer's operating system is like the wiring of the human brain.

Analogy is comparison, drawing a parallel between two seemingly different entities to illustrate a larger point due to their commonalities. It explains as well, through context and by providing an

↦ **6–15 UPS logo, Paul Rand, 1961.**

Rand combined elements from the brand's past logos (the shield) with a representation of what the company does (deliver packages).The client objected to the bow at first, because UPS discouraged the use of string on packages, but Rand successfully argued that the only way to make a rectangle read as a package is by putting a bow on it. That bow added an emotive quality to the logo. Don't we all get excited on receiving a gift?

↗↦ **6–16 Westinghouse logo, designer Paul Rand, 1959.**

Rand's logo for Westinghouse pulls off a design hat trick, referencing three separate electric elements (a circuit, wattage symbol, and wall outlet), jollied up by the arrangement of elements to resemble a human face. The analogous visual elements serve as a sort of Morse code transmitting different messages simultaneously: a scientific feel along with an emotive aura of warmth too.

↦↦↦ **6–17 and 6–18** How is a parking lot like a circuit board? They have little in common in terms of functionality or scale, but structurally and visually they are similar: orderly grids of lines interrupted by colorful rectangular units (parked cars or the blue resistors seen here).

explanation. Analogy is a bit more complex than metaphor, thanks to its explanatory function; it unpacks the topic in more detail to clarify the author's meaning.

One of the riddles posed by the Mad Hatter in *Alice's Adventures in Wonderland* is, Why is a raven like a writing desk? This is an odd analogy to be sure, and Alice refuses to reply, other than to say there is no possible answer. The Mad Hatter agreed. (In fact, author Lewis Carroll did not intend for there to be one, but he later provided this in an updated version of the book: "The answer is, 'Because it can produce a few notes, tho they are very flat; and it is never put with the wrong end in front!'")

The artistic use of imagery to create analogies aids authors in illustrating the deeper meaning of text concepts. Many familiar logotypes rely on visual analogies to help convey information about the company; for example, the CBS eye (which is also a symbol!) implies that the network founded on news reporting sees what's going on in the world and also says that people watch the broadcasts. The eye becomes a visual analogy for the abstractions of seeing and watching.

Visual analogy is helpful to distill abstractions into more easily understood concepts, especially for scientific or theoretical subjects. Learning that a computer's hard drive is divided into sectors just as a parking lot is divided into individual spaces allows a reader to easily imagine the chaos of a parking lot without lines and make a connection to how data are organized by an operating system. In this case, an image of an overhead view of a parking lot next to text discussing how computers manage files would work perfectly.

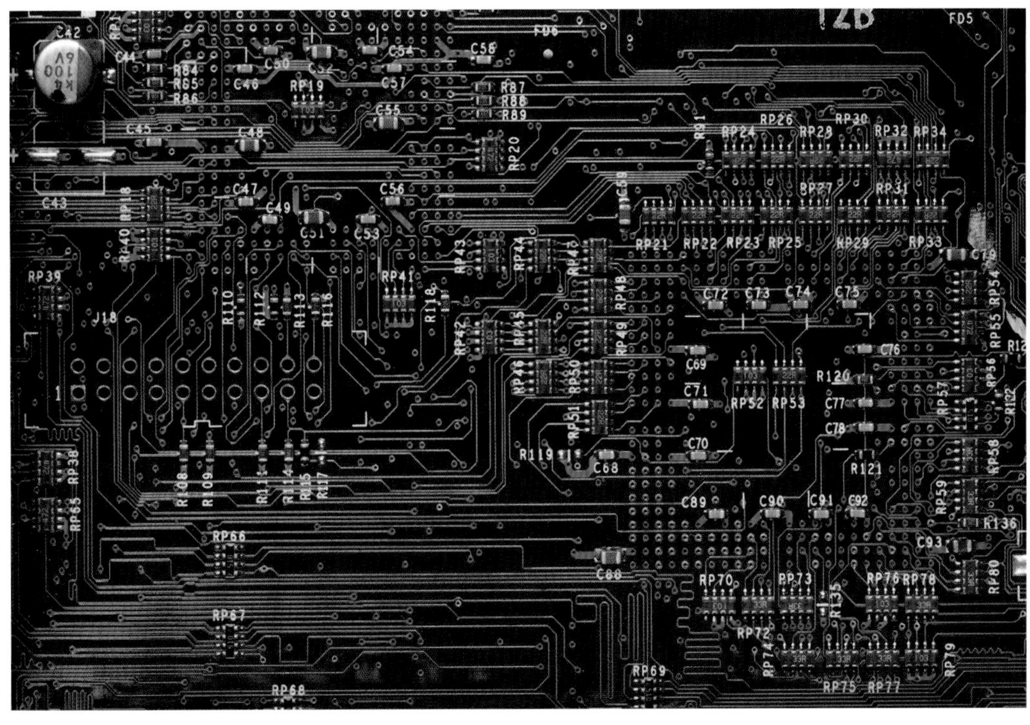
12B
FD5
C42
RP19
RP20
RP24
RP26
RP28
RP30
RP32
RP34
RP21
RP22
RP23
RP25
RP29
RP33
RP52
RP53
RP66
RP67
RP68
RP69
RP70
RP73
RP76
RP78
RP75
RP77

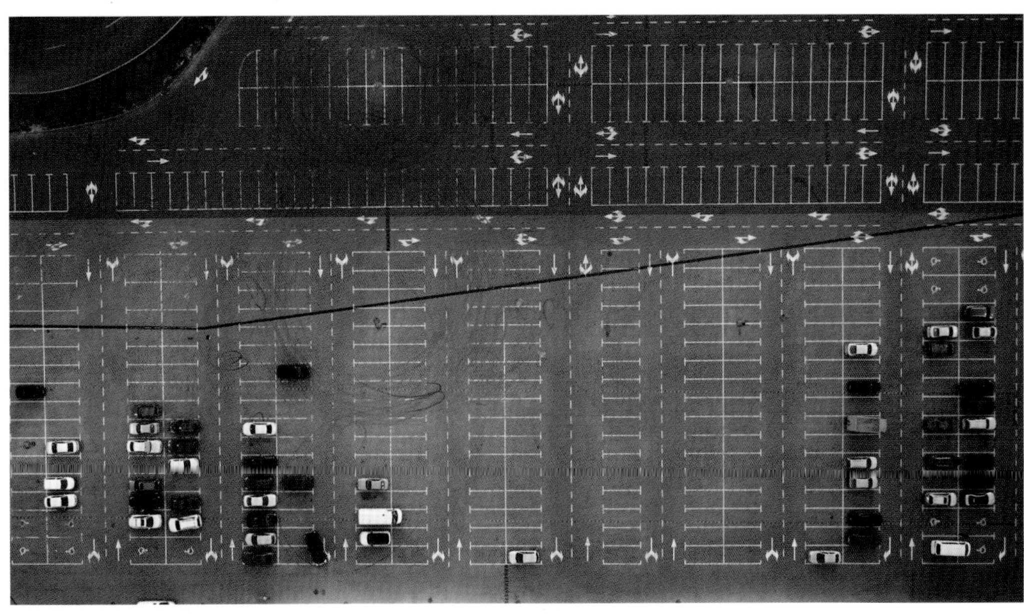

6–19 Owl of Athens, silver coin, ca. 480–420 BC.

The little owl is the avatar for Athena, the goddess of wisdom in Greek mythology (known as Minerva in Roman myths). The bird itself came to symbolize knowledge, wisdom, insight, and scholarship through its association with her. Consequently, owls are frequently used in design identities created for educational institutions, programs, and websites. Even if a viewer is not familiar with the classics, the iconography communicates its centuries-old message to all through familiarity and popular usage.

Iconography

Iconography refers to a range or system of images used to convey cultural or historical context or symbolic meanings.

> **Example:** the iconography of Greek mythology uses an image of an owl to represent the goddess Athena.

The word *iconography* derives from the Greek word *ikon*, or image. Beginning in the seventh century, icons were painted images of Christ used as devotional objects in the Greek Orthodox Church, and the term has gradually come to signify an image with especial significance or singularity. As with symbolism, iconic images can carry multiple meanings: an apple can represent a deadly threat to Snow White, or it can be the logo for a computer company.

Colors mean different things across various cultures, and iconography fluctuates across cultures too. For instance, in the Christian faiths, a snake stands for evil and temptation, the cause of Adam and Eve's expulsion from Paradise, and spark point for all the human suffering that came after. But in Chinese culture, the snake represents prosperity and is thought to bring good luck. For this reason, an awareness of general cultural context and the makeup

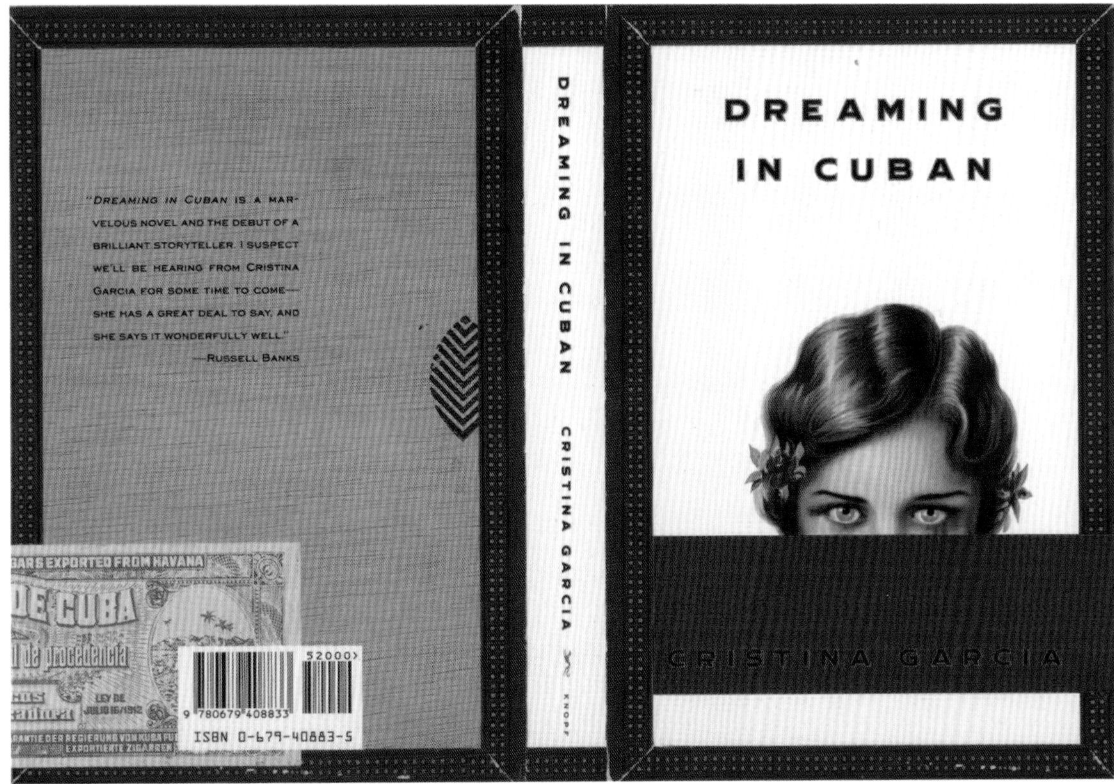

6–20 *Dreaming in Cuban*, by Cristina García, Alfred A. Knopf, designer Chip Kidd, 1993.

Just as an item of clothing can represent a specific person, in popular culture an object can come to represent the population, landscape, and consumer economy of an entire country. Cigars, that quintessentially Cuban product, have the added visual appeal of the beautiful, fragrant cedar boxes they come in. By evoking the iconographic design of a cigar box, Kidd immediately transports a viewer to Cuba at first glance.

of a text's main audience is crucial for authors considering the use of iconic images.

Iconography is distinctive, thanks to its cultural specificity and the relevance of its narrative to the demographic involved. It can be a bit difficult to define one's own personal iconography. For the artist Jeff Koons, it might be vast quantities of flowers or the mirrored surfaces of Mylar balloons; for artist Andy Warhol, it was cans of Campbell's soup. For authors, determining a visual iconography means pairing images with text in a way that feels definitive and highly individual—almost like a signature or an artist's unique style. Iconography that resonates positively with the culture of the audience connects the reader on a personal level with the author's themes and intentions.

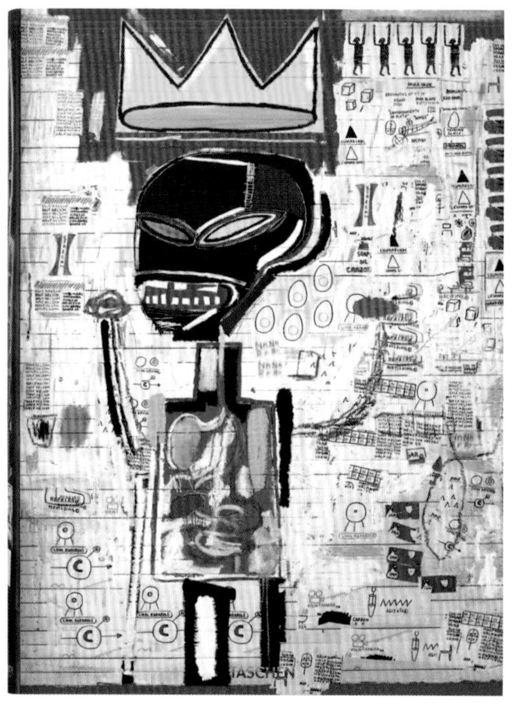

TASCHEN

WE SHALL SURVIVE, WITHOUT A DOUBT

6–21, 6–22, and 6–23 From left to right, *The Annunciation*, artist Fra Filippo Lippi, ca. 1435/1440; *Grillo* (detail), artist Jean-Michel Basquiat, 1984; "*We Shall Survive. Without a Doubt,*" artist Emory Douglas, 1971.

The religious iconography of halos has provided endless artistic inspiration throughout the ages. Venerable symbols such as crowns or halos confer exalted status to the heads they hover above, telling viewers there is something special, regal, or set apart about this person. In modern images, the function of the halo remains unchanged and easily understandable, even when it is shown as a crown or rays of light. All versions become a sort of visual shorthand for a VIP, alerting us to respect and pay homage to the exalted among us.

When mapping out the image selection strategy for your text (independent of whether you'll be using photography or illustration), ask yourself these questions:

- How can I use images to support and clarify an aspect of the text not directly stated?
- Is the connection between the images and text strong enough for a reader to understand the reason the images were chosen?
- Can images serve as a shorthand for a larger theme or context in my text?
- What is the overall tone of my text: direct and straightforward or more abstract?
- Does the strategy under consideration have the potential to be easily misinterpreted?

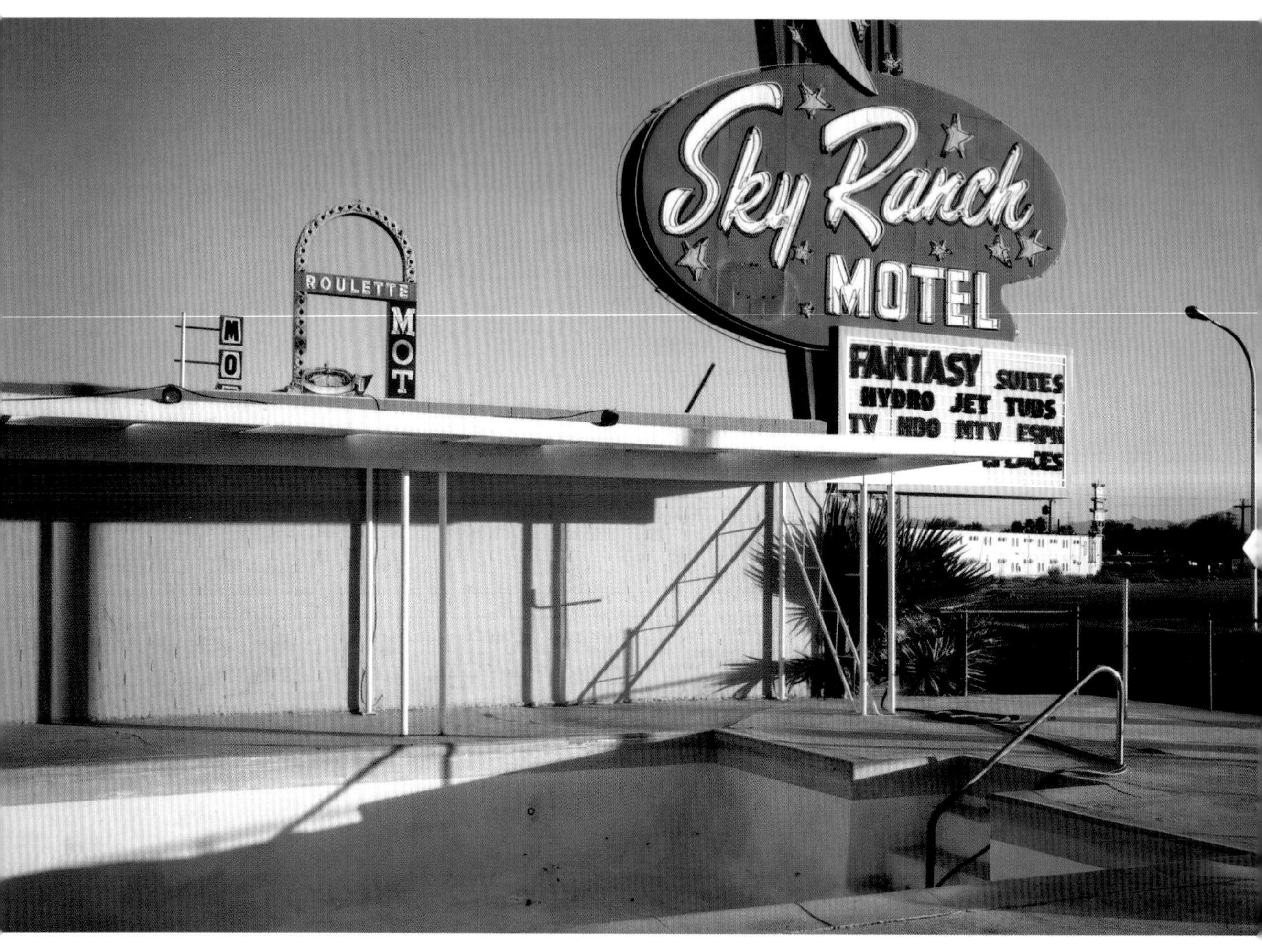

ROULETTE
MOT
MO
Sky Ranch
MOTEL
FANTASY SUITES
HYDRO JET TUBS
TV HBO MTV ESPN

07

Visual Grammar for Photography

7–1 Photographer David Graham, 1989.

The forlorn quality of an empty swimming pool at a deserted motel is emphasized by the angle of the late afternoon shadows. Night is approaching, in both a real and metaphoric sense. A cloudless blue sky and jaunty neon sign (and even the name of the place) bring in the optimistic aura of the 1950s, dimmed by the poignancy of the passage of time.

Within the basic image types of photography, illustration, and data visualization, each can have crossover functionality. For instance, a photograph can be entirely documentary (I was here and took a photo of this) to support a journalistic text, digitally collaged into a photo illustration of something not possible in the real world (a person with six arms), or from the world of fine art with more abstract and ambiguous imagery.

Why decide to use photography? In many instances, a photo or illustration will work equally well alongside text, and it's the author's preference that decides. If an author seeks to establish with precision what an object, person, or place looks like, it's usually better to opt for photographs, which will read as "realistic" to the viewer, not as an artist's interpretation. There are times when artistic interpretation is a better solution; for example, a text about the architectural history of Swedish fishing villages. Photos of the buildings will be viewed as realistic depictions of place, serving a valuable documentary function. Drawings of the same locales, however, can also bring in other,

7–2 Photographer Jonathan Bachman, 2016.

The best photos capture what pioneering early twentieth-century photographer Henri Cartier-Bresson called "the decisive moment": a split second that reveals the larger truth of a situation. Bachman's shot of twenty-seven-year-old nurse and activist Ieshia Evans standing tall against heavily armed cops during an anti–police brutality protest epitomizes brave dignity. She calmly faces down three officers who appear robotic and inhuman in their riot gear. There's something of classical sculpture in her pose and flowing gown; the officers seem to be recoiling backward from her power, as if she is radiating a force field. A truly decisive moment.

more intangible qualities (nostalgia, peacefulness, disruption, or decline) depending on the style of the artwork.

Editorial photography is created in service of a narrative; its intent from the get-go is to illustrate a specific story. It is not created to sell products or services as commercial photography is, though it can be argued that it sells a lifestyle or the editorial position of its publisher. Searching through stock photography can be an overwhelming experience. Many of the images available for licensing are purposely a bit generic, created as jack-of-all-trades meant to fit as broad a range of editorial usage as possible. Yet "master of none" applies to probably 85 percent of stock; you have to look really hard to find the good stuff.

Consider whether the image looks more like an advertisement (avoid these), or something you'd see as part of a main feature in a magazine or on a website. Photos for editorial use have a point of view and sense of narrative; they can be natural or hyperstylized; they feel specific and nongeneric. These very qualities can make it difficult to find a good match for your text (after all, the stock photo was not created with your text in mind), but it is possible to get close, with patience and a lot of digging.

Within the broader category of photography, imagery falls into these basic subtypes:

- Journalistic or documentary
- Illustrative
- Abstract or artistic

Journalistic or Documentary

Journalistic photos must be 100 percent authentic. They must show the viewer something that really happened, as it looked at that moment—*as it was*—or else they lose all credibility. The Associated Press Code of Ethics for Photojournalists puts it clearly:

> AP pictures must always tell the truth. We do not alter or digitally manipulate the content of a photograph in any way. The content of a photograph must not be altered in Photoshop or by any other means. No element should be digitally added to or subtracted from any photograph. The faces or identities of individuals must not be obscured by Photoshop or any other editing tool.

Photos can lie, and they always have; manipulation makes it possible for them to function more like illustrations, depicting things that don't exist in the real world. This has been true since the birth of the medium in the nineteenth century when spirit photos, purporting to show the ghosts of departed loved ones, were all the rage, especially since a public unfamiliar with the new technology had no idea that such a thing as a double exposure was possible. People were willing to accept the images as proof of the supernatural; they believed in the ghosts. We believe in all sorts of other ghosts now

7–3 *Free Solo* (trailer), photographer Jimmy Chin, 2018.

The feeling of vertigo is enhanced by the inclusion of the ground at the bottom; without it we'd have no way to judge the relative distance of the climber on his way up the mountain. Looking down the vertical rock face documents a point of view many of us would be too scared to attempt and so would never experience directly. Here we can imagine what it's like without risking life and limb.

that Photoshop has become a verb and Instagram filters allow everyone to look like anime versions of themselves (or like unicorns, or twenty-five pounds lighter and four inches taller, etc.).

In 1982, a *National Geographic* magazine cover brought to light one of the earliest high-profile public cases of inappropriate photo manipulation. Photographer Gordon Gahan's horizontally framed shot of Egypt's Great Pyramids of Giza, with dramatic silhouettes of men on camels in front of the pyramids, was too wide to fit the vertical cover. Solution? The magazine's art team cut the image apart to decrease the gap and move the two pyramids closer together (this was the pre-Photoshop era). The alteration was done without informing Gahan, who protested when he saw the published cover, as any cropping or alteration of images should not happen without the photographer's consent.

It's worth noting that Gahan reportedly paid the men on camels to ride back and forth multiple times to ensure he'd get exactly the photo he wanted. In other words, the camel riders were staged like extras in a film to add a picturesque local color narrative that wasn't true that day, but anyone seeing the magazine cover would have no way of knowing that.

Does this matter? Yes. If the image was presented as journalism, an authentic representation of a place and time, it matters a great deal. The image was art directed during the shoot and further manipulated in the production process. It was not reality as it exists; it was a narrative imposed by the photographer who believed his version of reality would make a better *National Geographic* cover, and by the magazine's art team that moved monumental ancient structures to fit the cover format. The problem is that the photo looks "real." Most people who saw it would likely not notice the alterations, and there is no way to know that the camel riders were props. The readers have been fooled.

7–4 *Street Arabs in Sleeping Quarters*, photographer Jacob Riis, ca. 1890.

In the late nineteenth century, Riis used his camera to document New York City's slums, populated mainly by poor immigrants. Images like this one, from his book *How the Other Half Lives*, forced the city's upper and middle classes to become aware of the appalling conditions endured by over one million poor people, including homeless children such as these. His work added tenement reform to the top of the list for New York's political agenda.

7–5 Associated Press, 2003.

It's difficult to bear witness to the dehumanization of this detainee at the Abu Ghraib prison in Baghdad. The anonymous, suffering figure appears almost crucified compared with the unconcerned ease of the soldier at the right, casually fiddling with what appears to be a camera. Small details such as the soldier's gold wedding ring are jarring when seen in context with the "rings" attaching wires to the detainee's fingers. Searing images like this are game changers, often driving protest and moving viewers to demand humanitarian action.

The moral of the story? Seeing is not always believing. Do your homework to be sure that any news-based or journalistic photo is authentic before you consider using it in your document. It's easier than ever before to create convincing fakes; don't be a sucker for it, and even more critical, don't allow your readers to be misled.

When a photo is not being presented as 100 percent truthful, the script shifts a bit. Magazine and advertising images in all media are typically altered to an incredible degree; people magically become years younger and remarkably blemish free, with brighter eyes and whiter teeth. During postproduction, the green shirt a celebrity wore to the photo shoot can be color shifted to any other hue, on a whim. Interiors often have the electric outlets, inset ceiling light fixtures, and other distracting features removed. This isn't journalism, however, so the line of what's permissible by way of alteration becomes more blurred. Here we aren't looking for reality and all its warts; we are looking for the magical and aspirational. We buy into the fantasy willingly. Legendary fashion photographer Irving Penn noted that his role was "selling dreams, not clothes."

Illustrative

Photo illustrations are a good way to evoke the impossible or ridiculously improbable; they can be satiric and pointed, lyrical and evocative, and pretty much anything in-between. They aren't bound by standards of authenticity and function more in the realm of illustration than photography. In other words, they are illustrations made using a camera instead of art media or design software. Photo illustrations rescue a dull subject by presenting it in a novel way while still providing elements of reality, albeit a new and improved reality. The difference between a photo and photo illustration is that the latter uses photographed elements as interchangeable components and recombines them to create a new narrative.

Here we aren't addressing hyperrealist drawings that look like photographs (to be discussed later) but rather images based on or collaged from photographs, deliberately altered for effect. Designers and artists such as El Lissitzky and Aleksandr Rodchenko began

7–6 Photographer Yuni Yoshida, n.d.

Every aspect of this photo adds to its narrative punch. The depiction of a human heart as fertile ground where emotions (love?) bloom is sweet and easily understood even when pictured as a dirty ball of roots. The shaggy bits of soil and the little red petals falling off hint at emotional difficulty and even pain. Those shed petals evoke drops of blood.

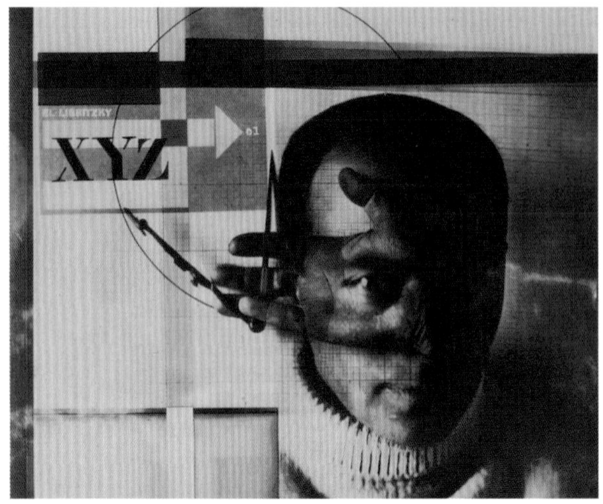

→ **7–7 *Self-Portrait*, artist El Lissitzky, 1924.**

Russian-born artist, designer, typographer, photographer, and architect El Lissitzky also created early twentieth-century Soviet exhibitions and propaganda. His experimentation with photographic printing and production techniques, developed in the 1920s and 1930s, has influenced graphic designers ever since. He was among the first to use layered transparent images blending real but disparate elements in order to express abstract thoughts or concepts.

↘ **7–8 *Kino Glaz (Film Eye)*, artist Aleksandr Rodchenko, 1924.**

Constructivist artist, writer, photographer, and designer of publications, packaging, and more, Rodchenko was one of the most prolific artists of the period following the Russian Revolution of 1917. His stark, limited-palette designs used photography in bits and pieces as graphic elements—a daring avant-garde approach at the time and a powerful technique still in use by graphic designers today.

→→ **7–9 Photographer Travis Rathbone, n.d.**

One fish can tell many stories. By showing the fish's head and tail in its natural state, Rathbone reminds us of its origin as a living thing. Moving the time line along to first a raw and then cooked fillet, accompanied by a chef's knife and seasonings, completes a viewer's mental transition of the fish from creature to ingredient to dinner.

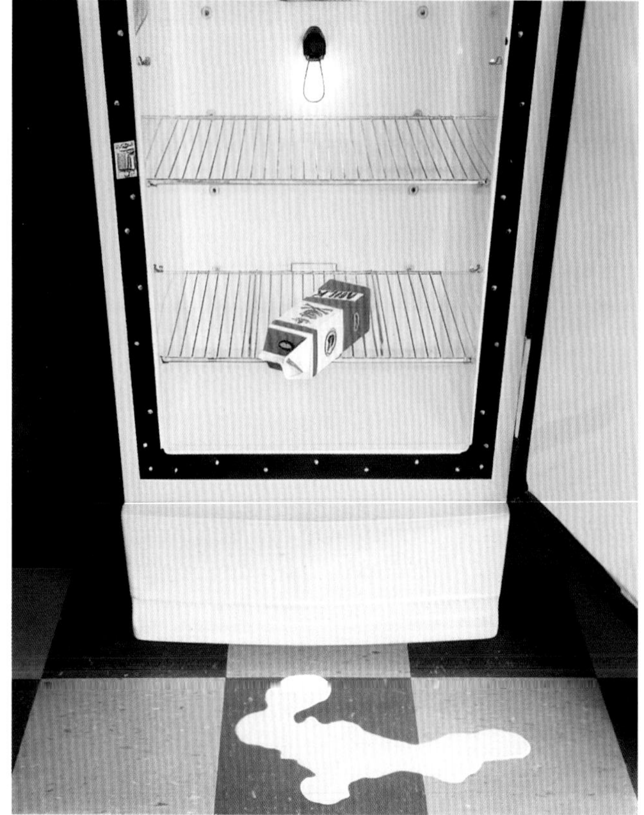

7–10 *Discover* magazine, photographer Dan Winters, n.d.

Image-editing software such as Photoshop has made it simple (and commonplace) to create an image like this out of existing digital bits and pieces. Still, it's hard to beat a studio shot that lays out a narrative in such a compelling manner; with just a few elements, the image feels believable yet mysterious. So many unanswered questions: Where's the rest of the food? Who spilled the milk? Is someone crying off-camera over it?

experimenting with photo collage techniques early in the last century, discovering a whole new use for a medium previously regarded as a way of recording reality, not altering or adapting it to fit an artist's vision.

This type of photo allows the image content to appear to defy gravity, change scale to a dramatic degree (imagine a six-hundred-pound mouse), put people who lived hundreds of years apart together at a party, or take on otherworldly colors. Photo illustrations have a pleasingly liminal quality, posed as they are between the observable world and human imagination. We know that the picture of a person with a giraffe's head and neck isn't a real creature, but because it's pieced together from "real" photos it has credibility and believability.

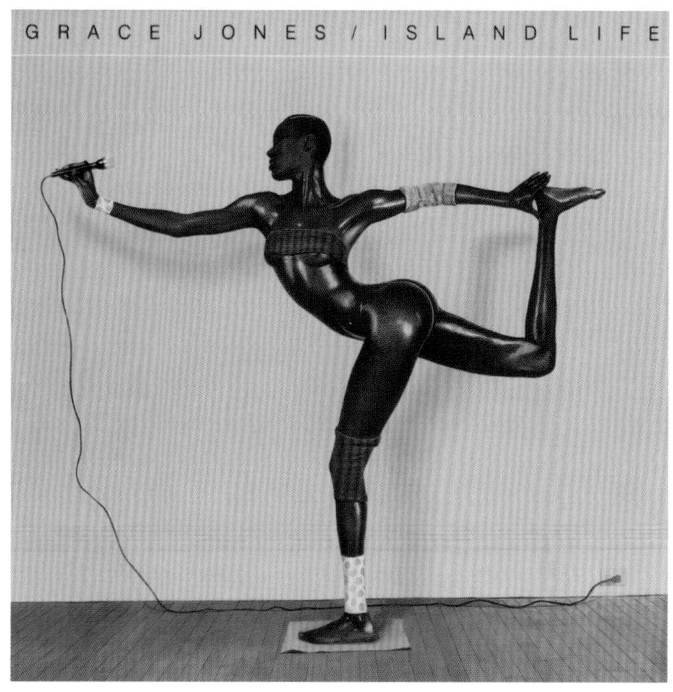

7–11 ***New York*** **magazine, photographer Jean-Paul Goude, 1978.**

Before Photoshop, there was airbrush image retouching, and before that, paint and brushes. The only way to achieve the anatomically unlikely human form seen in the finished photo of singer and model Grace Jones was to physically slice apart a montage of studio shots, puzzle them together, and fill in the missing transitions by hand. Images like this remind us how successfully photos can lie, but also how well they can succeed as illustrations.

→ 7–12 *McMansion*, photographer Jeremy Wolff, n.d.

↘ 7–13 Photographer USGirl, 2011.

The photo-collaged image of a house at top has personality and a story to tell, while the straightforward shot is dull and unengaging.

For fiction, essays, and poetry, photo illustrations bring sophisticated imagination to the marriage of image and text. They can also be used alongside reportage if the story warrants it: for instance, a news piece about the difficulty of selling a poorly built McMansion could be accompanied by a composite photo deliberately pieced together off-kilter and misaligned, hinting at the structure's shoddiness or any number of other interpretations suggested by the text. The approach accurately represents the scenario in an artful way that isn't misleading (viewers aren't likely to misunderstand what they see; they know the building isn't patched together like that) and is more interesting than a straightforward single photo.

Photo illustrations can be carefully set up to show a specific real-life situation that didn't (or couldn't) occur naturally or spontaneously. Let's say there was a mystery story where someone opened a refrigerator and found only a cat inside, gazing out. With a cooperative cat as model, this image could be generated in a studio, lit and staged for maximum effect with unnatural colors in the surroundings, deep and dramatic shadows, and otherworldly seeming light emanating from the cat that is actually being emitted by the refrigerator light bulb, and so forth. It's a photo that shows something that really happened (someone booked a studio, hired a photographer, and located the perfect cat to model), but as a deliberate, art-directed effort. Its function as a photograph is illustrative since every element was planned, staged, and editorialized in service of a specific narrative.

How is this different from taking pictures at an event for the local paper or shooting a celebrity in a photography studio for a magazine cover? In the first instance, the event photographer is documenting something that happens spontaneously in real time; it isn't art directed, and the photographer has creative agency and responsibility to search for and capture a narrative as they see it unfolding. In the second, the celebrity photos are not illustrating anything other than what the person looks like, aided by props chosen to enhance their preferred image for the public. The studio shots are documenting physical appearance in service of a narrative describing that person.

7-14 ***Argentina: Formalisms I*****, photographer José De Rocco, 2020.**

Abstract photography transforms its subject matter: a viewer doesn't really need to know what it's a picture of, but notices and appreciates other qualities of the image instead. Here, subtle grid and line patterns abound on all surfaces, joined by small but mighty pops of primary colors, capped off with a superassertive bright orange. It communicates joy as well as order, symmetry along with asymmetry.

Abstract or Artistic

7–15 *Dunes, Oceano*, photographer Edward Weston, 1936.

Weston was one of the first twentieth-century artists to champion photography as an abstract art form in itself; his influence on modern art was tremendous. In images such as this, light and shadow dramatically define forms and volumes, allowing the subject to escape its ordinary identity and become mysterious and alluring. Through his lens, sand dunes achieve a more exalted state of being.

There is no single definition for the ambiguous term *abstract photography*, sometimes referred to as nonobjective or concrete photography. Like its cousin abstract art, abstract photography ranges from representational images incorporating abstract elements to completely nonrepresentational images. The content of abstract photos focuses mainly on form, color, and texture. Many abstract photographers use imagery to relate to states of mind and emotion or depict elemental realities. A camera is not always involved in the creation of abstract photos, which can draw on a wide variety of photosensitive materials, equipment, and processes.

Abstract photography as an art form arose from late nineteenth-century scientific photographs of light rays dispersed by a spectroscope.

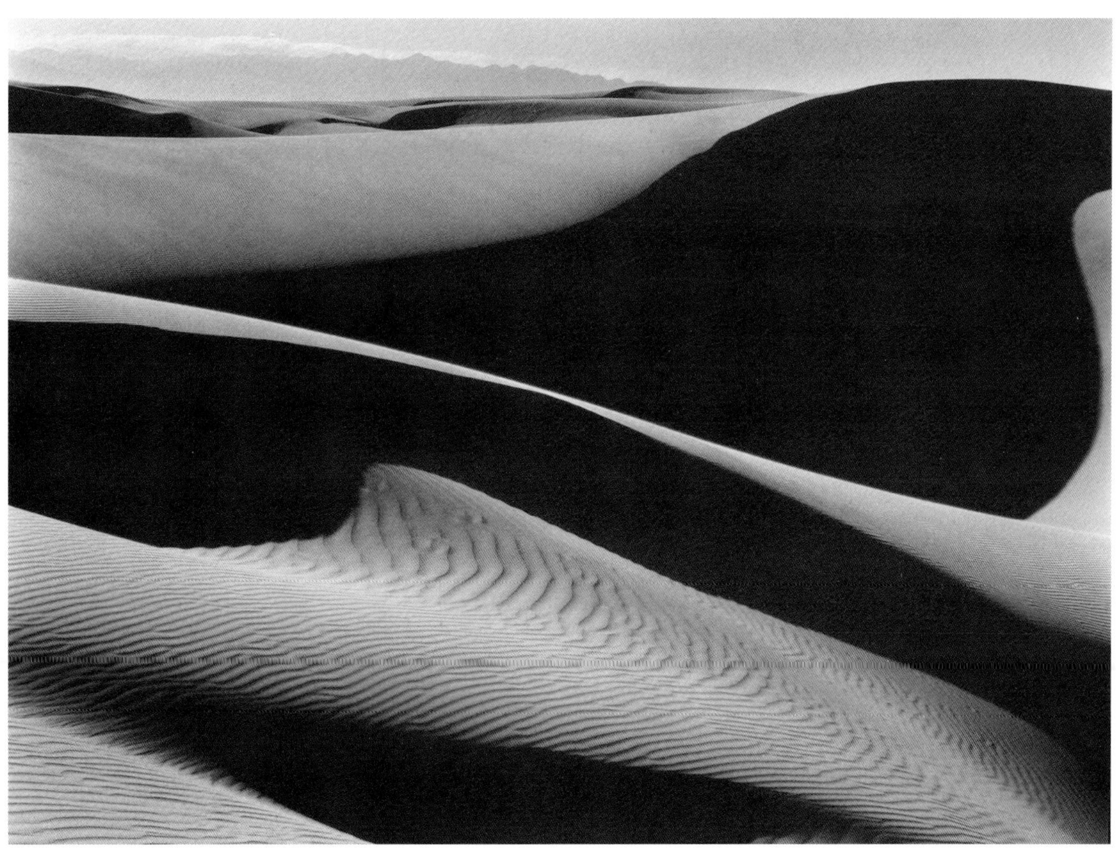

7–16 *New York Times*, photographer Andrew Moore, 2022.

Abstract photography gifts viewers with a new way of seeing the commonplace elements of everyday life, shifting the focus onto pure form rather than documentation of events or narrative. Moore framed this image of jutting balconies as strong geometric shapes of contrasting light and shadow punctuated by tiny staccato circles of drainage pipe openings—an original way to document a beachfront block of condominiums.

The beautiful patterns came to be appreciated as art by early twentieth-century avant-garde artists, who were inspired to experiment with abstraction in their own photography. Alfred Stieglitz's *Equivalents*, groundbreaking abstract photographs of clouds produced between 1922 and 1934, were described by art historian Sarah Greenough and artist Juan Hamilton as "photographs of shapes that have ceded their

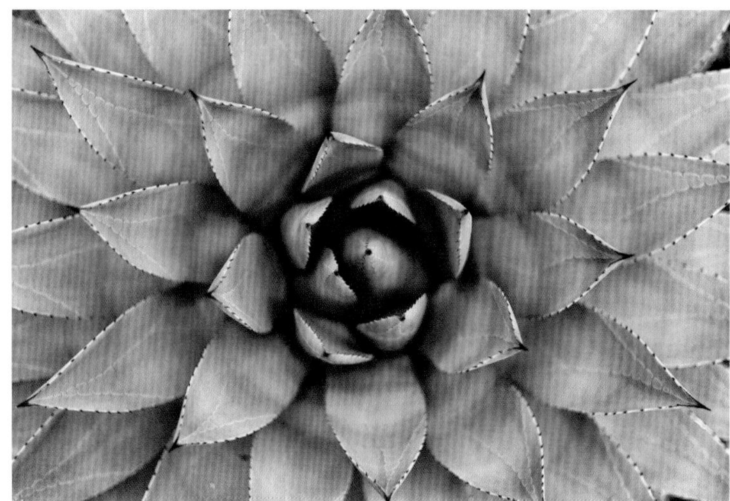

7–17 *Fractals*, photographer Genista/ Flickr, 2018.

Images shown in extreme closeup, cropped to remove all external sources of reference, present their subjects as pattern and rhythm separate from a main identity as a plant, mountain, or animal. Details that a viewer might overlook—the delicate spines on the leaves and Fibonacci spiral of growth—become important points of interest in their own right.

identity, in which Stieglitz obliterated all references to reality normally found in a photograph."

Abstract photographs lack a strict documentary function; while they often contain representational imagery, their formal effect is separate from the source subject matter. They are useful for creating visual parallels to text while not necessarily being specific to or directly illustrating it. In a scanning electron microscope picture of a fly's compound eye with its many facets, without the rest of the fly (wings, legs, and so on), the image cropped into a rectangle becomes less about the insect and more about pattern and texture, and can be used in a context other than the expected scientific literature. For this example, the image could pair with a text about modular architecture drawing inspiration from the natural world. Adding in a photo of the repeating balconies on a building facade, also cropped into a rectangle without other identifying details or landscape, allows the reader to quickly see the connection that the author is drawing in words. Photo captions fill in the missing information; without knowing the origin of the mystery texture in the fly's eye photo, the aspect of the architectural inspiration drawn from nature remains elusive.

As with abstract photography, the term *art photography* is not clearly defined. Art photos are created to express an artist's vision

RAILOWSK
RAILOWSK

← 7-18 ***Behind the Gare Saint-Lazare*, photographer Henri Cartier-Bresson, 1932.**

"For me the camera is a sketch book, an instrument of intuition and spontaneity, the master of the instant which, in visual terms, questions and decides simultaneously," Cartier-Bresson said when describing his approach to photography. His images capture life's surprising moments of grace with great precision; notice how the silhouetted figure is caught in midair with neither foot touching the ground, bringing to mind abstract thoughts of suspended time and gravity.

→ **7-19 Installation for the Berrydown Foundation, photographer Andy Goldsworthy, 2013.**

Goldsworthy's photos document his ephemeral outdoor sculptures made of leaves, twigs, rocks, and other organic material. The glowing arrangement of bright yellow leaves around the base of this tree's trunk seem to illustrate the primeval force of the forest or power of nature. There is just enough of a suggested narrative to make an image like this a fitting companion for fiction, poetry, or essays—with permission of the artist, of course.

using photography as the chosen medium; the camera becomes a studio tool in service of the imagination whether the artist is shooting landscapes or creating staged and scripted photos in a studio. They're sometimes, but not necessarily, abstract. They are often produced in narrative sequence—manipulated, pieced together, drawn or painted on, or otherwise altered to express an idea, emotion, or message unique to the artist. In other words, they are the heavily editorialized opposite of documentary photography.

A member of the Photographic Society of London, founded in 1853 when photography was just coming into use, protested at a meeting that the medium was "too literal to compete with works of art" because it did not "elevate the imagination." This sentiment, grounded in the notion that photography is a commercial, mechanical method of reproduction and so cannot be an art form, persisted until the mid-twentieth century. Part of the argument hinged on the fact that endless copies of a photo could be produced, effectively removing rarity and value, unlike a painting, which is a singular piece. Photographers simply began producing limited numbered and signed editions, much as printmakers had been doing for centuries, to increase the perceived value of the work.

Authors wishing to reuse an artist's photos need to be precise in describing the context when requesting permission since the work was not initially created to accompany the text. The artist must be given a right of refusal if they don't want the work repurposed. As with iconic journalistic photos, some art photos are too well-known to ever reuse. As a rule of thumb, if it's been used on a postcard, popular poster, screen saver, book jacket, or album cover, chances are there's a better, less familiar image option to pair with your text.

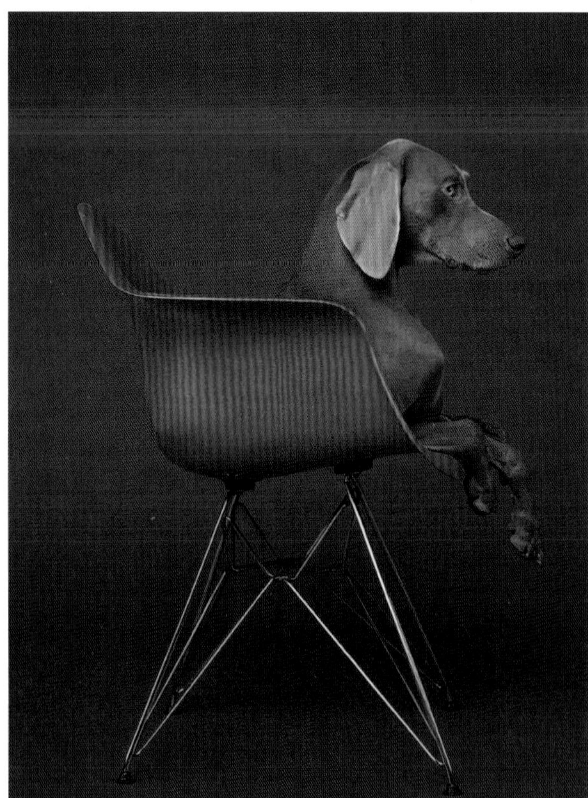

7-20 *Eames Low*, photographer William Wegman, 2015.

Wegman's photos of his Weimaraners over the years are charming, absurd, touching, and humorous. The images are the rare fine arts photos to be enthusiastically embraced by the general public, seen on tote bags, T-shirts, calendars, address books, note cards, and other merchandise. Their widespread familiarity means that such images may have been seen in other contexts very different from their intended use, and will perhaps spark an unintended interpretation or association for a viewer as a result.

7–21 *New York at Night*, photographer Berenice Abbott, 1932.

New York City is always wonderful lit up at night, but Abbott captured a rare moment: the quicksilver interval of time when night falls but office workers are still at their desks toiling away. The image speaks to the glamour and romance of New York as well as the reality: in Gotham, people work really, really hard in pursuit of success. Notice how this image is not just about the geometric forms of blocky buildings; it's also about human aspiration, even though there's nary a soul to be seen.

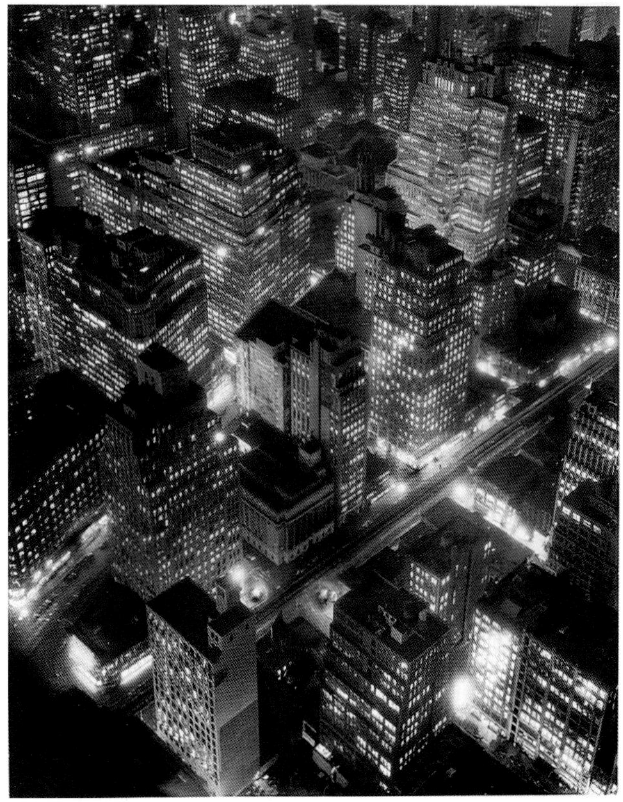

When weighing photo options, ask yourself these questions:

- Does the first image a viewer will see have a strong impact?
- Are the photos I'm considering well composed and in focus?
- Do the photo selections feel inspired or generic?
- Does the style of the photos feel like a good match for my text? Would black-and-white or full-color photos make for a better pairing?
- Do the photos add a level of understanding by "getting between the lines" of the text or do they simply mirror what is stated in the text?
- If I'm using multiple photos, does each image follow a separate and distinct step in my narrative arc?

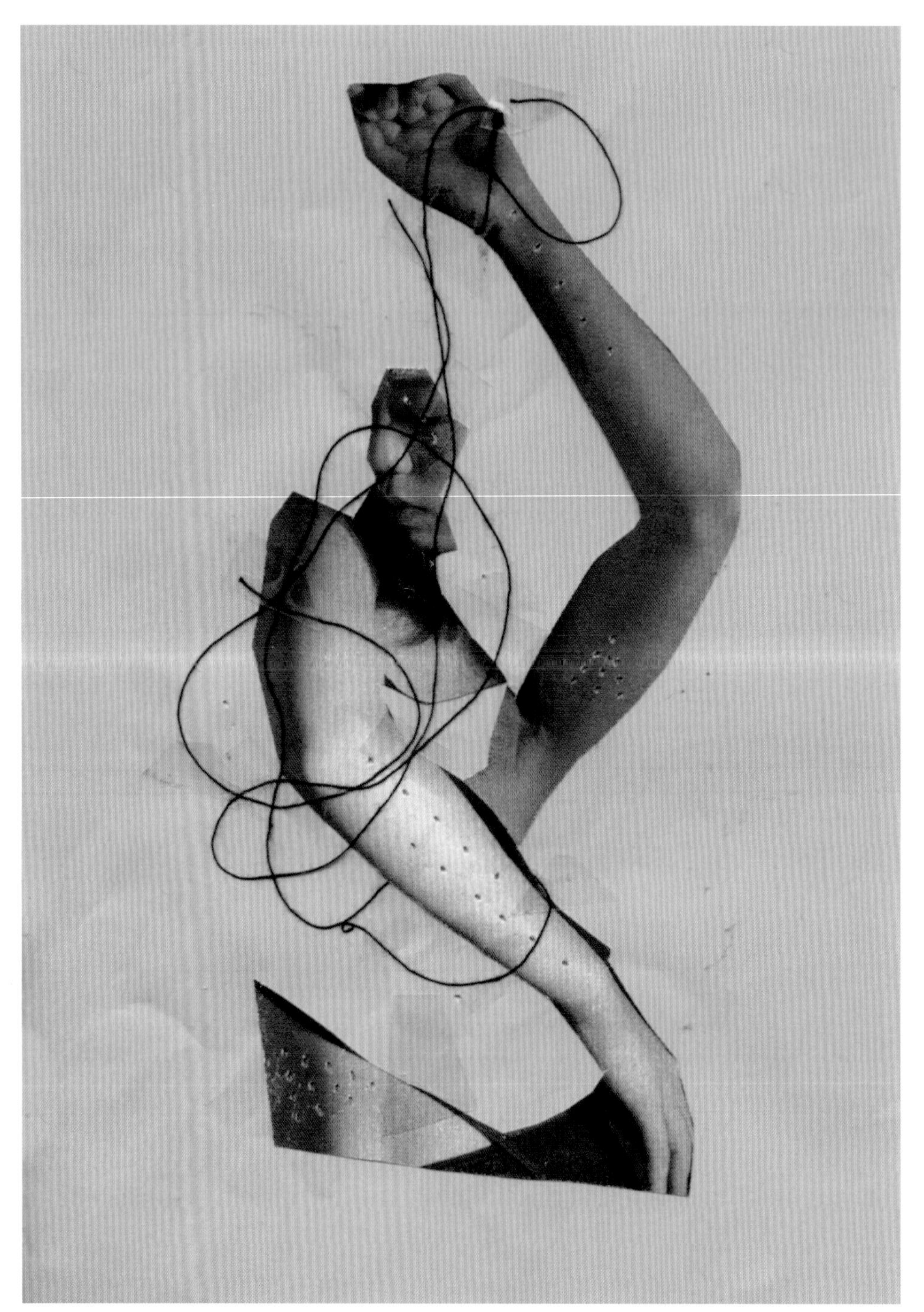

08

Visual Grammar for Illustrations

8–1 Artist Najeebah Al-Ghadban, 2020.

Like a haiku, this image speaks powerfully through minimal content. The fragmented female figure hints at alienation, violence, isolation, and damage—but her left hand pulling a long cord suggests agency, either to rescue herself by lassoing her parts back in or to purposely self-destruct. The neat rows of dots peppering her body are reminiscent of the eyelets in a corset. Is she lacing herself back together or coming undone?

Why use illustrations instead of photos? Illustrations are peerless at setting the mood and creating a sense of anticipation about the text alongside them. They add charm and humanity to publications, and depict both abstract ideas and realistic situations with equal success. Drawings can convey the impossible, improbable, and fantastic. They can also illuminate the real world in recognizable images stamped with the illustrator's personal artistic style, from rough and sketchy to super refined, realistic to expressive, hand drawn to digital, or some combination. An illustration can have a slick, tightly rendered surface or one rich with a variety of expressive marks. As a broad generalization, readers have predictable unconscious reactions to various illustration styles: finely rendered realistic work in pastel tones will feel calm and soothing, while hard-edged graphic work in bold, flat colors telegraphs urgency and excitement.

Illustration styles can either match or contrast the text; for instance, a serious message can be well served by humorous drawings

8–2 *8x8*, illustrator Ben Kirchner, Winter 2020.

Why use a realistic illustration when a photo would be more "real"? An illustration creates its own alternate universe and adds some special sauce: brighter colors, the charm of the artist's individual drawing style, or a pose that better matches the text. This drawing fits the cover format beautifully; the way the V for Victory hand sign bumps into the *8x8* logo neatly incorporates the logo into the overall composition.

if they help get the point across effectively. For authors, opting to use illustrations rather than photographs can be partly a matter of personal taste, like selecting a menu option for a side dish. Do you want the potatoes mashed or baked? They're still potatoes either way, but the style and end result are markedly different.

The golden age of US illustration began in the early 1900s. Before World War I, most magazine and newspaper publishers used illustrations rather than photographs to accompany articles and stories. Illustrations were familiar to the public and widely available, while photography for commercial printing was still in its infancy.

Printing methods for the accurate color reproduction of photographs were primitive, with unpredictable outcomes on press, while illustrations provided reliably superior results. Starting in the 1920s, however, growing industrial output and consumer demand created a boom in advertising and a need for new visual techniques to help products stand out from the rest of the pack. Technological advances in capturing and reproducing color images allowed a closer match of the original transparency to the printed result, and by the 1950s photography was the medium of choice for most print advertising.

While the use of illustration took a nosedive after photography became widely used in advertising, it has rebounded since. Digital illustrations and animations play such a large role in the technology of daily life that we barely take notice of them—yet every icon on phones, tablets, and websites is an illustration. Many illustrators use traditional art media, and just as many do all of their work on a computer or tablet. The method is immaterial; what matters is the finished result. Illustrator and designer Seymour Chwast says, "Drawing and drawings will never go out of style. The computer has made drawing—on it and on paper—more unique and personal. It is closer to the heart and hand than other methods."

Photo-illustrations using photography as a medium or tool for an illustrator (which are not the same thing as photographic images created with a camera for their own artistic value) function more as illustrations and should be thought of as such. (Conversely, hyperrealistic drawings function more like photographs due to the documentary nature of their appearance.) Choosing this style to depict imaginary circumstances or creatures sets up an uncanny valley sort of tension for the viewer that authors can put to good use, if the text warrants it.

Color palettes, drawing style, mood, and line quality all play a part in setting off one illustrator's work from another's. Some editorial illustrations are infused with the artist's opinion and personal point of view, while others, such as illuminated capitals and page borders, are purely decorative without inherent meaning of their own.

Commissioning illustrations allows authors to specify exactly what they need the art to show and do, and collaborate with the illustrator on the image development process. Yet most authors in

→ 8–3 ***Sensazioni*, artist Diego Koi, 2012.**

There's a certain delight experienced by a viewer who's been "fooled" into seeing a photo when in fact they're admiring an accomplished graphite rendering. But more critically, this style of illustration feels hyperreal; every aspect is planned and controlled with precision by the artist. The water in this image is doing exactly what the illustrator wanted it to; try achieving that with a camera!

→→ 8–4 ***The Really Big One*, illustrator Christoph Niemann, 2015.**

Illustrations are particularly effective expressions of metaphor, as in this understated but clear depiction of the danger posed to the US West Coast by the San Andreas Fault. Using very little specific detail, this piece definitively shows, metaphorically, the literal rift that a high-magnitude earthquake would create. The bright red overall color also telegraphs danger.

nondesign-adjacent fields will be more comfortable searching for stock illustrations, and the widespread availability of stock means that with a lot of patient sifting, it's possible to find images that will suit the text well enough, if not exactly match it.

Illustrations can be roughly grouped into these broad categories:

- Metaphoric
- Realistic
- Diagrammatic or instructive
- Data visualization

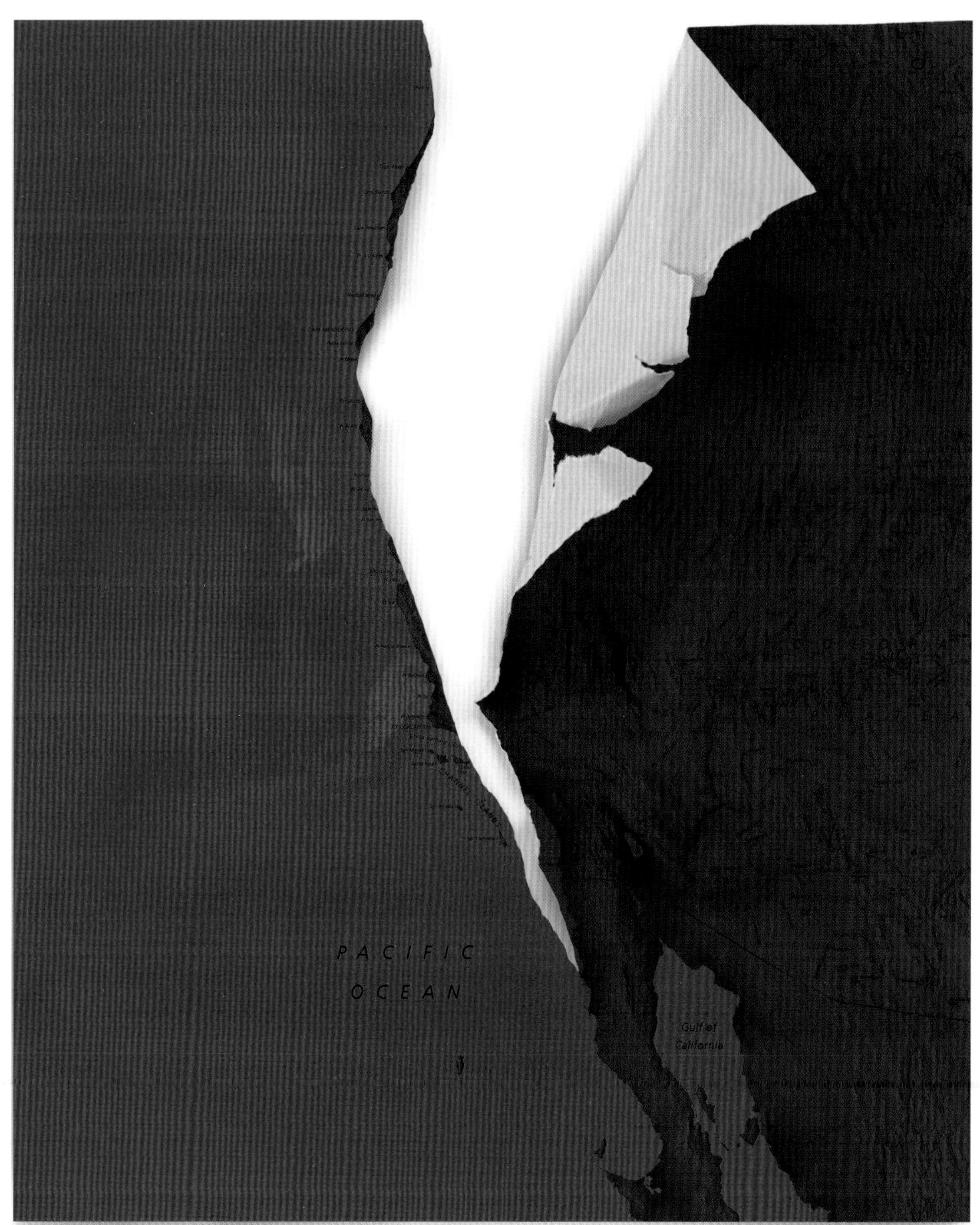
PACIFIC
OCEAN
Gulf of
California

Metaphoric

As mentioned in chapter 6, metaphor uses one thing to represent another, or symbolize abstract ideas or concepts. Illustration is especially adept at presenting visual metaphors since anything can happen in a drawing: alterations of scale, environment, character, color, extreme or exaggerated points of view, and more. Consider using this type of illustration when the real thing doesn't exist or you want to communicate information beyond literal appearances—for instance, a group of greedy corporate/political officials depicted as a single vulture carrying off an entire starving continent.

Metaphoric imagery is a sophisticated and thought-provoking tool to help readers visualize complex situations. The ways it can illuminate a concept are limited only by the imagination of the illustrator, and even when you think you've seen every possible way to visually depict a timeworn idea, an illustrator can always find another fresh option to beguile your readers. Metaphoric illustration is versatile. It can show or imply real or imagined activity—there can be flying cars—or it can find a way to visually represent the complex jumble of thoughts inside someone's head. It's also pretty much the sole method of visually depicting a feeling without being too literal or trite. The sentimental painting of a crying clown barely gets anyone's attention since we've already seen it millions of times before. Finding another metaphor for inner sorrow repurposed as humor will present the feeling in a far more interesting way for the viewer.

Metaphoric illustration is a natural fit for fiction, poetry, and essays, but with a little care it can support any type of writing so long as the connection between image and text is not too difficult for the reader to understand. A photo illustration of apples packaged as blister-pack pills would work for written content about replacing medications with natural foods, even if the text is scholarly and scientific in tone. Without taking away from the seriousness of the subject matter, this kind of image adds a bit of delight since the reader will feel clever for making the visual connection between the words and pictures. The image also quickly sums up information that the text may be laying out in a denser, slower-moving fashion.

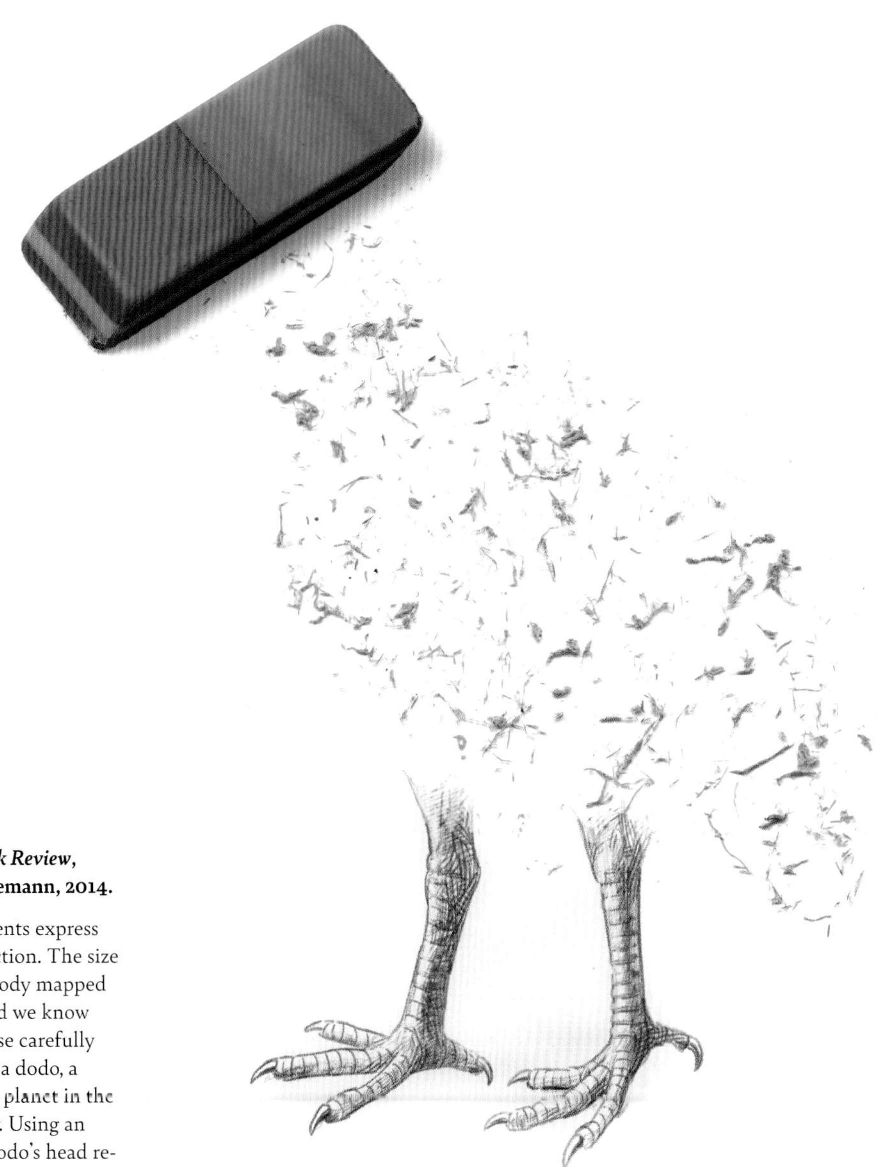

8–5 *New York Times Book Review*, illustrator Christoph Niemann, 2014.

Here, a few simple elements express the heavy topic of extinction. The size and shape of the bird's body mapped out in eraser crumbs (and we know it's a bird because of those carefully rendered feet) tell us it's a dodo, a creature erased from the planet in the late seventeenth century. Using an eraser to represent the dodo's head reinforces the resemblance. The drawing tells us what its subject is but also tells us what happened.

↦ **8-6 *Portfolio* magazine, illustrator Sam Weber, 2009.**

Even with the incendiary headline, using photos of the corporate and government officials being called out as vultures of profit would make for a dull layout. How much more exciting, then, to show an overscaled vulture making off with a continent, especially a continent made of money? The point is established, decisively and memorably, leaving the reader hungry to learn the rest of the story.

↘ **8-7 *Die Zeit*, photographer Reuters/Pool, 2009.**

The gridded columns of newspapers allow designers and authors to take advantage of the existing structure as a narrative device. By letting the red carpet continue out of the photograph (giving the photo a dual identity as an illustrative device) and spill down the page, the layout designer found a natural way to introduce a sidebar and maximize the visual impact of the red carpet. Here, text and image are practically inseparable, and both are better for it.

POLITIK 3

Gasputins Zittern

Russlands Härte im Energiestreit mit der Ukraine ist ein Zeichen der Schwäche. Das System Putin kämpft in der Wirtschaftskrise um sein Überleben

Ein Milliarden-Geschäft

Realistic

8–8 *Hyrcania*, artist Walton Ford, 2007.

As in John James Audubon's illustrations, this painting of a tiger contains a separate narrative of its own in addition to an accurate depiction of the animal. Such an approach to imagery feels rich and rewarding in its small details. The flowering tree tells us it's spring; the tiger's alert, crouched pose staring attentively off the edge of the frame makes us wonder what they see. Friend or foe? And what are they guarding in their front paws?

Here we return to the original question that started out this section, with a new adjective thrown in: Why use *realistic* illustrations instead of photos? A realistic drawing style can lend credibility to imaginary scenarios and creatures, depicting them in any way the author prefers, with great credibility. A drawing will often feel warmer and more organic than a photograph because a viewer knows that a human created the image from nothing rather than capturing an image with a camera. The representational nature of realistic illustrations lends them credibility; we believe that what they are showing is real (or will be) because it *seems* real.

Let's start with nondiagrammatic drawings: realistic illustrations that follow the rules of the natural world in terms of form, color, light, and perspective. In this way they are akin to photographs, but while a photo of a house at the beach tells a viewer exactly what the house looks like, a realistic watercolor of the same house implies a bit of extra information too, hinting at its proximity to the sea simply by the quality of the marks left by its watery medium on the

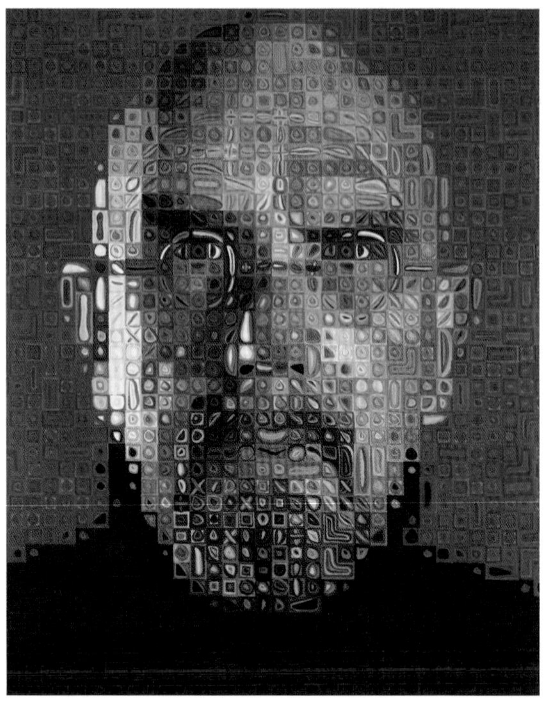

8–9 and 8–10 From left to right, *Lady Agnew of Lochnaw*, artist John Singer Sargent, 1892, and *Self-Portrait*, artist Chuck Close, 2004–5.

Realistic illustration—that is, art that accurately depicts its subject—varies greatly according to an artist's individual technique. These two examples demonstrate how it's possible to create a portrait of someone via entirely different methodologies. Neither approach is strictly realistic: Sargent's paintings combine sharply rendered features with loosely sketched areas, while Close's later style used a grid to create a likeness. Each style is as individual as the artist's fingerprint.

paper. Realistic illustrations can be metaphoric; these two categories are not mutually exclusive. In fact, the strength of a metaphor can be amplified if presented in a drawing that looks "real."

Even highly accurate, representational drawings depend on an artist's individual style to relay information through a distinct visual vocabulary. Think of a portrait by John Singer Sargent and one by Chuck Close. Sargent's lush brushstrokes in oil depicted the rich fabrics and luxurious interiors, the shining hair and flawless complexions of his Gilded Age subjects with a tactile sensuality, putting the leisure and excess of the era on full display. Close's midcareer portraits changed from his earlier realistic monochromatic acrylic paintings to daubs of color arranged in a grid to create a likeness of his subjects. The bright shiny blobs of plastic-based paint feel as cold as the pixels on a screen. Both artists produced realistic, accurate representations of specific people, but one's work would never be mistaken for the other's; it all comes down to style.

8–11, 8–12, and 8–13 "Tribal Rites of the New Saturday Night," *New York* magazine, illustrator James McMullan, 1976.

Nik Cohn, the author of this story later adapted for the silver screen as *Saturday Night Fever*, was not accompanied by a photographer during his journalistic research outings to the Brooklyn disco 2001 Odyssey. These realistic (but not photorealistic) watercolors fill in the gaps, setting the scene and showing us details to help visualize a specific time, place, and set of characters. They also bring something of their own to the party in the illustrator's artful handling of the medium.

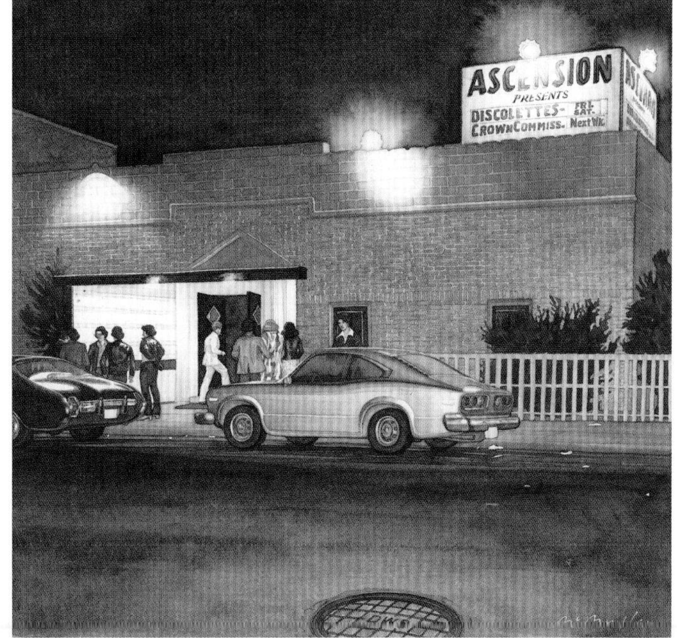

8–14 ***Audrey Irmas Pavilion*****, architect Rem Koolhaus, 2021.**

Architectural renderings illuminate future reality. For anything that doesn't exist except in the mind of its creator, realistic illustration styles allow viewers to see exactly what an imaginary object, place, or creature is meant to look like. The literal rendering of form and volume, perspective, and surface qualities gives credibility to the depiction and makes it a believable part of the known world.

When there is a need to depict an event that has already happened, or a historic moment or person from the past, a drawing will accurately present scenes that were never documented with a camera (or that happened centuries before the invention of photography). Realistic illustrations can also follow along the author's narrative with precision: here is the scene inside a disco in 1976, here is the building from the outside, or here are the kings of the dance floor. Such illustrations make the text come alive for the reader, adding specific detail to everything from the furnishings to manner of dress to mode of transportation and more. Realistic illustrations step in to visualize the future as well. Architectural renderings, for example, serve a valuable purpose by projecting the vision of a soon-to-be built structure onto a muddy vacant lot years before the building's completion.

Diagrammatic or Instructive

Just as floor plans help visualize the alignment and arrangement of a three-dimensional architectural space, diagrams of all kinds support text of a complex instructional nature. They show the reader a collection of parts (everything from anatomy to automobiles can be diagrammed) and how they relate to one another. Diagrams can portray how things happen in stages, such as a baby's growth from egg cell to birth, or an assembly line manufacturing process from raw materials to finished product.

Diagrams break intricate activities into manageable steps, and often don't need any language to explain them at all. Most of us are familiar with the wordless instructions included with IKEA flat-pack furniture, which need to be legible to people speaking a wide range of languages in the sixty-two countries where the store

8–15 *Topographic Map of the Moon*, designer Eleanor Lutz, 2019.

Here, a tiny surprise challenges a viewer's first assumption—that this is a representation of the earth, whose oceans are almost always shown in tones of blue. This diagram, however, shows the moon, which we expect to see in pearl gray. That little bit of dissonant information acts as an irresistible lure to keep our attention focused and appreciate the drawing's carefully mapped out details.

→ 8-16 *The Butterfly*, artist Paul Sougy, 1953.

Diagrams are a subcategory of literal illustration, meant mainly to provide information (sometimes at the expense of style). Not in this case, though; these drawings, specific and scientific yet colorful, arranged in a pleasing composition, help a reader understand the complicated structures of butterfly wing scales and mouth parts through instruction that's simple to grasp and rewarding to look at.

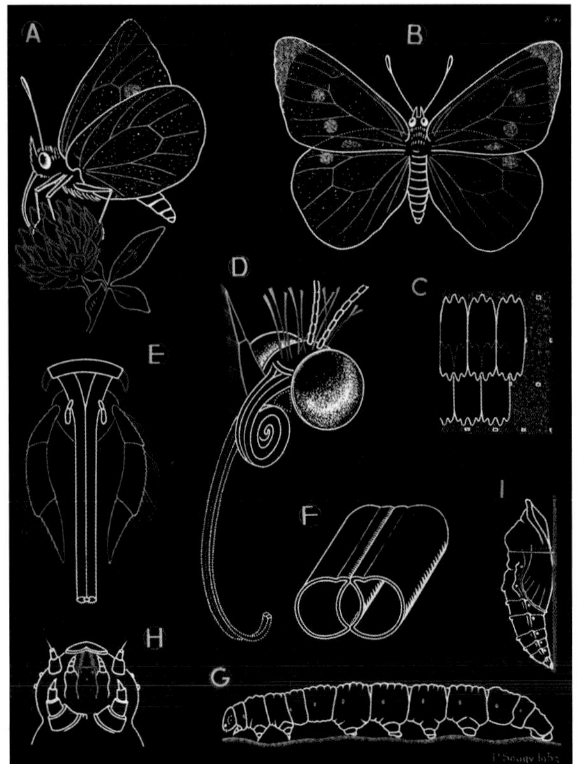

↘ 8-17 *Canadian Family* magazine, illustrator James Provost, n.d.

Explanatory illustrations are more effective when they're also charming. Goldenrod yellow circles enliven spare, simple black-and-white line drawings and set them off from the page background. Pointers calling out parts of the drawings tie the art to text describing how to shell a lobster or loop two rubber bands together, and make it easy for a reader to follow the instructions.

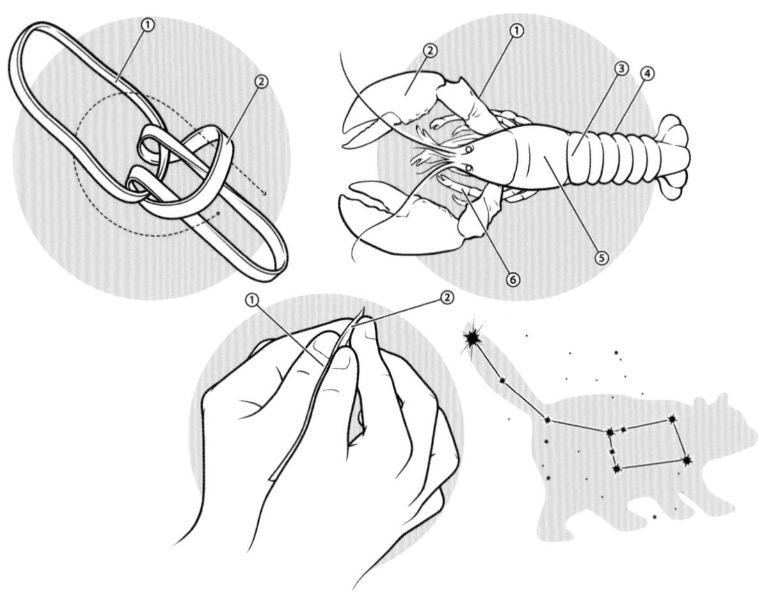

demystifier

London's New Arrival

In the works since 1989, British Airways' Terminal 5 finally opens this spring with a radical design aimed at eliminating Heathrow hell

...

by Carlye Adler

Baggage The handling process includes 11 miles of conveyor belts and an optical-scanning system that speeds late luggage from check-in to planes without being touched (or lost) by handlers. Maximum capacity: 12,000 bags an hour.

Design Departing passengers enter on the top level and don't go to the gate until their flight is called. The building has no interior columns, a design strategy meant to make the space seem more open and less confusing.

Retail B.A. is hyping the terminal's shopping options. All 112 stores, including Paul Smith, Tiffany & Co., and Coach, were asked to create a product sold nowhere else (which is why Krispy Kreme will offer the exclusive Terminal 5 doughnut).

PORTFOLIO.COM

VIEW AN INTERACTIVE GRAPHIC AND TIMELINE AT PORTFOLIO.COM/MAG/HEATHROW.

Write to CARLYE.ADLER@GMAIL.COM.

LONDON'S HEATHROW airport is a place of superlatives. It sees the most international passengers of any airport in the world. It also routinely has the worst delays in Europe and some of the longest lines. (They once snaked out the door and onto the roofs of the parking garages.) Its main airline, British Airways, loses more bags than almost any other carrier—an average of 3,000 a day in 2006. In 2007, fuming passengers hit the carrier with a class-action lawsuit over lost luggage.

While increased security since 9/11 has exacerbated what travelers have come to call Heathrow hell, the main cause is more fundamental: The airport was designed to handle about 45 million passengers a year, and it now serves more than 66 million. Because the system is so overtaxed, even the most minor glitch—a late arrival, a lazy baggage handler, a broken X-ray machine—throws everything off.

But in March, Heathrow will open Terminal 5, an $8.6 billion project spurred by British Airways, which will be the sole carrier in the new space. In development since 1989, the terminal was designed by British architect Richard Rogers, who won the 2007 Pritzker Prize, the Nobel Prize of architecture. It has become the biggest construction project in Europe (two rivers had to be rerouted to make way for it), and B.A. hopes to dazzle passengers with the details. A look at some key features.

Check-in Passengers arriving up to 45 minutes before a flight can check in at one of 96 self-service kiosks.

Transportation A rail station with Tube connections sits below the terminal. About half of all passengers are expected to arrive on mass transit.

FUTURE

Heathrow, which is owned by Spanish construction firm **Grupo Ferrovial,** is undergoing a complete renovation. Terminal 2 will be demolished later this year and rebuilt as **Heathrow East,** designed by architect Norman Foster. Terminals 1, 3, and 4 will be spruced up, and the entire project is scheduled to be completed by 2012.

68 Condé Nast Portfolio.January.08

ILLUSTRATION *by* BRYAN CHRISTIE

January.08.Condé Nast Portfolio 69

8–18 ***Portfolio*** **magazine, illustrator Bryan Christie, 2008.**

A cutaway diagram of Terminal Five at London's Heathrow airport allows a quick overview of how the different service areas relate and connect to each other, giving a sense of the streamlined improvements offered by the new terminal. Portraying a complex structure in cross-section helps readers comprehend three-dimensional space, and text callouts add to the diagram's scope of information.

operates. Eliminating the need for words in order to comprehend and follow the assembly instructions was a wise move on IKEA's part, if not always foolproof for the customer trying to put together a dresser.

Even in our age of YouTube videos that teach everything from deboning a duck to fixing a dishwasher, step-by-step how-to diagrams are valuable to help readers understand instructions or stages of a process without a live demonstration (and they offer the advantage of not having to hit pause on a video every few minutes while puzzling out the next step). It's one thing to try to explain in words how to tie nautical knots; for someone who's never attempted it before in real life, the how-to diagram is a lifesaver.

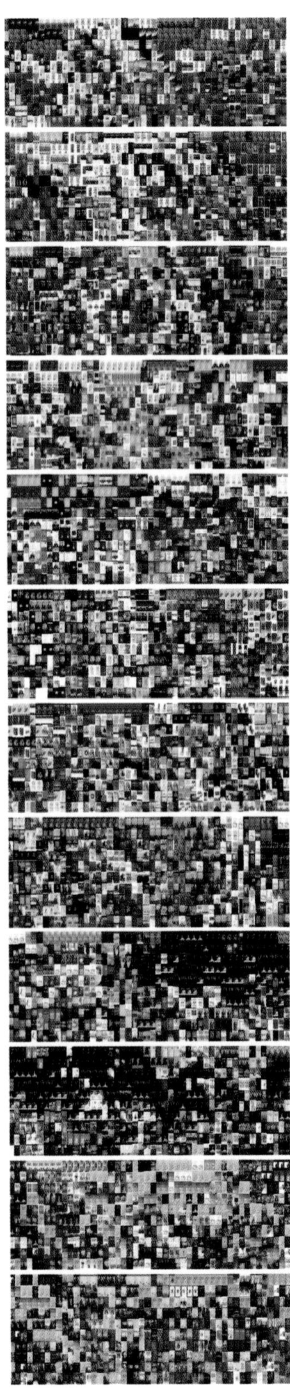

Authors should consider adding diagrams (which are not charts and graphs, discussed next) to their texts when additional clarification of complex processes or systems is needed. These illustrations supply information about the internal workings of things, frequently providing a peek via hidden views. Diagrams, being obvious and literal, can even take the place of part of a main text to clarify instructions and smooth things out for the reader. There's no need to overexplain; simple captions for each step of the diagram and a basic reference within the text such as "see diagram at right" are usually sufficient.

How-to sequences can also be accomplished with a series of photographs, but line art tends to be simpler to follow and cleaner looking, without shadows and photographer's props to distract the eye. There are so many ways to diagram activity; think of footprints and arrows showing dance steps, overhead-view drawings showing how to braid a loaf of bread dough before popping it in the oven, or the flow charts that illustrate abstract information architecture. All lead the viewer to a clear understanding of the subject at hand.

Data Visualization

The term *data visualization* is a fancier way of saying charts and graphs. Certain kinds of information become far easier to understand when displayed as data. Graphed data conveys authority since it demonstrates facts, rather than opinions or an author's personal conclusions, in a visual format. Information designer Georgia Lupi says, "If you see data the way I see data, data can be a lens, or a filter to parse the stories of a brand, of an institution, of a community of people, and then as a design material for communication design projects of different kinds. . . . [E]xploring new types of data can be unearthed to tell more hand-crafted stories."

Charts and graphs can be beautiful pieces of artwork in their own right, not just dry little things generated by software. Data visualization expert Edward R. Tufte says, "To envision information—and what bright and splendid visions can result—is to work at the intersection of image, word, number, art."

← 8–19 *If We Assume*, author James R. A. Davenport, 2012.

Each week's top ten–selling book covers placed in an annual grid creates a visual record of trends in book cover design over a twelve-year period. Some years a preponderance of black-covered books linger on the top ten list for weeks; other years the top-selling titles feature brighter yellow or green covers. Visualizing data in this manner creates a record that can be cross-compared to other events of that year—artistic, social, political, and cultural—to see if any insights arise.

→ 8–20 Feltron annual reports, designer Nicholas Felton, 2006, 2009, and 2014.

Between 2005 and 2014, the designer created a personal "annual report" using data gathered from his day-to-day existence to generate maps, graphs, and statistics pertaining to his life. Each year's report analyzed a slightly different data set. Applying formal visualization techniques to not-very-serious data (such as logging eating, drinking, reading, and mood) is a playful strategy to draw readers into texts.

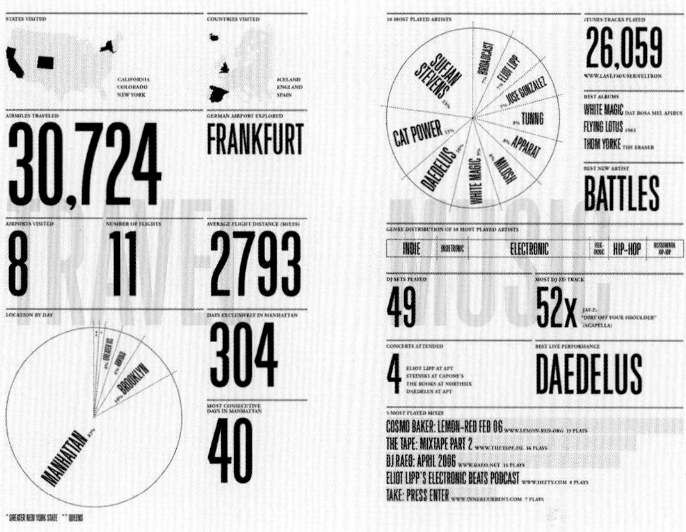

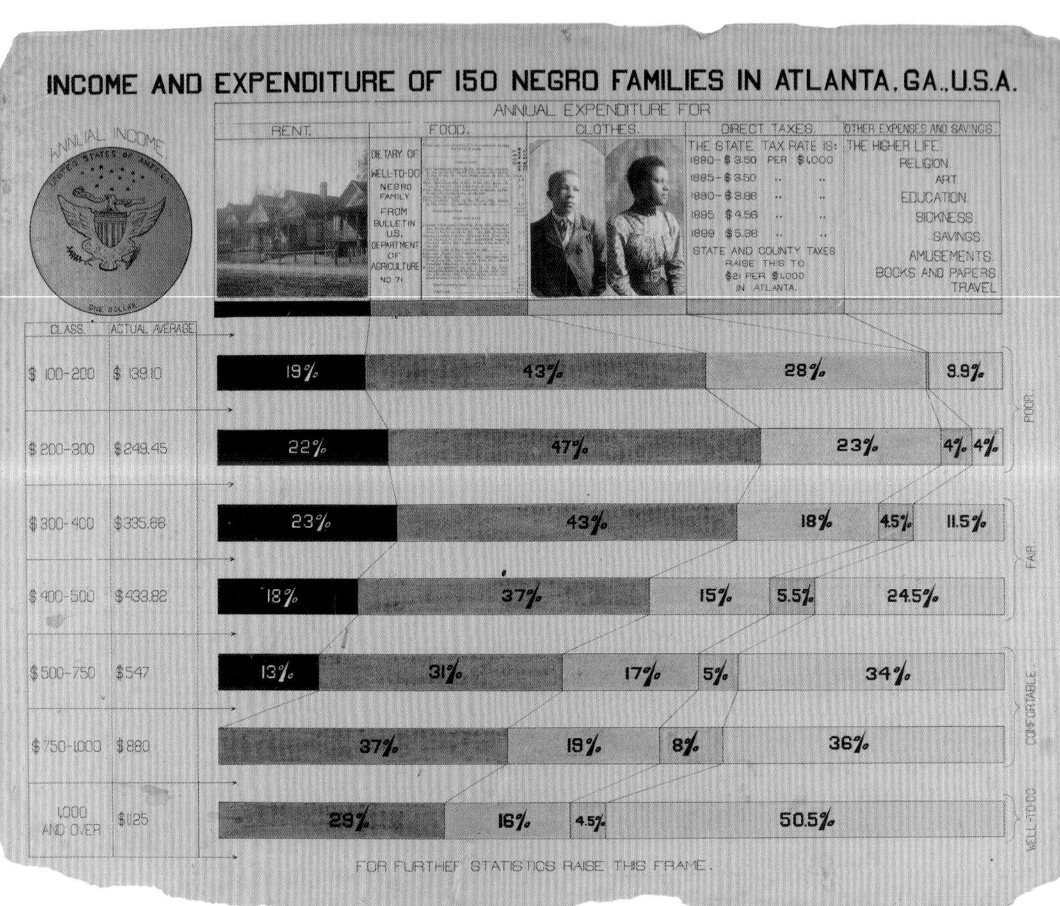
INCOME AND EXPENDITURE OF 150 NEGRO FAMILIES IN ATLANTA, GA., U.S.A.
ANNUAL INCOME.
UNITED STATES OF AMERICA
ONE DOLLAR
ANNUAL EXPENDITURE FOR
RENT.
FOOD.
CLOTHES.
DIRECT TAXES.
OTHER EXPENSES AND SAVINGS
DIETARY OF WELL-TO-DO NEGRO FAMILY FROM BULLETIN U.S. DEPARTMENT OF AGRICULTURE NO 71
THE STATE TAX RATE IS:
1880-$3.50 PER $1,000
1885-$3.50 " "
1890-$3.86 " "
1895 $4.56 " "
1899 $5.38 " "
STATE AND COUNTY TAXES RAISE THIS TO $21 PER $1,000 IN ATLANTA.
THE HIGHER LIFE.
RELIGION.
ART.
EDUCATION.
SICKNESS.
SAVINGS.
AMUSEMENTS.
BOOKS AND PAPERS.
TRAVEL.
CLASS.
ACTUAL AVERAGE.
$ 100-200
$ 139.10
19%
43%
28%
9.9%
$ 200-300
$ 249.45
22%
47%
23%
4%
4%
POOR.
$ 300-400
$ 335.66
23%
43%
18%
4.5%
11.5%
$ 400-500
$ 433.82
18%
37%
15%
5.5%
24.5%
FAIR.
$ 500-750
$ 547
13%
31%
17%
5%
34%
$ 750-1000
$ 880
37%
19%
8%
36%
COMFORTABLE.
1,000 AND OVER
$ 1,125
29%
16%
4.5%
50.5%
WELL-TO-DO
FOR FURTHER STATISTICS RAISE THIS FRAME.

8–21 ***The Exhibit of American Negroes*****, designer W.E.B. Du Bois, 1900.**

Gathering statistics and data, analyzing them, and translating the findings into a visual format revealing previously hidden information is a powerful tool for communication. Data sets come alive when expressed visually; what is invisible seen as rows of numbers suddenly becomes clear. This chart shows that as income rises, the percentage of money a family has to spend for such things as art, education, and amusements also rises—by 500 percent.

These are the main forms of data visualization:

- **Tables:** rows and columns used to compare variables
- **Pie charts and stacked bar charts:** graphs divided into sections representing parts of a whole in order to organize data and compare the relative sizes of each component
- **Line graphs and area charts:** these plot a series of data points over time so as to track change; line graphs are exactly what they sound like, while area charts use line segments to connect data points and color to separate variables
- **Histograms:** a distribution of numbers using a bar chart (without any space dividing the bars), showing a quantity of data falling within a specified range
- **Scatter plots:** these are useful to identify the relationship between two variables expressed as data points plotted (scattered) across a field
- **Heat maps:** a method of visualizing behavioral data by location
- **Tree maps:** a display of hierarchical data drawn as a set of nested shapes, usually rectangles, used for comparing the proportions between categories via their area size

Use data visualization to help a reader sort a pile of dense numbers or facts into real and vivid information, such as an up or downward trend, vast inequity in population or income, or species of animal rapidly becoming extinct over the past decade. Tufte warns his readers to beware of "chartjunk," which he defines as unimpactful data dressed up in ornamental ways as opposed to meaningful data presented in easily understood formats. All of this is to say that if the data are less than overwhelming when presented in chart form, rethink the notion of charting them. If they don't pass the "Wow, look at that, I had no idea!" test, perhaps those data don't need to appear as a chart or graph.

Data pulled from public sources or reports are valuable information but not usually particularly pleasing to look at in their original format. This kind of image is deadening to the eye as well as the

Mrs. K____ has been taken to the emergency room of a renowned hospital on Manhattan's Upper East Side. The doctors "work her up." More than $200 worth of blood tests are ordered ("emer rm lab," "lab serology out"), $232 worth of X-rays taken, $97.50 worth of drugs administered. I never saw Mrs. K____, she wasn't in my hospital, I don't know her medical history. But I am a doctor, and can reconstruct from her hospital bill what is going on, more or less. She is sick, very sick.

Mrs. K____ has been moved to the Intensive Care Unit ("room ICU"). It costs $500 a day to stay in the ICU, base rate. California has the highest average ICU rates in the country: $632 a day. In Mississippi, the average is $265. ICUs were developed in the 1960s. They provide technological life-support systems and allow for extraordinary patient monitoring. An inhalation blood-gas monitor ("inhal blood gas mont") is being used to keep a close check on the amount of oxygen in her blood. Without the attention she is receiving in the ICU, Mrs. K____ might already be dead.

Mrs. K____ has been running a high fever. The doctors have sent cultures of her blood, urine, and sputum to the lab to find out why. She is put on gentamicin ("lab gentamycin troug"), a powerful antibiotic. Such strong drugs can have toxic side effects. Gentamicin kills bacteria, but can also cause kidney failure.

It is Mrs. K____'s fifth day at the hospital, and she is slipping closer to death: her lungs begin to fail. She is put on a respirator ("inhal respirator"), which costs $119 a day to rent and requires a special technician to operate. A hospital can buy the machine for about $15,000.

BILL TO	INSURANCE COVERAGE
JOHN K____	BLUE CROSS STD 21

DATE	DESCRIPTION		TOTAL CHARGES
DETAIL	OF CURRENT CHARGES AND PAYMENTS		
09/23	EMER RM OTHER	5009000	119.00
09/23	EMER RM LAB	5006000	172.00
09/23	LAB SEROLOGY OUT	1406800	35.00
09/23	EMER RM EKG	5007000	61.00
09/23	X-RAY ABDOMEN	1501001	58.00
09/23	X-RAY CHEST RTN	1501009	58.00
09/23	X-RAY CHEST RTN	1501009	58.00
09/23	X-RAY CHEST RTN	1501009	58.00
09/23	PHARMACY	2601000	2.25
09/23	EMER RM PHARMACY	5002000	46.00
09/23	PHARMACY	2601000	49.25
09/23	ROOM ICU		500.00
09/24	LAB AUTO BLOOD CT	1402101	17.00
09/24	LAB ACT PAR THROM	1404001	27.00
09/24	LAB PROTH DETER	1404011	17.00
09/24	LAB BLOOD CULT	1405002	37.00
09/24	LAB BLOOD CULT	1405002	37.00
09/24	LAB CHEM-20	1401104	31.00
09/24	SP HEM CBC	1602010	28.00
09/24	SP HEM RETIC CT	1602046	17.00
09/24	SP HEM PLATELET CT	1602090	17.00
09/24	LAB SEROLOGY OUT	1406800	35.00
09/24	LAB MAGNES	1401042	27.00
09/24	LAB RTN URINAL	1403001	16.00
09/24	LAB RTN CULT	1405003	37.00
09/24	LAB BACTERIA SM	1405011	16.00
09/24	LAB RTN CULT	1405003	37.00
09/24	LAB DIFF	1402099	15.00
09/24	LAB PROT ELEC	1401049	53.00
09/24	LAB FUNGUS	1405008	31.00
09/24	LAB FUNGUS	1405008	31.00
09/24	LAB TBC CULT	1405014	42.00
09/24	LAB DIFF	1402099	15.00
09/24	LAB AUTO BLOOD CT	1402101	17.00
09/24	X-RAY CHEST-BED	1501128	74.00
09/24	PHARMACY	2601000	10.00
09/24	PHARMACY	2601000	8.00
09/24	PHARMACY	2601000	8.00
09/24	PHARMACY	2601000	4.50
09/24	SPECIMEN MUCUS TRAP	2709085	3.00
09/24	SPECIMEN MUCUS TRAP	2709035	3.00
09/24	INHAL BLOOD GAS MONT	2101034	354.00
09/24	ROOM ICU		500.00
09/25	LAB SALICYLATE	1401050	49.00
09/25	LAB AMMONIA	1401006	40.00
09/25	LAB CHEM-20	1401104	31.00
09/25	LAB PROTH DETER	1404011	17.00
09/25	LAB CHEM-8	1401111	31.00
09/25	LAB BACTERIA SM	1405011	16.00
09/25	LAB AUTO BLOOD CT	1402101	17.00
09/25	LAB AUTO BLOOD CT	1402101	17.00
09/25	LAB ACT PAR THROM	1404001	27.00
09/25	LAB TBC CULT	1405014	42.00
09/25	LAB TBC CULT	1405014	42.00
09/25	LAB FUNGUS	1405008	3L.00
09/25	LAB RTN CULT	1405003	37.00
09/25	LAB RTN CULT	1405003	37.00
09/25	CARDIO ROUTINE EKG	1801001	61.00
09/25	X-RAY CHEST-BED	1501128	74.00
09/25	X-RAY ABDOMEN	1501001	58.00
09/25	X-RAY CHEST-BED	1501128	74.00
09/25	X-RAY CHEST-BED	1501128	74.00
09/25	PHARMACY	2601000	13.50
09/25	PHARMACY	2601000	39.00
09/25	PHARMACY	2601000	3.70
09/25	PHARMACY	2601000	16.50
09/25	PHAR IV SOLUTIONS	2601003	16.00
09/25	PHARMACY	2601000	2.50
09/25	PHAR IV SOLUTIONS	2601003	13.50
09/25	PHAR IV SOLUTIONS	2601003	13.50
09/25	PHARMACY	2601000	3.35
09/25	PHARMACY	2601000	2.25
09/25	INHAL BLOOD GAS MONT	2101014	354.00
09/25	ROOM ICU		500.00
09/26	LAB PROTH DETER	1404011	17.00
09/26	LAB CHEM-8	1401111	31.00
09/26	LAB AUTO BLOOD CT	1402101	L7.00
09/26	LAB UR SODIUM	1401077	27.00
09/26	LAB UR POTASS	1401076	27.00
09/26	LAB DIFF	1402099	15.00
09/26	LAB CHEM-8	1401111	31.00
09/26	LAB GENTAMYCIN TROUG	1401112	27.00
09/26	CARDIO ROUTINE EKG	1801001	61.00
09/26	X-RAY CHEST BED	1501128	74.00
09/26	PHARMACY	2601000	31.20
09/26	PHARMACY	2601000	3.70
09/26	PHARMACY	2601000	13.50
09/26	PHARMACY	2601000	39.00
09/27	LAB CHEM-8	1401111	31.00
09/27	LAB PROTH DETER	1404011	17.00
09/27	LAB DIFF	1402099	15.00
09/27	LAB AUTO BLOOD CT	1402101	17.00
09/27	LAB ACT PAR THROM	1404001	27.00
09/27	LAB CHEM-8	1401111	31.00
09/27	LAB CHEM-20	1401104	31.00
09/27	LAB CHEMISTRY OUT	1401800	10.00
09/27	LAB FECES CULT	1405007	40.00
09/27	CARDIO ROUTINE EKG	1801001	61.00
09/27	BLD BK ANTIBDY SCRN	1701004	23.00
09/27	BLD BK ADMIN FEE	1701028	69.00
09/27	PHAR IV SOLUTIONS	2601003	37.50
09/27	PHAR IV SOLUTIONS	2601003	11.00
09/27	PHAR IV SOLUTIONS	2601003	26.00
09/27	PHAR IV SOLUTIONS	2601003	13.50
09/27	PHAR IV SOLUTIONS	2601003	63.50
09/27	PHARMACY	2601000	40.50
09/27	PHARMACY	2601000	11.00
09/27	PHARMACY	2601000	9.00
09/27	PHARMACY	2601000	13.50
09/27	PHARMACY	2601000	39.00
09/27	PHARMACY	2601000	3.70
09/27	PHARMACY	2601000	2.50
09/27	PACK CE 250 PROC FEE	1701018	46.00
09/27	25 NSA 50MU PROC FEE	1701077	35.00
09/27	INFUSION PUMP	2705027	30.00
09/27	INHAL RESPIRATOR	2102015	119.00
09/27	ROOM ICU		500.00
09/28	OPER OP RM 150	1001005	521.00
09/28	LAB OCC BLOOD	1403021	16.00
09/28	LAB GENTAMYCIN TROUG	1401117	27.00
09/28	LAB DIFF	1402079	15.00
09/28	LAB RTN CULT	1405003	37.00
09/28	CARDIO ROUTINE EKG	1801001	61.00
09/28	BLD BK GROUP RH	1701002	28.00
09/28	BLD BK X MATCH	1701006	46.00
09/28	BLD BK ANTIBDY SCRN	1701004	23.00
09/28	X-RAY CHEST-BED	1501128	74.00
09/28	X-RAY CHEST-BED	1501128	74.00
09/28	PHARMACY	2601000	11.00
09/28	PHAR IV SOLUTIONS	2601003	13.50
09/28	PHAR IV SOLUTIONS	2601003	50.00
09/28	PHARMACY	2601000	3.70
09/28	PHARMACY	2601000	39.00
09/28	PHARMACY	2601000	9.00
09/28	PHARMACY	2601000	13.50
09/28	ANEST ANEST DRUGS	1103001	12.40
09/28	INHAL RESPIRATOR	2102015	119.00
09/28	OPER OP RM SUPPLY	1002000	198.00
09/28	SUCT MACHINE-CONT	2704015	22.00
09/28	DIAL SOLN 1.5-CASE	2709040	24.00
09/28	INHAL BLOOD GAS MONT	2101034	354.00
09/29	LAB CHEM-8	1401111	31.00
09/29	LAB CHEM-20	1401104	31.00
09/29	LAB AUTO BLOOD CT	1402101	17.00
09/29	LAB DIFF	1402099	15.00
09/29	LAB DIAG SM/MILL	1407002	40.00
09/29	LAB AUTO BLOOD CT	1402101	17.00
09/29	LAB AUTO BLOOD CT	1402101	17.00
09/29	LAB DIFF	1402099	15.00
09/29	LAB DIFF	1402099	15.00
09/29	LAB GENTAMYCIN TROUG	1401112	27.00
09/29	LAB SP FL CELL CT	1402018	26.00
09/29	LAB CHEM-8	1401111	31.00
09/29	LAB CHEM-8	1401111	31.00
09/29	LAB CHEM-8	1401111	31.00
09/29	LAB FUNGUS	1405008	31.00
09/29	LAB BACTERIOLOGY OUT	1405800	35.00
09/29	LAB OVA & PARASITES	1405018	31.00
09/29	LAB SM&CELL BLOCK	1407003	53.00
09/29	LAB FIBRIN QUAN	1404007	40.00
09/29	LAB COAG FIBRIN SPLT	1404018	49.00
09/29	LAB ACT PAR THROM	1404001	27.00
09/29	LAB AUTO BLOOD CT	1402101	17.00
09/29	LAB FROZEN SECT	1408004	119.00
09/29	LAB RTN CULT	1405003	37.00
09/29	BLD BK COLD AGG	1701007	18.00
09/29	BLD BK ADMIN FEE	1701028	23.00
09/29	X-RAY CHEST-BED	1501128	74.00
09/29	X-RAY ABDOMEN	1501001	58.00
09/29	PHARMACY	2601000	13.50
09/29	PHARMACY	2601000	11.00
09/29	PHAR IV SOLUTIONS	2601003	50.00
09/29	PHARMACY	2601000	39.00
09/29	PHARMACY	2601000	3.70
09/29	ISOLATION GLOVES-BOX	2709025	7.00
09/29	HEEL-ELBOW PROTECTOR	2706025	9.00
09/29	HEEL-ELBOW PROTECTOR	2706025	9.00
09/29	DIAL-PERID KIT 87110	2708015	14.00
09/29	DIAL SOLN 1.5 CASE	2709040	24.00
09/29	SPECIMEN MUCUS TRAP	2709085	3.00
[illegible]	[illegible]	[illegible]	[illegible]
09/29	INHAL BLOOD GAS MONT	2101034	354.00
09/29	INHAL BLOOD GAS MONT	2101034	354.00
09/29	ROOM ICU		500.00
09/30	LAB AUTO BLOOD CT	1402101	17.00
09/30	LAB CHEM-8	1401111	31.00
09/30	LAB CHEM-8	1401111	31.00
09/30	LAB DIFF	1402099	15.00
09/30	SP HEM COAG STDY COM	1602007	239.00
09/30	SP HEMATOLOGY	1600000	49.00
09/30	SP HEM RETIC CT	1602046	17.00
09/30	SP HEM CBC	1602010	28.00
09/30	LAB BACTERIA SM	1405011	16.00
09/30	LAB ACT PAR THROM	1404001	27.00
09/30	LAB PROTH DETER	1404011	17.00
09/30	LAB FIBRIN QUAN	1404007	40.00
09/30	LAB AUTO BLOOD CT	1402101	17.00
09/30	LAB CHEM-20	1401104	31.00
09/30	LAB TBC CULT	1405014	42.00
09/30	LAB CHEM-20	1401104	31.00
09/30	LAB RTN CULT	1405003	37.00
09/30	LAB RTN CULT	1405003	37.00
09/30	BLD BK ADMIN FEE	1701028	207.00
09/30	X-RAY CHEST-BED	1501128	74.00
09/30	X-RAY CHEST-BED	1501128	74.00
09/30	PHAR IV SOLUTIONS	2601003	16.00
09/30	PHARMACY	2601000	39.00
09/30	PHAR IV SOLUTIONS	2601003	21.00
09/30	PHAR IV SOLUTIONS	2601003	16.00
09/30	PHARMACY	2601000	3.70
09/30	PHARMACY	2601000	13.50
09/30	PHARMACY	2601000	11.00
09/30	PHARMACY	2601000	2.25
09/30	PHAR IV SOLUTIONS	2601000	21.00
09/30	PHAR IV SOLUTIONS	2601000	21.00
09/30	PHAR IV SOLUTIONS	2601003	18.50
09/30	PHARMACY	2601000	2.50
09/30	PLAT CONC PROC FEE	1701014	180.00
09/30	FRSH FR PLA PROC FEE	1701019	26.00
09/30	INHAL RESPIRATOR	2102015	119.00
09/30	DRESSING SET-DISP.	2708041	7.00
09/30	VEST RESTRAINT	2709032	12.00
09/30	INHAL BLOOD GAS MONT	2101034	354.00
09/30	ROOM ICU		500.00
10/01	LAB CHEM-20	1401104	31.00
10/01	LAB CHEM-8	1401111	31.00
10/01	LAB CHEM-8	1401111	31.00
10/01	LAB CHEM-8	1401111	31.00
10/01	LAB DIFF	1402099	15.00
10/01	LAB AUTO BLOOD CT	1402101	17.00
10/01	BLD BK ADMIN FEE	1701028	23.00
10/01	X-RAY CHEST-BED	1501128	74.00
10/01	PHAR IV SOLUTIONS	2601003	37.50
10/01	PHARMACY	2601000	13.50
10/01	PHARMACY	2601000	11.00
10/01	PHARMACY	2601000	3.70
10/01	PHARMACY	2601000	31.20
10/01	PHARMACY	2601000	2.40
10/01	PHARMACY	2601000	27.20
10/01	PHAR IV SOLUTIONS	2601003	13.50
10/01	25 NSA 50MU PROC FEE	1701077	35.00
10/01	INHAL RESPIRATOR	2102015	119.00
10/02	PHARMACY	2601000	27.20

Mrs. K____'s first week in Intensive Care ends in a flourish of blood tests. She has five Chem-8s ("lab chem-8")—tests that measure the levels of sodium, potassium, and six other chemicals in her blood. The hospital charges Mrs. K____ $31 for each Chem-8. Most independent labs charge about half as much; some hospitals charge up to $60. The *New England Journal of Medicine* has said: "The clinical laboratory [is] a convenient profit center that can be used to support unrelated deficit-producing hospital operations." The *Annals of Internal Medicine* estimates that the number of clinical lab tests being done is rising 15 percent a year.

Mrs. K____ has started peritoneal dialysis ("dial-perid kit 87110"). Her kidneys are failing. She is still hooked up to the respirator. She is being kept alive by what Lewis Thomas calls "halfway technologies" — "halfway" because kidney dialysis machines and respirators can support organ systems for long periods of time, but can't cure the underlying disease. Some doctors are beginning to question this practice. A recent study at the George Washington University Medical Center concluded: "Substantial medical resources are now being used in aggressive but frequently futile attempts to avoid death."

Mrs. K____ has been put in a vest restraint. Restraints are used in Intensive Care to keep patients from thrashing about or pulling their tubes out. Many ICU patients develop what is called "ICU psychosis." They become disoriented, begin hallucinating. The condition is brought on by lack of sleep, toxic drugs, the noise of the ICU staff and machines, and pain.

8-22 ***The Slow, Costly Death of Mrs. K*****, redrawn by Edward Tufte, 1984.**

Originally published in *Harper's* magazine. A typically dense hospital bill for an ICU patient contains a wealth of buried data—ordering a certain test indicates that the doctor suspected a heart condition, for instance—information not stated directly in the rows of abbreviated charges and numbers. This annotation unpacks the data by deciphering the progression of an illness and its severity through the bill's details about the treatments, procedures, and medications.

soul and doesn't add to the visual appeal of your text. When faced with information-packed but unattractive charts, consider hiring a graphic artist to redraw them if your budget allows.

When deciding whether illustration is the best image strategy for your project, ask yourself:

- Would a drawing bring some level of understanding to the text that a photo would not?
- Does the illustrator's style feel like a good fit for my text?
- Do I need to depict something that is impossible in the real world or an event that is already past?
- If I'm considering data visualization, will it clarify my information and make it easy for a viewer to understand?

イギリスの、アメリカの女の子が泣いて感激した 唄いまくるビートルズ！ギラギラする青春のリズムが爆発する!!
ビートルズがやって来る
ヤァ！ヤァ！ヤァ！
YEAH....
YEAH....
YEAH....
ポール・マッカートニー ジョン・レノン
ジョージ・ハリスン リンゴー・スター
yeah!
yeah!
yeah!
yeah!
THE BEATLES
新らしい歌6曲を加えて
唄いまくる、ビートルズ

09

Putting It All Together

9–1 *A Hard Day's Night* film poster (Japanese release), designer anonymous, 1964.

The energy in this poster comes from so many directions: the leaping Beatles, each shown in a single bright color; the exuberant type treatment; and the small line drawings scattered throughout of girl fans screaming with joy, all of it grounded by the strong horizontals of the musical staff and tritone stripe of audience at the bottom. The Latin and Japanese typefaces work especially well together (notice how the gray exclamation points at the right, together with the small "Yeah Yeah Yeahs," fit neatly into the vertically set Japanese type). A densely layered image like this can be hard to pull off but richly rewarding.

Finalizing a selection of images feels like standing on a high diving board after a long climb up the ladder; here's where many authors pause before taking the plunge. Gazing on the selection of images you've curated can be confounding. Well, here they are. Now what?

The good news is that the biggest and most challenging part of the work is behind you. Your last remaining task is to merge images with text into a cohesive narrative. Although it's a big step, it can be the most enjoyable part of the process. How many images to use, at what size, and how to sequence them for good narrative pacing is more of an art than a science. Like stepping stones, images guide the reader through to a conclusion. It's wise to play around with various combinations and methods of sequencing images until you're satisfied. Remember, the first pancake is almost always a throwaway.

The "kill your darlings" approach applies to visual grammar as well as the written word. To paraphrase William Strunk Jr. and E. B. White's *The Elements of Style*, vigorous writing is concise. So is vigorous visual grammar. Ruthlessly culling a wide initial pool of images down to only the most essential ones yields the most impressive results. Allow the images to suggest, hint, underscore, and show in order to tell. Don't attempt to illustrate every single text point. A haiku can land with the same impact as an epic, in far less space. That said, know when you have an epic on your hands and don't be afraid to deploy a suitably epic image strategy. If you have lots of beautiful photos and the room to use them large, go for it. An epic text demands nothing less.

This chapter discusses varying strategic approaches for building narrative structures according to the rules of visual grammar, including:

- Grid structures
- What are you going for?
- Image editing
- The lead versus supporting image
- Sequencing and pacing

Grid Structures

Grid-based design is logical and functional as well as aesthetically pleasing because the human eye is subconsciously attuned to balance, ratio, and proportion. Using a grid to organize visual information is most often associated with midcentury Swiss design, but its earliest roots date to the thirteenth century, when French architect Villard de Honnecourt based his constructions on geometric grids. His principles were later adapted and applied to publication design by Bauhaus typographers and designers at the beginning of the twentieth century, and later on to designs for screens.

In the early days of the internet, graphic design possibilities for computer screens were extremely limited. Tablets and smartphones had not yet been invented. At that point it was impractical to use a grid for web design (and no one did) due to technological restraints, but increasing technical improvements led web designers to embrace the grid, making a centuries-old system of creating order in print a prerequisite of user interface design as well.

9–2 Festival poster, Josef Müller-Brockmann, 1961.

Grids divvy up visual space neatly and impose visual order onto content. The consistent placement of text allows readers to orient themselves on the page and locate information quickly, with a minimum of fuss. As in this example, grids often provide balance; the large headline and "air" around it are welcome contrasts to the nine dense columns of small type below.

Because website displays are responsive to different browsers and devices (monitors, tablets, and smartphones), image sizes are fluid yet retain similar proportional relationships independent of device screen aspect ratios.

In his authoritative book *Grid Systems in Graphic Design*, Josef Müller-Brockmann wrote that:

> by arranging the surfaces and spaces in the form of a grid . . . [t]he pictorial elements are reduced to a few formats of the same size. The size of the pictures is determined according to their importance for the subject. The reduction of the number of visual elements used and their incorporation in a grid system creates

→ **9-3 Crate & Barrel, 2022.**

The grid layout of this consumer site allows a shopper to quickly compare models, prices, and color options at a glance. It's bothersome to have to hunt and click and keep searching through a website for different versions of the same item, and it would be a mess to show so many on a single page without the order imposed by the grid. The lack of color in the site design allows the user to focus on the products without distraction.

↘ **9-4 Grids Are Good, designers Khoi Vinh and Mark Boulto, 2016.**

The vast majority of publications and websites on the planet are laid out according to an underlying grid system, be it complex or simple, that directs where the content falls as well as the relative size and position of its visual and text elements. The main grid columns here are overlaid in pink, separated by thin white gutters. Photos in varying sizes easily conform to the widths offered by the multiple column structure, and all the different kinds of text—sidebar, navigation, articles, and footers—have a logical place within the hierarchy.

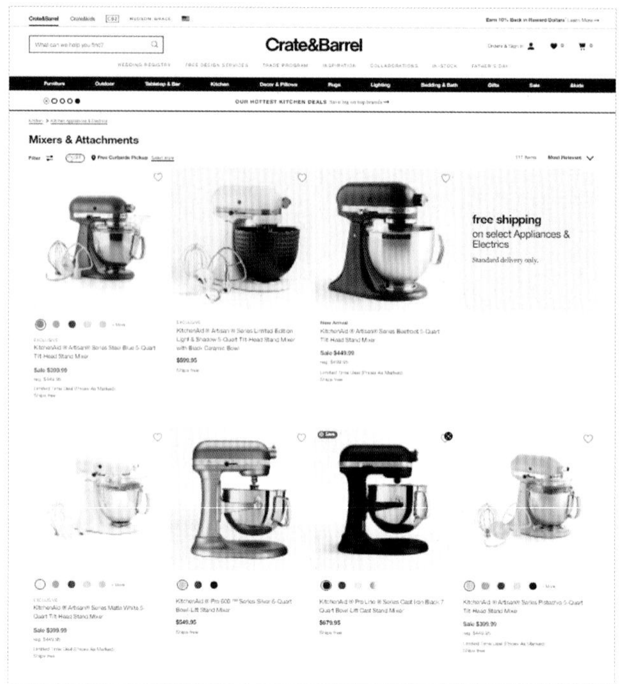

> a sense of compact planning, intelligibility and clarity, and suggests orderliness of design. This orderliness lends added credibility to the information and induces confidence. Information presented with clear and logically set out titles, subtitles, texts, illustrations and captions will not only be read more quickly and easily but the information will also be better understood and retained in the memory.

Luckily, authors don't need encyclopedic knowledge of Bauhaus principles to successfully apply a few basics of grid-based design; a little order goes a long way. Each page doesn't require its own unique layout. In fact, using a consistent underlying grid with varied but mathematically proportional image sizes will aid your audience's ability to follow along by creating the expectation that similar information will be presented in parallel structures. For instance, set up a multichapter printed document by opening each chapter with a full-page image, followed by a couple of half-page images on the following spreads, and some quarter-page images sprinkled throughout.

What Are You Going For?

Selecting and planning images has intellectual underpinnings—analyzing the text, and thinking about what sort of images match its tone and content—but there are also process-related and emotional components to the endeavor. Perhaps during your search you come across an odd image that unexpectedly sparks a new direction as you move forward. Or you find an image that you respond to strongly from the heart instead of the head—you just like it but can't necessarily say why. All of these considerations are valid and should be given equal weight until you've gathered more images than you think you'll need and are about to begin culling them down. At this point, revisit your original strategy and be sure you have enough images that support the goals and intentions.

Reviewing a preliminary image set will start to suggest possible groupings and similarities among the options. (If it doesn't, try

→ 9-5 *Dairy Today*, photographer Randal Ford, 2008.

A comparison of four image strategies will demonstrate the very different results possible with a single topic—in this case, the cow. The text dictates which way to go when selecting images. Here, a soft and lovely glamour shot of a cow depicts the animal as a personality, a celebrity in their own right. Photographed on a pink seamless studio background, the image has none of the typical bovine environment we'd expect to see, such as barnyards, stalls, milking machines, and pastures. By shooting the cow in the same manner as a supermodel on a fashion magazine cover, the image conveys a tongue-in-cheek humor that would make it a fitting accompaniment for a philosophical essay about the various forms of beauty or article supporting animal rights. This humanized portrait confers great dignity and gravitas on its subject.

↙ **9-6** Cows don't even make an appearance in this image; their presence is merely implied by the lone cowhand. The breathtaking landscape sets up a viewer to ponder the romantic appeal of a life spent outdoors on horseback instead of staring into a computer monitor or laboring on an assembly line. The image transmits a feeling of wide open space, freedom, and possibility that references cows obliquely, as an afterthought.

↗ **9-7 *National Geographic*, photographer Chris Johns, 1989.**

Here is the opposite of a glamour portrait of a cow or dramatically beautiful landscape that might have cows somewhere in it; this is the dusty reality of cowhands managing a herd. It looks like hard work for them, and not particularly pleasant for the cattle either. The image is an honest view of a difficult and dangerous occupation, with none of the romance often associated with tales of the US West.

→ **9-8 Anonymous, n.d.**

And finally, the cow transformed into carcasses for consumption. Stripped of individuality and natural environment, the sides of beef bear no resemblance to living creatures. This photo's pleasing regularity and order lend it a certain visual appeal, even as it presents the harsh realities of the slaughterhouse. It could easily be used to make a point about animal rights or vegetarianism, not by celebrating the cow's life, but by showing its stark end. Conversely, it could support an article about the cleanliness and efficiency of modern meatpacking facilities.

pulling in a few more images to fill in any gaps you notice.) Rearrange the groupings a few times until the image narrative dovetails well with the text. The most important thing to keep in mind is the original overall objective—the image strategy—for what you want the images to do for your text: Explain? Document? Prove? Decorate?

As you begin to assemble the final image list, consider these points:

- Do these images feel like a set, varied yet cohesive?
- Do they match the tone and mood of my text?
- Is there a strong opening image?
- Do I have the right amount of images to fit my narrative? Is anything missing?
- Are each of the images equally compelling?
- If I removed one of these, would I miss it?

Final Image Editing

Here, we're not talking about making visual adjustments using image-editing software but instead about reviewing a collection of images to select the final options. A tight edit ensures crisp pacing where each image contributes to the overall impact of the text, and nothing feels repetitive or extraneous. The excellent Strunk and White advice concerning text—*make every word tell*—applies to images as well.

Editing doesn't compel you to limit the number of images you choose or rush a reader through the narrative's detail, but every image should tell. During the editing process ask yourself: Do these images relay the same story as my text, both individually and as a group? Is any one of them off topic? Does the image selection have a narrative arc that matches the text's flow and progression? Do these images feel right? This last question is the most subjective part of the process, but you'll know it when everything falls into place. You will feel it.

If you plan on using a variety of image sizes as described earlier (full, half, and quarter page or their on-screen equivalents), keep in mind that large images need to be more forceful and arresting than small ones. Even if you really love a certain picture, be sure it is up to the task of communicating at the size you plan to use it. Detailed images should not be run at small sizes; the detail will be hard to appreciate, and the image will just look overbusy.

How consistent or varied your image edit is will depend on the nature of your text. For example, an architectural text about a specific building might show different angles of the exterior, interiors, and floor plan, and perhaps gardens, allowing the reader to take a narrow but deep view of a single structure. A text about a specific style of architecture, such as Georgian or Palladian, might show several different buildings to demonstrate how the style is expressed across a variety of structures. An effective strategy for this type of text is variety plus consistency: decide how many images and what view (exterior, interior, or floor plan) you want to show for each building, and follow this structure throughout the document. It allows the reader to understand the architectural style by seeing how it plays out over different buildings shown in a predictable way.

In photographer David Graham's multiple shots of a blazing red tree, house, trailer, and Harley, his final selection fulfills his original reason for taking the picture in the first place as well as addressing other aesthetic and conceptual considerations. Small details that weren't quite right in some shots, or the need to stand five feet to the right or left to balance the image the way he wanted it, weighed into his decision-making process. He says, "At first, I thought a portrait of one of the guys in the doorway of the trailer would be totally great, but, ultimately, I liked the quieter image that didn't pin the picture down to 2021. I wanted the picture to show how these folks lived, juxtaposed to nature's gorgeous tree at a gorgeous time of year with a small reference (the upside-down American flag) to the conflict amongst Americans."

← 9-9 RIVER ROAD, photographer David Graham, 2022.

Whether you've hired a photographer or taken your own pictures, consider each element, the overall composition, and the point of view as you review the images to select the best one to accompany your text. Graham was drawn to the exploding color of the autumn leaves as well as intrigued by the juxtaposition of house, trailer, and Harley. This image is his final choice from all the options he shot that day.

↗ **9-10** Here a viewer gets more of a narrative about the trailer's occupant and their politics than about what initially captured the photographer's eye. It's also an image fixed in 2021; the selected shot has more of a timeless quality.

→ **9-11** In this image, everything is more or less centered, making for a dull composition.

↘ **9-12** This one is all about the trailer and motorcycle, without giving a bigger picture of the odd combination of nature plus house plus extra house parked at the curb. Considering that the tree was a main attraction for the photographer, there is not enough of it shown here to give it VIP status.

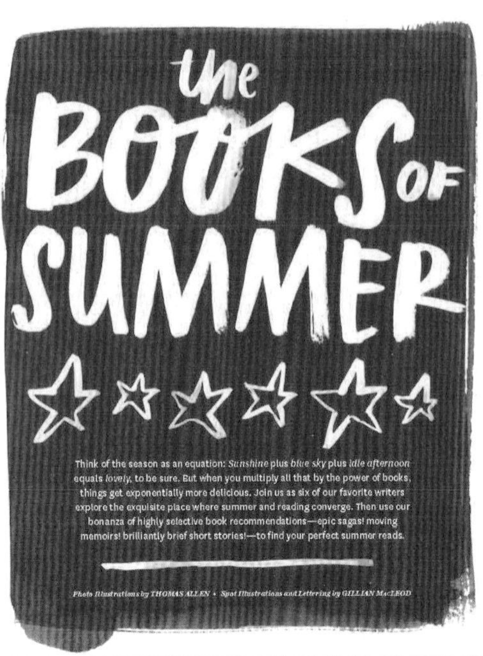

the BOOKS OF SUMMER
Think of the season as an equation: *Sunshine* plus *blue sky* plus *idle afternoon* equals *lovely*, to be sure. But when you multiply all that by the power of books, things get exponentially more delicious. Join us as six of our favorite writers explore the exquisite place where summer and reading converge. Then use our bonanza of highly selective book recommendations—epic sagas! moving memoirs! brilliantly brief short stories!—to find your perfect summer reads.
Photo Illustrations by THOMAS ALLEN • Spot Illustrations and Lettering by GILLIAN MacLEOD

CONFESSIONS of a PATHOLOGICAL READER

ZADIE SMITH is the author of *White Teeth*, *The Autograph Man*, *On Beauty*, *NW*, and the essay collection *Changing My Mind*.

ZADIE SMITH offers an ode to bibliomania, a happy disorder nicely accommodated by this forgiving time of year.

QUITE OFTEN I AM ASKED TO RECOMMEND, as a practice, the habit of "reading." I like to do this, though I always feel a little phony. To recommend something implies that its presence in your life is a positive choice, like playing tennis or avoiding gluten. For me, being a reader, in summer or at any other time, isn't a "lifestyle choice." Rather, I made the choice—if that's what it was—so long ago, it has taken on an inescapable character in my mind. I think that if I were a very good swimmer, I would be proud to be so, but being proud of being a reader, in my case, is like being proud you have feet. I don't feel much pride when, on the way to somebody's house for dinner, I stuff several books into my handbag for...well, for what? Can I really not manage a brief subway ride without textual support? Is that normal? Are there other people who, when watching a documentary set in a prison, secretly think, as I have, *Wish I had all that time to read?*

What I'm describing is a condition that might be termed "pathological reader syndrome." My acquisition and digestion of books is, to be frank, absurd. Just get a Kindle, everyone advised me a few years ago. Yet here I am, packing for a short flight between London and Belfast, with my Kindle, certainly, but also with four or five hardback books jammed into my hand luggage, just in case. Just in case we happen to fly through a wrinkle in time in which an hour expands to accommodate infinity.

While I'm not sure I can recommend living this way, I can say that if you are similarly afflicted, summer is your season: The beach is one of the few places pathological readers can pass undetected among their civilian cousins. Of course, summer calls for a particular kind of book. In August, in a hammock, I find that one sentence must flow unobstructed to the next, and the people I'm reading about should struggle and die and confess their eternal love for one another. **Tolstoy is excellent for hammock reading,** especially *Anna Karenina*, *War and Peace* (skipping over the essays at the end), and any of his shorter stories. Flaubert's *Madame Bovary* is, likewise, utter heaven. More recently I forgot I had a life while reading of lives torn apart by the Biafran war in Chimamanda Ngozi Adichie's *Half of a Yellow Sun*. The epic inaction of our summer holidays is perhaps what makes them suitable for the reading of epics, especially those set in times of war. When I am doing nothing but watching a 4-year-old dig a large hole in the sand, it's nice to know that somewhere else the Russian army is advancing. I once went to the Bahamas with my mother and brothers, but in truth I went on holiday with *Daniel Deronda*. A decade later, I still remember Eliot's sentences better than the charms of the company.

Though the length of Tolstoy's massive masterpiece War and Peace *has been the butt of many a joke, the novel is not nearly the world's longest. Proust's seven-volume* In Search of Lost Time *is triple the size.*

I have also experienced much summer reading joy sinking into the epic lives of real people. Adrian Nicole LeBlanc's *Random Family: Love, Drugs, Trouble, and Coming of Age in the Bronx* gave me one of the greatest, most immersive summer reading experiences of my life. This summer I hope to read *Common Ground: A Turbulent Decade in the Lives of Three American Families* by J. Anthony Lukas, which gives us Boston in the '60s and '70s, with all its racial and political turmoil. I say "hope" because all reading now, pathological or otherwise, is dependent on my two children giving me time to do it. Epics begin to look daunting when you're measuring your time in teaspoons. For this reason, among many others, I do not sniff at true crime, which you can read even while your children are talking to you. And the grandfather of that genre, Truman Capote's *In Cold Blood*, is still, to me, the finest.

My name is Zadie Smith, and I am a 38-year-old pathological reader. I would like to say in my defense that I don't really get the appeal of **YOLO.** I live many times over. Hypothetical, subterranean lives that run beneath the relative tedium of my own and have the power to occasionally penetrate or even derail it. I find it hard to name the one book that was so damn delightful it changed my life. The truth is, they have all changed my life, every single one of them—even the ones I hated. Books are my version of "experiences." I'm made of them. But every summer I hope to take a book to a beach and pretend that it's only an occasional thing, a seasonal indulgence, which will be put down come September, as I return, like any civilian, to real life.

A sort of carpe diem for the younger set, YOLO, meaning "You only live once," was popularized by rapper Drake in his 2011 song "The Motto."

LINDA BROWNLEE/CORBIS OUTLINE

THE SAGA OF THE SUMMER

A God in Every Stone
By Kamila Shamsie (Atavist)

A sweeping novel of love, empire, and rebellion set in Turkey, England, and British India during and after World War I by a writer short-listed for the Orange Prize.

NEW LINES WE LOVE

"She comes out of the house and sees FRESH SHAPES in the GRASS, a GEOMETRICAL WARNING she does NOT UNDERSTAND."

From ***Song of the Shank*** By Jeffery Renard Allen

⟵ **9–13 *O, the Oprah Magazine*, designer Angela Riechers, 2014.**

For these commissioned images, the illustrator was asked for a full-page opener artwork to communicate the relaxed pleasure of reading a book outside on a warm summer day, followed up by a series of genre-specific secondary images. The opener creates an overall feeling of the joys of reading so vital to the book review section, while the following images serve as quick visual guides to locating a reader's favorite topics.

⟶ **9–14 *Vanity Fair*, photographer Helmut Newton, 1989.**

Either of these two photos could have opened this article. The second image shows Lauren Hutton as we expect to see her—hair, makeup, breasts, and a couture gown. The first image, however, is a killer—completely weird and delightful. The model, always glamorous and beautifully dressed, wearing a gold bracelet in the form of an alligator, is presented as a superhero. Her wide-stance posture shows how difficult it is to hold up the heavy reptile, but her grin says, "Ain't life a hoot?" The alligator, hanging limp, appears completely defeated. He has succumbed to her powers; she is triumphant.

THE PRIME OF Lauren Hutton

Twenty years ago the swamp queen with a gap between her front teeth was the hottest model in the world. Now, reports MAUREEN ORTH, she's become the baby-boomers' pinup. She's the woman who wasn't born yesterday and looks better for it

Photographs by HELMUT NEWTON
Styled by MARINA SCHIANO

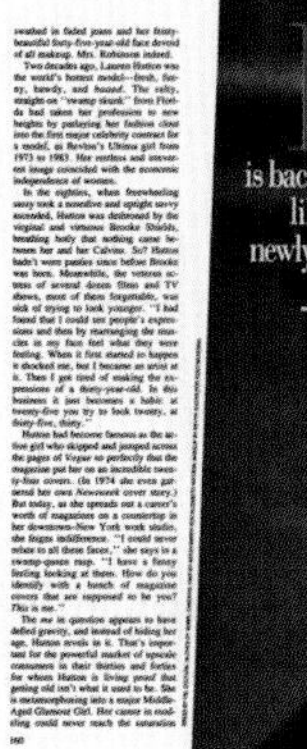

Hutton is back, taunting the libidos of the newly middle-aged.

Lead/Hero Image versus Secondary Images

If a publication was a movie, the lead or hero image would fill the starring role: grabby, attention getting, with a powerful wallop of mood or main theme. The secondary images take the role of a movie's costars: explaining and supporting the narrative without taking front and center stage.

The lead image for your publication or presentation should be the most memorable visual in the set of images you've gathered. Which is the one you think of first? Which elicits the strongest emotional reaction? Which best sets up the reader's expectations for what the text will deliver? A thoughtfully curated set of images

⟵ 9-15 ***The Collected Works of Jim Morrison*, Pentagram / Michael Bierut, 2021.**

The first image a viewer will see in any format, print or digital, should be showstopping. Called the opening or lede image, a good one is a powerful magnet to draw readers in. If we were talking about a film, the lede photo would get top billing as the main star. The opener sets up expectations for the rest of the text; ideally it doesn't give everything away but tells just enough to leave us hungry for more. In this example, either photo could function as the lede; notice how the narrative shifts. If we first see Morrison driving and then walking away from a crash, there's just been an accident. But if we see the crash first and then the driver back behind the wheel, it's either a flashback to a moment before an accident or possibly the driver has found another vehicle to continue on his way.

⟶ 9-16 ***Esquire*, designer George Lois, 1968.**

Esquire's cover of Muhammad Ali (which incidentally has been called the greatest magazine cover of all time) posing as the martyr Saint Sebastian unites three big topics with great precision: the boxer's persecution for his personal religious beliefs, racism, and the Vietnam War. This image depicting a single, isolated subject without context or background expresses multiple ideas with great force.

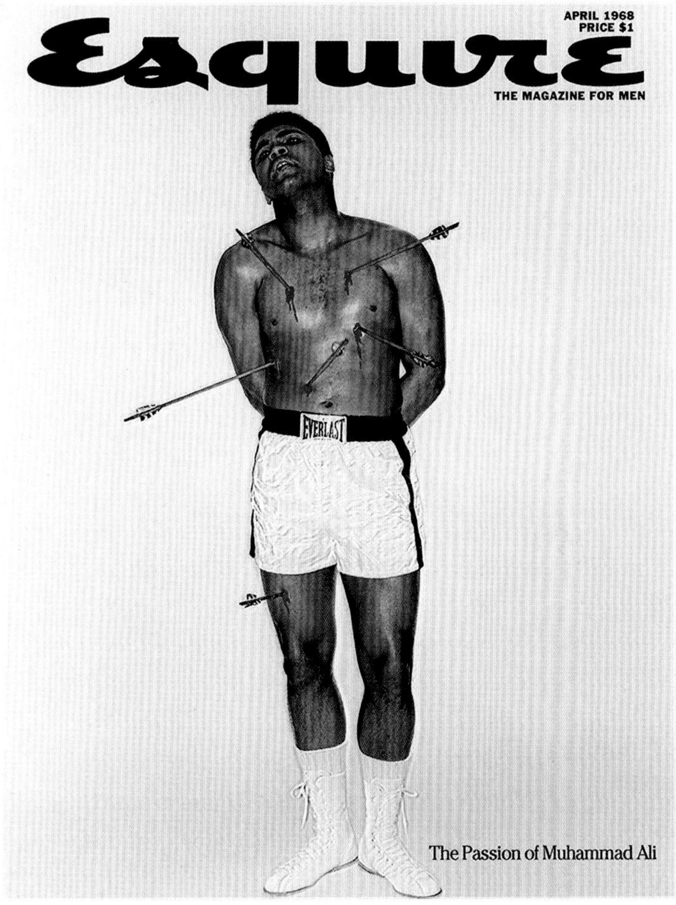

often has more than one contender for the starring role; if time allows, experiment with all the possibilities before choosing the winning option. How do you know which is the winning option? Again, it's the one that feels best. Don't overthink it.

After the establishing shot provided by the lead image, choosing the secondary images is mostly a matter of how well they move the narrative along. Feature the strongest images early on, and end on a strong image as well; in vaudeville theaters, the first act always closed with a great performer to put the audience in the right frame of mind to stick around for the second act. While image selection isn't

9–17 *The Animal Kingdom*, photographer Randal Ford, 2018.

A porcupine, that shy critter quietly munching on pine needles high up in a conifer, attains a more dignified status when shown as a nearly perfect ball of quills radiating out around a pointy snout. The lowly creature becomes classic geometry in animal form. An image such as this gains impact from the lack of distracting elements and its novel point of view, presenting the subject in a new and pleasing manner.

quite the same as vaudeville, sending the reader off with a strong visual at the conclusion of the text will aid retention of the material.

Sequencing and Pacing

Different media call for slightly different image strategies, but the underlying visual grammar principles remain unchanged. When it comes to sequencing images, if you're using just a few, the gap between them will be greater; the reader will scan the image narrative from beginning to middle to end in bigger increments. Using more images allows for a slower narrative buildup, perhaps with more nuanced travel from point to point. You can choose to have images transport your readers from A to B in a straight line or map out a more indirect route.

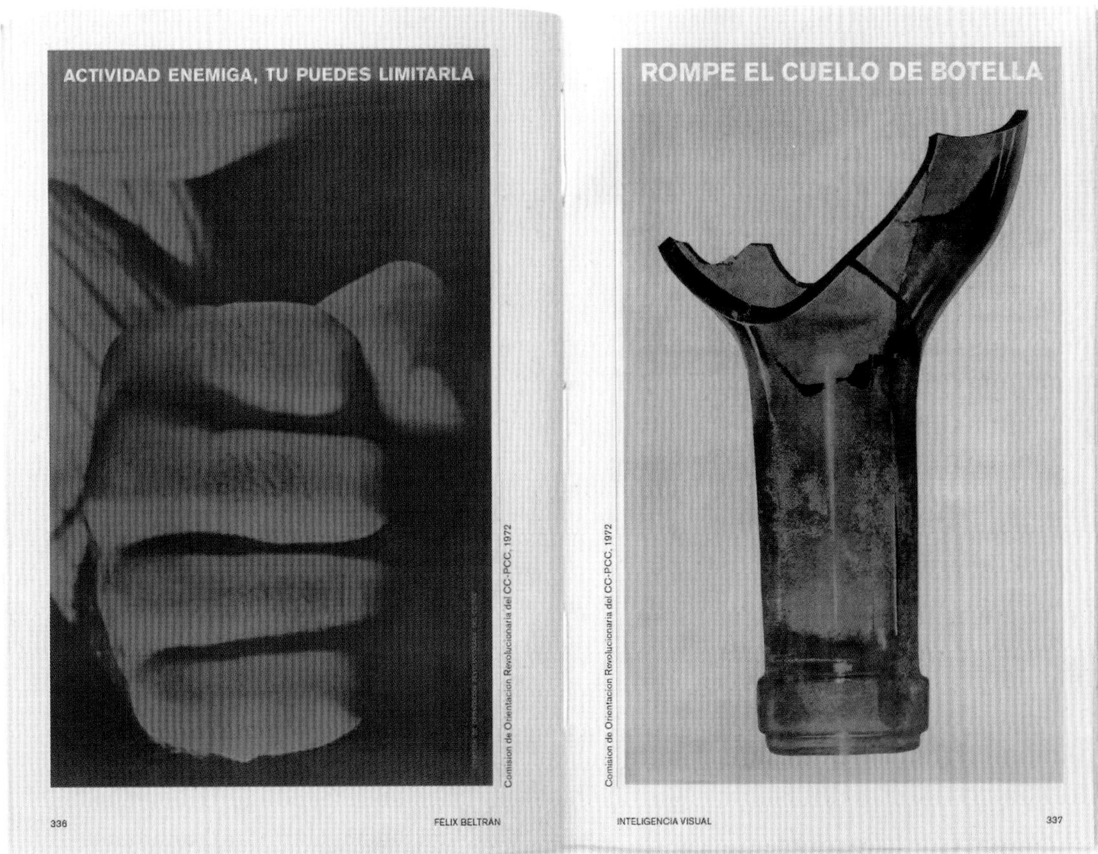

9–18 *Inteligencia Visual*, designer Felix Beltrán, 2021.

An image does not need to be complicated or overthought to speak with a direct and compelling voice. Simple subjects—a clenched fist and broken bottle—become icons of power and violence when shot in tight close-ups. These photos would complement a detailed narrative about war and revolution, for instance, by serving as a potent distillation of theme and letting the text fill in the facts.

In a paper or presentation of limited length, frequently the direct route works best (two or three well-curated images), but if you have the space, the scenic route (several images with a wider range of visual content) will add extra flair toward an enjoyable visual journey along the way. Rearranging the image sequence will alter the narrative arc with each reposition; try a few versions before you settle on image order.

Selecting just one image to use from a number of options is a slightly different process than curating a group of images to spread throughout over a publication. That single image has to function in much the same way that a poster or book cover does, succinctly representing the whole of a larger endeavor, without support from

→ 9-19 *Girls in the Windows*, photographer Ormond Gigli, 1960.

With apologies to Bauhaus architect Ludwig Mies van der Rohe, who famously uttered the phrase "Less is more," sometimes you have to pile it on. An image such as this—rich with detail and color, and a spirit of fun—adds a spark to the text by giving the reader plenty to see, enjoy, and even wonder about. What are those models doing in the windows anyway? Formal aspects of the composition (rhythm, pattern, and even a Bauhausian grid) form a solid foundation for the lighthearted subject matter.

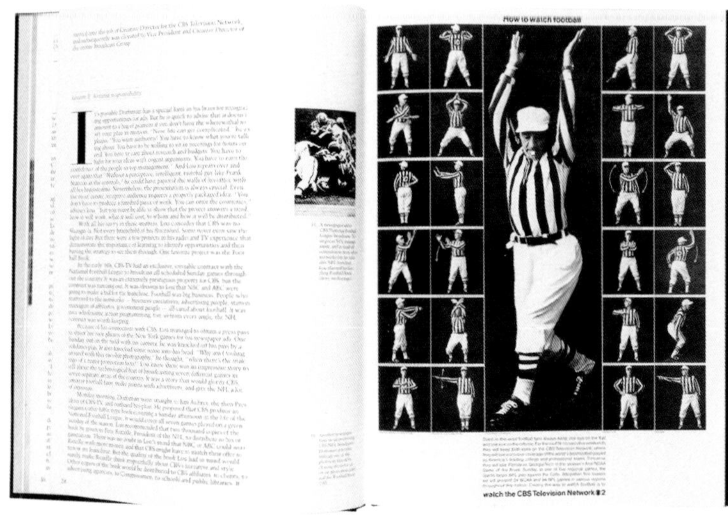

How to watch football

watch the CBS Television Network 2

↘ 9-20 Lou Dorfsman and CBS, *How to Watch Football*, designer Lou Dorfsman, 1964.

In this guide to football referee signals, stacks of ten different small images flank the largest photo of the ref, focusing the entire composition. The high-contrast black and white creates a stark gallery of images, with each pose clearly distinct from those around it. Showing everything together allows for quick side-by-side comparisons; imagine how hard it would be to comprehend if the information was laid out as a single pose per page, requiring a reader to flip back and forth.

9–21 *99 Cents*, photographer Andreas Gursky, 1999.

Whoever arranged the merchandise for sale in this 99-cent store had a real eye for color. The image feels overwhelming—a consumerist fever dream. Despite the rigid order of the shelves, there is almost too much to look at. A viewer can practically hear the buzzing fluorescent lights overhead. Be mindful that visually crowded images often evoke claustrophobia and anxiety; if these emotions match the mood of your text, it will make for a powerful strategy.

other images. It has to be eye-catching and provocative, with a similar emotional impact as the rest of the larger work. Think of this strategy as putting all of your money at the racetrack on a single horse to win.

Single and Multiple Subjects

Images where a lone subject is treated iconically, with a central focal point and limited background elements, will focus attention like a magnifying glass; the eye locks into place and stays there while the reader ponders the meaning of this strong single image.

The polar opposite is the image with a busy surface—in other words, a picture where there's a lot going on. This sort of image attracts through sheer volume; it captures a viewer's eye with the lushness and detail of its content and will not let go until it has been studied at great length. These are best used at large sizes so that the amount of detail can be fully appreciated. Usually one such image

9–22 *Lifeguard*, photographer Joseph Szabo, 1990–2015.

The same images can be rearranged to relay completely different narratives. This sequence suggests sighting a swimmer in distress, a team leaping into action, a rescue, and exhaustion afterward. The narrative shifts if we move the final image of the napping lifeguard before the images where the action starts; this new sequence implies that he was slacking off. In the first instance we don't begrudge him his sleep; on the contrary, we feel he deserves it. But in this retelling, a viewer might judge him to be literally asleep on the job; his inattention could have had dire consequences for a swimmer in trouble.

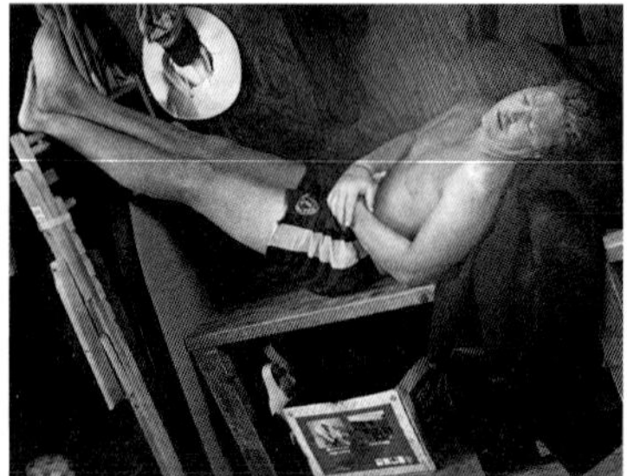

is enough, making the notion of seeing it as a multiple somewhat oxymoronic. Essentially, it's a single that acts as a multiple.

For a set or grouping of images, here are some key considerations to bear in mind: Do they feel like they belong together in terms of mood, tone, content, or coloration? Does each tell a separate part of the narrative? Are they varied yet cohesive? If they were all from a single source such as one photographer, the task is somewhat narrower since those first criteria are satisfied, but choosing the best grouping of the shots and determining their order can be a challenge. Not sure about one or the other of your options? Take it out and consider the rest again. Do you miss the deleted one? If not, you have your answer.

Pacing is a crucial element of structuring an effective image progression, yet it is often not given the consideration it deserves. A well-paced set of images provides interest through lively changes of scale, image dimension, and variety; it doesn't feel too dissimilar

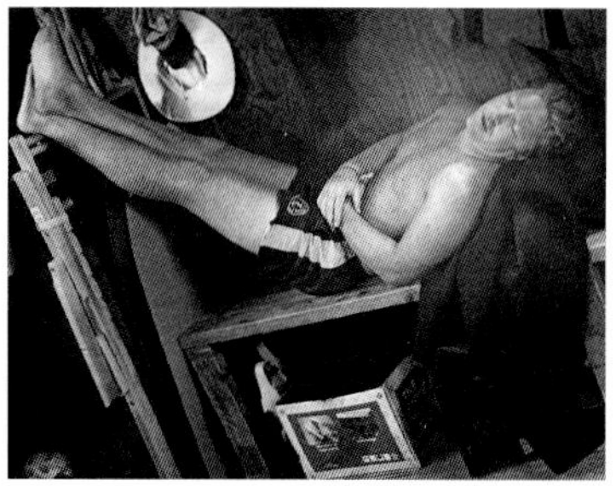

throughout, nor is it repetitive. The first and last images in a sequence should always be spectacular; start and end with a bang. It's difficult to visualize in your head how well the image-text marriage is functioning. Make a draft of the document or presentation combined with a selection of images and give it a hard look. Trust your gut if something feels off, and don't be afraid to add or subtract an image or two, or rearrange all of them yet again.

Just as each human possesses a unique writing style and manner of speaking, designers and nondesigners alike have the ability to express creativity, individuality, and mastery of the subject at hand via imagery. Text accompanied by an imaginative and thoughtfully chosen set of images is far more alluring for the reader than vast oceans of words, and will have a greater, longer-reaching impact. We all love a good story. Purposefully chosen images will enrich your narrative and carry it along to a memorable and satisfying conclusion.

Bibliography

"Abstract Photography." Art Story. https://www.theartstory.org/movement/abstract-photography/history-and-concepts/. Accessed April 24, 2022.

Adams, S., and Stone, T. L. *Color Design Workbook: A Real-World Guide to Using Color in Graphic Design*. Rev. ed. Beverly, MA: Rockport, 2017.

Albers, J. *Interaction of Color*. Abr. ed. New Haven, CT: Yale University Press, 1971.

Alexa, A. "Meet Pentagram's Newest Partner: Information Designer Giorgia Lupi." Core77. May 20, 2019. https://www.core77.com/posts/88383/Meet-Pentagrams-Newest-Partner-Information-Designer-Giorgia-Lupi.

Anderson, C. "Haddon Sundblom: Santa Paintings." Oglethorpe University Museum of Art. March 2, 2020. https://museum.oglethorpe.edu/exhibitions/sundblom/.

Argent, P. "Seymour Chwast on Milton Glaser, the Importance of Illustration + the State of Contemporary Design." AIGA Eye on Design. December 3, 2020. https://eyeondesign.aiga.org/seymour-chwast-on-milton-glaser-the-importance-of-illustration-the-condition-of-contemporary-design/.

"Basic Facts about Homelessness: New York City." Coalition for the Homeless. September 12, 2022. https://www.coalitionforthehomeless.org/basic-facts-about-homelessness-new-york-city/.

Berger, J. *Ways of Seeing*. London: Penguin Books, 1972.

Blake, R. "Disraeli and Gladstone: Opposing Forces." BBC. February 17, 2011. https://www.bbc.co.uk/history/british/victorians/disraeli_gladstone_01.shtml.

Burnett, D. "The Real Story behind This Iconic Olympics Photo." *Runner's World*, July 24, 2020. https://www.runnersworld.com/runners-stories/a33367218/mary-decker-zola-budd-1984-olympics/.

Carroll, L. *Alice in Wonderland: The Original 1865 Edition with Complete Illustrations by Sir John Tenniel*. Independently published, 2021.

Chao, D. "The Snake in Chinese Belief." *Folklore* 90, no. 2 (1979): 193–203. https://doi.org/10.1080/0015587x.1979.9716142.

Chu, J. "An Extinction in the Blink of an Eye." *MIT News*, February 10, 2014. https://news.mit.edu/2014/an-extinction-in-the-blink-of-an-eye-0210.

Corbusier, L. A., J. Goodman, and J. Cohen. *Toward an Architecture*. Los Angeles: Getty Research Institute, 2007.

"Color." Getty Research Institute. June 10, 2019. https://www.getty.edu/research/exhibitions_events/exhibitions/bauhaus/new_artist/form_color/color/#:%7E:text=Itten%20identified%20seven%20fundamental%20categories,meridians%E2%80%9D%20radiating%20from%20their%20circumference.

Copyright.gov. May 2021. https://www.copyright.gov/fair-use/more-info.html.

Cronin, D. A., E. H. Hall, J. E. Goold, T. R. Hayes, and J. M. Henderson. "Eye Movements in Real-World Scene Photographs: General Characteristics and Effects of Viewing Task." *Frontiers in Psychology* 10 (January 14, 2020). https://www.frontiersin.org/articles/10.3389/fpsyg.2019.02915/full.

"Data Visualization." IBM. February 10, 2021. https://www.ibm.com/cloud/learn/data-visualization.

"Egypt's Desert of Promise." *National Geographic*, February 1982, cover. https://www.amazon.com/National-Geographic-Magazine-February-1982/dp/B000PCFDSM.

Elliot, Andrew J. "Color and Psychological Functioning: A Review of Theoretical and Empirical Work." *Frontiers in Psychology* 6, no. 368 (April 2, 2015). doi:10.3389/fpsyg.2015.00368.

"5.3: Symbolism and Iconography." LibreTexts Humanities. March 9, 2021. https://human.libretexts.org/Bookshelves/Art/Book%3A_Introduction_to_Art_-_Design_Context_and_Meaning_(Sachant_et_al.)/05%3A_Meaning_in_Art/5.03%3A_SYMBOLISM_AND_ICONOGRAPHY.

"Glossary." National Gallery. https://www.nationalgallery.org.uk/paintings/glossary/foreground#.

Gombrich, E. H. "Moment and Movement in Art." *Journal of the Warburg and Courtauld Institutes* 27 (1964): 293–306. https://doi.org/10.2307/750521.

Gurtner, L. M., M. Hartmann, and F. Masta. "Eye Movements during Visual Imagery and Perception Show Spatial Correspondence but Have Unique Temporal Signatures." *Science Direct* (May 2021). https://www.sciencedirect.com/science/article/pii/S0010027721000160.

"Henri Cartier-Bresson." Magnum Photos. November 19, 2020. https://www.magnumphotos.com/photographer/henri-cartier-bresson/.

Hess, D., M. Muller, and L. Dorfman. *Dorfsman and CBS*. 1st ed. Webster, NY: American Showcase, Inc., 1987.

"How Red and Green Became the Colors of Christmas." NPR One. December 20, 2016. https://one.npr.org/?sharedMediaId=506215632:506337240.

Itten, J. *The Art of Color: The Subjective Experience and Objective Rationale of Color*. Hoboken, NJ: John Wiley and Sons, 1974.

Laja, P. "10 Useful Findings about How People View Websites." CXL. February 23, 2021. https://cxl.com/blog/10-useful-findings-about-how-people-view-websites/.

Lange, A. "Can Data Be Human? The Work of Giorgia Lupi." *New Yorker*, May 25, 2019. https://www.newyorker.com/culture/culture-desk/can-data-be-human-the-work-of-giorgia-lupi.

"Latest Stories." Christie's. Christie's. https://www.christies.com/features.aspx.

Le Poidevin, R. "Time and the Static Image." *Philosophy* 72, no. 280 (1997): 175–88. http://www.jstor.org/stable/3751098.

"Literary Devices and Terms." Literary Devices. August 8, 2020. https://literarydevices.net.

Marly, P. "Designing Faster with a Baseline Grid." Teehan+Lax. https://teehanlax.com/blog/designing-faster-with-a-baseline-grid/. Accessed December 3, 2022.

McFadden, C. "9 Animals That Can Actually See in UV." Interesting Engineering. March 10, 2022. https://interestingengineering.com/9-animals-that-can-actually-see-in-uv.

Melina, R. "Why Is the Color Purple Associated with Royalty?" LiveScience. 2011. https://www.livescience.com/33324-purple-royal-color.html.

Miller, B., and C. O'Donnell. "Opening a Window into Reading Development: Eye Movements' Role within a Broader Literacy Research Framework." *School Psychology Review* 42, no. 2 (2013): 123–39. Practice and Cognitive Processes. Frontiers. Retrieved September 18, 2022, from https://www.frontiersin.org/articles/10.3389/fpsyg.2020.00394/full.

Morley, M. "Cover Story: What the Stack Awards Winner Tells Us about the New Rules of Magazine Design." AIGA Eye on Design. November 21, 2017. https://eyeondesign.aiga.org/cover-story-what-the-stack-awards-winner-tells-us-about-the-new-rules-of-magazine-design/.

Müller, J., and J. Wiedemann. *The History of Graphic Design, Vol. 2, 1960–Today*. Multilingual ed. Cologne: Taschen, 2018.

Müller-Brockmann, J. *Grid Systems in Graphic Design*. 4th ed. Sulgen, Switzerland: Verlag Niggli AG, 1996.

Newhall, N. *The Photographs of Edward Weston*. 1st ed. New York: Museum of Modern Art, 2022.

"Painting Your Historic House, a Guide to Colors and Color Schemes." Historic Ipswich. November 18, 2021. https://historicipswich.org/colors/.

Pavan, A., L. F. Cuturi, M. Maniglia, C. Casco, and G. Campana. "Implied Motion from Static Photographs Influences the Perceived Position of Stationary Objects." *Vision Research* 51, no. 1 (2011): 187–194. https://doi.org/10.1016/j.visres.2010.11.004.

Perich, S. "New York City at Night, 76 Years Ago." Picture Show, NPR. December 20, 2010. https://Www.Npr.Org. https://www.npr.org/sections/pictureshow/2010/12/20/132143636/nyc.

"Photography and Print Advertising." Harvard Business School, Baker Library, Historical Collections. 2022. https://www.library.hbs.edu/hc/naai/03-photo-print-ads.html#:%7E:text=By%20the%201930s%2C%20photography%20would,choice%20for%20most%20print%20advertising.

"Positive and Negative Space: Explore and Experiment with Positive and Negative Space." Whitney Museum of American Art. https://whitney.org/education/forteachers/activities/115. Accessed September 18, 2022.

"Principles of Design." Getty.edu. 2011. https://www.getty.edu/education/teachers/building_lessons/principles_design.pdf.

Prodger, M. "Photography: Is It Art?" *Guardian*, June 25, 2021. https://www.theguardian.com/artanddesign/2012/oct/19/photography-is-it-art.

Rand, Paul. *Speaking Out on Annual Reports*. New York: S. D. Scott Printing Company, 1983.

"Reading and the Brain." Harvard Medical School. https://hms.harvard.edu/news-events/publications-archive/brain/reading-brain. Accessed September 18, 2022.

"The Rise of Color." *Harvard Magazine*, March 3, 2014. https://www.harvardmagazine.com/2010/07/rise-of-color#:%7E:text=%E2%80%9CColor%20photography%20made%20its%20appearance,and%20three%2Dcolor%20printing%20processes.

"The Science of Movement: Eadweard Muybridge." Europeana. April 9, 2012. https://www.europeana.eu/en/blog/the-science-of-movement-eadweard-muybridge.

Smith, J. T. *Remarks on Rural Scenery: With Twenty Etchings of Cottages, from Nature: and Some Observations and Precepts Relative to the Pictoresque*. Legare Street Press, 2022.

Strunk, W., Jr., E. B. White, and M. Kalman. *The Elements of Style (Illustrated)*. 4th ed. London: Penguin Books, 2007.

Thomson, T. J., D. Angus, and P. Dootson. "3.2 Billion Images and 720,000 Hours of Video Are Shared Online Daily. Can You Sort Real from Fake?" November 3, 2020. https://theconversation.com/3-2-billion-images-and-720-000-hours-.of-video-are-shared-online-daily-can-you-sort-real-from-fake-148630.

Tillyard, R. J. *The Biology of Dragonflies*. Charleston, SC: Nabu Press, 2010. Originally published 1917.

Tinbergen, N. *Animal Behavior*. New York: Time-Life Books, 1965.

Tufte, Edward R. *Beautiful Evidence*. 1st ed. Cheshire, CT: Graphics Press, 2006.

Tufte, Edward R. *Envisioning Information*. Cheshire, CT: Graphics Press, 1990.

"Visuals." Associated Press. March 1, 2022. https://www.ap.org/about/news-values-and-principles/telling-the-story/visuals.

Wasserman, R. "The Case of the Colorblind Painter." *New York Review of Books*, September 12, 202. https://www.nybooks.com/articles/1987/11/19/the-case-of-the-colorblind-painter/?lp_txn_id=1330664.

Illustration Credits

Copyright © Adam Hillman: 3-31
Copyright © Alexandra Rowley: 3-17, 3-18, 3-19, 3-20
Copyright © Andreas Gursky/ARS, New York, 2022, courtesy of Sprüth Magers: 9-20
Copyright © Andrew Moore: 7-16
Copyright © Andriy Sarymsakov / Alamy Stock Photo: 6-17
Copyright © Andy Goldsworthy, courtesy Galerie Lelong & Co., New York: 7-19
Copyright © Anthony Acosta: 2-16, 3-32
Copyright © Ascent/PKS Media Inc., Getty Images: 3-4
Copyright © Audrey Flack, image courtesy of Louis K. Meisel Gallery, NY: 3-2
Copyright © Berenice Abbott/Getty Images: 7-20
Photograph by Biz Herman: 4-10
Copyright © Boston Globe, Getty Images: 0-4
Copyright © Cássio Vasconcellos: pages xviii–1, 3-29, 3-34
Copyright © Center for Creative Photography, Arizona Board of Regents: 7-15
Copyright © Chris Johns: 9-7
Copyright © Christoph Niemann 2022: 6-11, 8-4, 8-7
Copyright © Chuck Close: 8-10
Copyright © Constantine Poulos: 5-10
Copyright © Dan Winters Photography: 7-10
Copyright © David Burnett: 1-3
Copyright © David Carson: 0-1
Copyright © David Graham Photography: 7-1, 9-9
Copyright © Diego Koi: 8-3
Copyright © Dougie Wallace: 2-25
Reprinted by permission, © Edward R. Tufte, Envisioning Information (Graphics Press LLC, Cheshire, CT): 8-22
Copyright © Eight by Eight Magazine (8by8.com); designers: Grace Lee, Robert Priest; illustrator: Diego Patiño: 5-22
Copyright © Eleanor Lutz: 8-15
Copyright © Estate of Jean-Michel Basquiat. Licensed by Artestar, New York: 6-22
Copyright © EyeEm/Alamy Stock Photo: 3-13, 3-28
Copyright © Federico Tardito: 5-11
Copyright © Fondation Henri Cartier-Bresson/Magnum: 7-18
Copyright © Fred Ramos: 5-20
Copyright © Getty Images: 2-7
Copyright © Glenn Hunt Photography: 5-5
Copyright © Gooldteeth & Co.: 2-11
Creative directors/designers: Grace Lee and Robert Priest; illustrator: Ben Kirchner: 8-2

Copyright © Helmut Newton: 9-14
Courtesy of the artist and i8 Gallery, Reykjavik. Photograph by Ari Magg: 2-20
Copyright © J. Grant Brittain Photos, www.jgrantbrittain-photos.com: 2-19, 2-23, 3-28
Copyright © Jack Davidson: 5-14
Copyright © James McMullan: 8-11, 8-12, 8-13
Copyright © James Provost: 8-17
James R. A. Davenport, IfWeAssume blog—The Top-10 Best Seller Book Covers from 2000–2011: 8-19
Copyright © Jeremy Wolff: 7-12
Copyright © Jimmy Chin Productions: 7-3
Copyright © John Filo / Getty Images: 5-19
Copyright © Jonai Gibson-Selix, RISE: Philadelphia (2020). Designs by Jonai. Cover image by Andrea Hu: 5-1
Copyright © Jonathan Bachman Photography; reprinted by permission of Thomson Reuters: 7-2
Copyright © José De Rocco: 7-14
Copyright © Joseph Ford: 0-2
Copyright © Joseph Szabo/Trunk Archive: 9-22
Courtesy of the artist and Kasmin Gallery: 8-8
Copyright © Kate Mathis: 4-12
Copyright © Kelly Marshall: 4-7
Copyright © KennyNemes: 9-15
Copyright © Kevin Carter/Getty Images: 5-21
Copyright © Levi Brown/Trunk Archive: 3-7, 3-8, 3-16
Copyright © Loes Heerink: 2-1
Design/art direction by Louise Fili; illustrations by Kelly Thorn: 5-16
Photo: Luke Stettner; art direction: 2x4, New York: 0-8
Copyright © Maija Isola: 3-6
Copyright © Max Aguilera-Hellweg: 4-17
Illustration: Melinda Beck; art direction: Matt Dorfman; client: The New York Times Book Review: 6-20
Copyright © Mike Krautter: 2-17
Copyright © Mikkel Vang: 5-18
Copyright © 2010 MIT. Courtesy of MIT Museum: 3-24
Copyright © The Museum of Modern Art/Licensed by SCALA/Art Resource, NY: 1-12, 4-1
Copyright © Najeebah Al-Ghadban: 8-1
Copyright © Nathan Vieland: 1-7
Copyright © New School: 2-24
Copyright © Nicholas Felton: 8-20
Copyright © OMA: 8-14
Copyright © Paul Szakacs/EyeEm, Getty Images: 2-8
Copyright © Peter Mendelsund: 4-9
Copyright © Philip Mimaki: 3-9
Copyright © Popperfoto, Getty Images: 4-21
Copyright © Ramsay de Give: 3-12
Copyright © Randal Ford Photography: 9-17
Copyright © Randal Ford Productions: 2-26
Copyright © Rob Tringali/Stringer, Getty Images: 2-15
Design director: Robert Priest; art director and designer: Grace Lee; illustrator: Sam Weber: 8-5
Design director: Robert Priest; design: Grace Lee; infographic director: John Grimwade; illustrator: Bryan Christie: 8-18
Copyright © Robin Knight, Getty Images: 3-14
Copyright © Ruth Fremson: 5-7
Copyright © Science Museum Group: 5-13
Copyright © Shawn Pridgen: pages 96–97
Copyright © simonkr, Getty Images: 3-5
Sudeep Jesani / Alamy Stock Photo: 9-6
Copyright © Thom Atkinson: 2-18
Photo illustrations by Thomas Allen (thomasallenonline.com): 9-13
Copyright © T.O.K./Alamy Stock Photo: 2-6
Copyright © Travis Rathbone/Trunk Archive: 7-6
Copyright © US Girl/Getty Images: 7-12
Copyright © v.Horn/Stockimo/Alamy Stock Photoo: 3-33
Copyright © Visual Arts Press: 0-5
Copyright © William Wegman: 7-21
Copyright © Yon Marsh/Alamy Stock Photo: 6-16
Copyright © Zentrum Paul Klee, Bern, Image archive: 4-3

Index

Page references in italics refer to figures.